Bloom's Modern Critical Views

African American Poets: Wheatley–Tolson
African American Poets: Hayden–Dove
Edward Albee
Dante Alighieri
American and Canadian Women Poets, 1930–present
American Women Poets, 1650–1950
Hans Christian Andersen
Maya Angelou
Asian-American Writers
Margaret Atwood
Jane Austen
Paul Auster
James Baldwin
Honoré de Balzac
Samuel Beckett
Saul Bellow
The Bible
William Blake
Jorge Luis Borges
Ray Bradbury
The Brontës
Gwendolyn Brooks
Elizabeth Barrett Browning
Robert Browning
Italo Calvino
Albert Camus
Truman Capote
Lewis Carroll
Willa Cather
Cervantes
Geoffrey Chaucer
Anton Chekhov
Kate Chopin
Agatha Christie
Samuel Taylor Coleridge
Joseph Conrad
Contemporary Poets
Julio Cortázar
Stephen Crane
Daniel Defoe
Don DeLillo
Charles Dickens
Emily Dickinson
John Donne and the 17th-Century Poets
Fyodor Dostoevsky
W.E.B. DuBois
George Eliot
T.S. Eliot
Ralph Ellison
Ralph Waldo Emerson
William Faulkner
F. Scott Fitzgerald
Sigmund Freud
Robert Frost
William Gaddis
Johann Wolfgang von Goethe
George Gordon, Lord Byron
Graham Greene
Thomas Hardy
Nathaniel Hawthorne
Robert Hayden
Ernest Hemingway
Hermann Hesse
Hispanic-American Writers
Homer
Langston Hughes
Zora Neale Hurston
Aldous Huxley
Henrik Ibsen
John Irving
Henry James
James Joyce
Franz Kafka
John Keats
Jamaica Kincaid
Stephen King
Rudyard Kipling
Milan Kundera
Tony Kushner
D.H. Lawrence
Doris Lessing
Ursula K. Le Guin
Sinclair Lewis
Norman Mailer
Bernard Malamud
David Mamet
Christopher Marlowe
Gabriel García Márquez
Cormac McCarthy
Carson McCullers
Herman Melville
Arthur Miller
John Milton
Molière
Toni Morrison
Native-American Writers
Joyce Carol Oates
Flannery O'Connor
Eugene O'Neill
George Orwell
Octavio Paz
Sylvia Plath
Edgar Allan Poe
Katherine Anne Porter
Marcel Proust
Thomas Pynchon
Philip Roth
Salman Rushdie
J.D. Salinger
José Sarramago

Bloom's Modern Critical Views

Jean-Paul Sartre
William Shakespeare
George Bernard Shaw
Mary Wollstonecraft Shelley
Percy Bysshe Shelley
Alexander Solzhenitsyn
Sophocles
John Steinbeck
Robert Louis Stevenson
Tom Stoppard
Jonathan Swift
Amy Tan
Alfred, Lord Tennyson
Henry David Thoreau
J.R.R. Tolkien
Leo Tolstoy
Ivan Turgenev
Mark Twain
John Updike
Kurt Vonnegut
Derek Walcott
Alice Walker
Robert Penn Warren
H.G. Wells
Eudora Welty
Edith Wharton
Walt Whitman
Oscar Wilde
Tennessee Williams
Thomas Wolfe
Tom Wolfe
Virginia Woolf
William Wordsworth
Jay Wright
Richard Wright
William Butler Yeats
Emile Zola

Bloom's Modern Critical Views

ROBERT HAYDEN

Edited and with an introduction by
Harold Bloom
Sterling Professor of the Humanities
Yale University

CHELSEA HOUSE
PUBLISHERS
A Haights Cross Communications Company
Philadelphia

A Haights Cross Communications Company

http://www.chelseahouse.com

Printed and bound in the United States of America.
10 9 8 7 6 5 4 3 2 1

Library of Congress Cataloging-in-Publication Data

Robert Hayden / Harold Bloom, ed.
p. cm. — (Modern critical views)
Includes bibliographical references and index.
ISBN 0-7910-8127-3 (alk. paper)
1. Hayden, Robert Earl—Criticism and interpretation. 2. African Americans in literature. I. Bloom, Harold. II. Series.
PS3515.A9363Z87 2004
813'.52—dc22
2004013051

Contributing Editor: Jesse Zuba

Cover designed by Keith Trego

Cover photo:

Layout by EJB Publishing Services

All links and web addresses were checked and verified to be correct at the time of publication. Because of the dynamic nature of the web, some addresses and links may have changed since publication and may no longer be valid.

Every effort has been made to trace the owners of copyrighted material and secure copyright permission. Articles appearing in this volume generally appear much as they did in their original publication with little to no editorial changes. Those interested in locating the original source will find bibliographic information in the bibliography and acknowledgments sections of this volume.

Contents

Editor's Note

My Introduction is an intense appreciation of Robert Hayden's poetic achievement, and I regret passing over so many wonderful poems to center upon only a few: the famous *Middle Passage* and *Runagate Runagate* sequences, the equally poignant *John Brown*, and the prophetic final [*American Journal*] which closes the *Collected Poems of Robert Hayden* (1996).

Constance J. Post begins the chronological sequence of critical essays by analyzing the deliberate paradoxes of Hayden's imagery, after which Lewis Turco accurately characterizes Hayden's style as "Protean."

Middle Passage, founded upon the *Amistad* Munity, is praised by Fred M. Fetrow for its understated ironies, after which Robert B. Stepto learnedly contrasts Michael Harper, Hayden, and the great poet Jay Wright as allied responses to Ralph Ellison's call for a mature African-American literary art.

Wilburn Williams, Jr. traces Hayden's poetic lineage to Emersonian tradition, while the late and much-missed Charles T. Davis adumbrates Hayden's very complex stances towards African-American history.

The Yeatsian strain in Hayden is meditated upon by Fritz Oehlschlaeger, after which Vera M. Kutzinski powerfully returns us to *Middle Passage* in order to show how Hayden's revision of the sequence's closing lines improved its moral power.

Pontheolla T. Williams surveys the poems of *A Ballad of Remembrance* (1962) and notes their continuous moral discernment, while Brian Conniff suggests that Hayden (like Hart Crane) set out to answer Eliot's *The Waste Land*, though Conniff neglects Crane's role in aiding both Hayden and Jay Wright in their emancipation from Eliot's poetic procedures.

In Frank Rashid's return to Hayden's early Detroit poems, we are given a useful account of how intricately the mature artistry of the poet ultimately stemmed from populist origins.

Edward M. Pavlić concludes this volume on a major American poet with a discussion centering upon "The Diver", and showing its continuity with [*American Journal*].

HAROLD BLOOM

Introduction

I met Robert Hayden only once, when sometime in the early 1970s I lectured at Ann Arbor, and had the privilege of a personal conversation with him for rather more than an hour or so. We talked about the Baha'i gardens in Haifa, which I had visited in the later 1950s, and also about the poetry of W.B. Yeats, on which I had recently published a long book, and of Hart Crane, who still seems to me an unexamined presence in several of Hayden's strongest poems.

Like Jay Wright, Hayden is a major modern American poet, as well as forming a quartet, together with Ralph Ellison, Toni Morrison, and Jay Wright, one that seems to me the crown of African-American literary achievement up to this moment (I write in May, 2004). Hayden (1913–1980) is a permanent poet, canonical in a sense that current politicism continues to deride. Cultural fashions fade away, and literary survival always depends upon three criteria: aesthetic splendor, cognitive power, and wisdom. If the United States emerges from the triumphalism of George W. Bush, a time will come when much current rant and cant will dwindle into period pieces, at best. Hayden, a maker and not an image of political correctness, will be read long after louder voices have vanished into the void.

Hayden was at his best in poetic sequences, though some of his lyrical poems are as rewarding. Like Yeats and Hart Crane (and the young Jay Wright of *The Homecoming Singer*), at his most memorable, Hayden is an incantatory poet. His characteristic rhetorical movement is invocation, rather as Yeats invokes his Tower or Hart Crane, Brooklyn Bridge. Most of Hayden's critics regard him as invoking black history, but they over-simplify the basis for his rhetorical art. You can be a very bad poet no matter how incessantly you call upon the West African past, or the horrific sadism of the English, Spanish, and Portuguese slave traders and owners of the Americas. Hayden matters because he is an authentic poet, one of the best of his generation (which included Elizabeth Bishop, Theodore Roethke, May Swenson, and the still overesteemed Robert Lowell). He told me, with a reticence worthy of his best poems, that he was fascinated by the *impacted* quality of Hart Crane's rhetoric, and in some respects he resembles Crane more than he does Yeats, whom his teacher W.H. Auden had commended to him as a model.

Like Crane, who hymned an Unknown God, Hayden was a religious poet, but of the highly eclectic Baha'i persuasion, a heresy from Iranian Islam. Inwardness and aesthetic elitism mark Hayden's highest achievements, as they do the Pindaricism of Jay Wright, for whom Hayden's freedom from spuriously black ideological "criticism" provided a beacon. Hayden's poetic integrity, like Jay Wright's, was absolute, and invariably courageous, in the mode of Ralph Ellison, who insisted that the American and European literary traditions were as much his possession as was the example of Richard Wright.

All this is merely preamble to a rather rapid survey of a few of Hayden's superb sequences, of which *Middle Passage* is the most famous. Both Hart Crane and T.S. Eliot are both drawn upon and evaded in Section III in particular, where an Eliotic allusion, in *The Waste Land*, to Shakesepeare's *The Tempest*, fuses with the high rhetoric of Crane's Columbus approaching the New World in the "Ave Maria" canto of *The Bridge*:

> Shuttles in the rocking loom of history,
> the dark ships move, the dark ships move,
> their bright ironical names
> like jests of kindness on a murderer's mouth;
> plough through thrashing glister toward
> fata morgana's lucent melting shore,
> weave toward New World littorals that are
> mirage and myth and actual shore.
>
> Voyage through death,
> voyage whose chartings are unlove.
>
> A charnel stench, effluvium of living death
> spreads outward from the hold,

where the living and the dead, the horribly dying,
lie interlocked, lie foul with blood and excrement.

Deep in the festering hold thy father lies,
the corpse of mercy rots with him,
rats eat love's rotten gelid eyes.

The dispassionate tonalities of this extraordinary passage stem from Hayden's poetic reticence, his characteristic rhetoric of litotes or understatement, in a reaction-formation against Crane's ecstatic hyperboles and Eliot's hyperbolic ironies. For Crane, Columbus is a mystical (if cruel) disciple of the prophet Isaiah, while Eliot's Tiresias is death-in-life desperately waiting for the grace of Anglican conversion. Hayden, a black Baha'i, longs for a more universal salvation. His Cinquez, hero of the *Amistad* Mutiny, is the emblem of all those, of whatever origin, who sought the Blessing that America ought to constitute, however far from that ideal it continues to fall:

Voyage through death
to life upon these shores.

Runagate Runagate is not as intricate and fully written as *Middle Passage*, but it too dares and sustains a high rhetoric:

Tell me, Ezekiel, oh tell me do you see
mailed Jehovah coming to deliver me?

My late friend, the great poet-novelist Robert Penn Warren, fiercely hated John Brown, upon whom he had written his first book. One day, at lunch with Warren, I commended John Brown as a prophet, though violent in the extreme, yet in the best of causes. Warren, too urbane to argue, presented me at the next week's lunch with a copy of his *John Brown: The Making of a Martyr*. Loving and honoring Warren's memory, I still follow Emerson and Thoreau and vote for Hayden's sequence, *John Brown*, which honestly admits the prophet's responsibility for "Bleeding Kansas":

Doing The Lord's work with saber
sharpened on the grindstone
of The Word:
Bleeding Kansas:

the cries of my people the cries
of their oppressors harrowed
hacked—poison meat for Satan's
maw.
        I slew no man but blessed
the Chosen, who in the name
of justice killed at my command.

Bleeding Kansas:
                        a son martyred
there: I am tested I am trued
made worthy of my servitude.

Oh the crimes of this guilty
guilty land:
            let Kansas bleed.

Of John Brown, Hayden says simply: "he died/for us". Few American poets have understood so well their hopelessly paradoxical country. Hayden, in the concluding stanza of his *American Journal*, joins Walt Whitman in apprehending what may be beyond comprehension:

confess i am curiously drawn unmentionable to
the americans doubt i could exist among them for
long however psychic demands far too severe
much violence much that repels i am attracted
none the less their variousness their ingenuity
their elan vital and that some thing essence
quiddity i cannot penetrate or name

CONSTANCE J. POST

Image and Idea in the Poetry of Robert Hayden

In Robert Hayden's "Kodachromes of the Island,"[1] the speaker of the poem roams about, thinking of Yeats' passionate search for a theme while seeking one of his own. For both men the search came long after their careers as poets had been established. Yeats, it will be recalled, wrote "The Circus Animals' Desertion," the poem in which he discusses his search for a new theme, fifty years after the publication of his first book of poetry. In Hayden's case, the search came in the middle of his career after he had already written some of his most celebrated poems, such as "Middle Passage," "Runagate Runagate" and "Frederick Douglass." These and other poems were included in his first book of poetry, *A Ballad of Remembrance*, published in 1962, ten years before the collection in which "Kodachromes of the Island" appears, entitled *Words in the Mourning Time* (1972).

Both men pursued the quest with dogged persistence. According to Yeats, the search preoccupied him daily for more than a month and culminated in his enumeration, resignedly, of old themes, among them the reconciling of what he called the three islands of incompatible things, "Vain gaiety, vain battle, vain repose." Hayden, eschewing any such enumeration, leaves it up to the reader to judge the degree of his success. Elsewhere, however, a clue is provided in an interview conducted with him by John O'Brien. Having acknowledged how stale and repetitious he thought his

From *CLA Journal* 20, no. 2 (December 1976). © 1976 by the College Language Association.

poetry had become, Hayden affirms that *The Night-Blooming Cereus* represented a real breakthrough for him.[2] After that, he says, "I began to move in a new direction and to consolidate my gains, such as they were."

A careful study of Hayden's poetry will reveal, I believe, that any new direction he might have taken was primarily in the area of consolidation, if only to look at his old themes from a new angle. By his so doing, a thread of continuity is woven throughout his entire work, giving it a unity and a coherence it otherwise would lack. This is true in general of his themes and the means he uses to develop them, especially of his imagery. Considered together, his lyrics take on an almost epic quality. They therefore support Donald Stauffer's thesis that the imagery of some poets, whether consciously or unconsciously, is organized in such coherent patterns that an epic effect is achieved.[3]

Struggle, for example, is a common theme running through Hayden's poetry, fortified not only by his choice of imagery but through his use of paradox. His chief symbol for it is the star. In the poem entitled "Stars," he refers to the starlight which "crosses eons of meta-space to us" and asks, "How shall the mind keep warm save at spectral fires—how thrive but by the light of paradox?" (12). The light of paradox *is* the light of the star since, by crossing eons of meta-space, it challenges our expectations about speed, distance and time just as paradox, literally meaning "beyond opinion," contradicts our expectations. (*Meta* and *para* share the same meaning of *beyond.*)

The star, moreover, is a paradox because of its physical properties. It exists only because of the careful balance of contradictory forces whereby "the energy generated by nuclear reactions in the interior is balanced by the outflow of energy to the surface"; similarly, "the inward gravitational forces are balanced by the outward-directed gas and radiation pressure" (*American Heritage Dictionary*). When such a balance of opposites is no longer present in the star, it collapses within itself. Starlight can thus be seen as a means of keeping the mind warm and thriving.

What additional meanings does Hayden attach to the stars? Of central importance in understanding the significance of the stars to him is the connection he makes between them and the Baha'i faith.[4] In Section V of "Stars," he mentions many different kinds of stars and then singles out the Nine-Pointed Star, "sun-star in the constellation of the nuclear Will" (15). A symbol commonly used by the Navaho Indians, the nine-pointed star represents perfection according to Baha'ism, since after nine all numbers are repetitious. Furthermore, the number nine is seen as the numerical manifestation of the Greatest Name, Baha, says A.Q. Faizi, who gives the numerical value of the name Baha, based upon the Arabic alphabet, as follows: B = 2, A = 1, H = 5, A = 1 for a total of 9.[5]

In Section III of "Stars" the number nine also assumes importance as Hayden, in groups of two, three and four, mentions the names of nine stars of various colors and constellations. All share one thing in common, however, and that is brightness. Five of the nine stars—Aldebaran, Arcturus, Altair, Vega and Polaris—are among the brightest stars in the sky, visible at latitude 40° N. Another two, Betelgeuse and Algol, are two of the brightest variable stars; even though their brightness fluctuates, it nevertheless exceeds that of most of the other 6,000 stars in the sky which are visible to the naked eye. Also visible without the use of a telescope are the last two, Almaak (also known as Almach) and Maia, the star for whom Hayden's daughter is named.

The significance of nine for Baha'ism, other than that already mentioned, varies somewhat. Because every Baha'i temple has nine openings and since the one in the United States, located in Wilmette, Illinois, has nine sides, a common interpretation among Western Baha'is is that each side represents one of the major religions of the world: Hinduism, Confucianism, Taoism, Buddhism, Judaism, Islam, Christianity, Zorastrianism and Baha'ism.[6] The last religion, that of Baha'ism, is considered therefore by some as the latest in a series of manifestations of God, though not necessarily his final revelation to man. Baha'u'llah himself gave a different interpretation to the significance of the nine openings. According to his teachings, the temple of wood or stone is but a correspondence of the human body, itself the temple of God, which has nine openings. In either interpretation, the salient point is that God is not limited in the ways he manifests Himself. Our minds can thus be illuminated by any one of the nine stars or by the Nine-Pointed Star itself "whose radiance filtering down to us lights mind and spirit, signals future light."

That explains why in Section I of the poem, Orion, the giant hunter who pursued the Pleiades, is praised. As the lover of Eos, the Greek goddess of dawn, he represents, in a larger sense, those who love the dawning of this new manifestation of God. In "Baha'u'llah in the Garden of Ridwan," he is equated with the auroral darkness. Aurora, the Roman equivalent of Eos, figures importantly in the Baha'i faith since the term "Dawnbreaker" has often been used to refer to thousands of early Persian Baha'is who were martyred. (A literal translation of the term from Arabic is "The Rising Place of the Lights of the Sun.") In the garden, all of nature joins in praising the Dawnbreaker Baha'u'llah. "Energies like angels dance glorias of recognition," their radiance as much an illumination as the pulsars and quasars of Section IV in "Stars."

Coming down to earth, we find that even the rocks praise Baha'u'llah as "Within the rock the undiscovered suns release their light" (117). A mineral silicate, common in igneous and metamorphoic rock, is called mica. The word *mica* is influenced by the Latin *micare*, meaning *to shine*. Bearing a brightness similar to that of the stars, it participates in the general awakening of nature which accompanies the arrival of the Dawnbreaker.

Mica is used elsewhere by Hayden to refer to the sea and to the sky. In "Gulls" (102), for instance he speaks of the "mica'd fall of the sea," using mica to describe the dark sea as the waves, breaking upon it, appear as little suns. Thus mica, based upon a metaphor derived from the stars, is first transferred to rock and then to the sea and finally, to complete the circle, back to the sky again.

"The birds explode into mica sky" writes Hayden in "A Plague of Starlings" (71), a poem which describes the attempts of workmen at Fisk University to get rid of the troublesome birds by shooting into the leaves at evening time. Starlings themselves are reminders of the stars in their dark, often irridescent plumage. The irony which they present is not lost upon the speaker in the poem as he tries to avoid their carcasses while walking to class to lecture on what Socrates had told his friends about the migratory habits of the soul.

Not only do the rocks and the sea reflect the light of the stars. So do people. In "Runagate Runagate" (128) Hayden praises Harriet Tubman, leader of the Underground Railroad, as a "woman of earth, whipscarred, a summoning, a shining." She, like Sojourner Truth, is a star, summoning others to her light as well as being the light. Similarly, Akhenaten in "Two Egyptian Portrait Masks" is spoken of as, "O Lord of every land shining forth for all." Finally, Baha'u'llah is the supreme reflection of that light. Of him Hayden says, "who by the light of suns beyond the suns beyond the sun and stars ... alone can comprehend ... and stars and stones and seas acclaimed."

Hayden's theme of struggle draws support not just from his imagery of the stars and other celestial bodies, as well as their correspondences in other aspects of Nature. Equally significant is his use of oxymorons whereby he achieves the maximum effect of combining opposites with a minimum number of words. For example, Sojourner Truth is called a 'childless mother' in Section III of "Stars" (13). An apparent contradiction, it can be resolved by one's remembering that Hayden refers to this freed slave, originally called Isabella, as one who was following the star, her mind a star. Believing that she had received a special message from heaven, she left her job in New York, adopted the name Sojourner Truth and travelled throughout the North preaching emancipation and women's rights. By shedding light upon others, she consequently became the mother of countless children even though she physically did not give birth to any.

Likewise, the apparent contradiction contained in Hayden's reference to Akhenaten as "multi-single like the Sun" can be resolved by the examination of the image closely in the poem "Two Egyptian Portrait Masks" (116). Akhenaten, King of Egypt from c. 1375–c. 1358 B.C.E., believed, as the name he adopted suggests (*Aten* meaning *sun*), that the sun was god and god alone. The universe was filled with his beneficent light and by it everything that lived had its being. So convinced was Akhenaten of the truth of his solar monotheism that in addition to taking a new name he also established a new capital. The spirit in his heart, says Hayden, was that of "Aten Jahveh Allah God." Akhenaten can therefore be multi-single because he contains within himself the spirit of God in several of its manifestations besides his own: that of Yahweh, worshipped by Jews; Allah, by Moslems; and God, by Christians, among others. Akhenaten is thus seen as one of the royal prophets in the progressive revelation of God.

Two of Hayden's oxymorons are somewhat similar in content although the position of the terms has been reversed. A striking contrast can thus be observed between "eudaemonic pain" in the poem "Witch Doctor" and "pained amusement" in the poem "The Sphinx." In the first of these two poems the witch doctor, a religious leader, is considering what new device he can use in order to "enmesh his flock in theopathic tension" (107). The degree of his success is attested by the "cries of eudaemonic pain" from the audience, a pain that is happy since it comes from having a good spirit.

Just as pain may be accompanied by happiness, so happiness may be accompanied by pain, according to Hayden. The latter is illustrated in the second poem in which the Sphinx says that eventually "you will come to regard my questioning with a certain pained amusement" (35). Causing pain, the Sphinx's riddle may concomitantly be a source of gaiety, enabling a person to tolerate a paradox. By the poet's own admission, this poem suggests that "something fundamentally negative, or apparently so, may be used in a positive, a creative way" (Interview with John O'Brien, p. 120). Turning adversity into advantage is vintage Brer Rabbit, of course, and serves to remind us of the degree to which folk material from Hayden's Afro-American tradition permeates his poetry.

An apparently insolvable question also puzzles the participants in "Electrical Storm" (77). In that poem the speaker muses over whether it was chance or choice that saved himself and others in the storm which killed several persons. While he is content to leave the question dangling as are the electrical wires strewn about the ground, he feels confident that he knows "what those cowering true believers would have said." True believers—the phrase is used by Eric Hoffer as the title of his book on religious fanaticism—supposedly do not find it necessary to cringe or shrink in fear. In this case, the speaker in the poem appears certain that the believers would have insisted that heavenly design determined who would be saved. The irony in this poem is that those who don't know the answer to the riddle can nevertheless live with it better than those who are so sure they have the answers.

The oxymorons in "Theme and Variation" will serve as the final examples of the compact paradox as used by Hayden. In this poem the speaker, identified as a stranger, ponders life's ephemerality. Referring in the first line to the four major categories of life—animal, plant, insect and man—and in the second to the four elements (earth, air, water and fire), the stranger avers that these "Are the revelling shadows of a changing permanence" (115). This idea, at least as old as Heraclitus, has been advanced more recently by the twentieth-century philosopher Henri Bergson. According to his views, change takes on the pervasive character of reality. Such a constantly altering state of things makes man a voyeur, spying "upon the striptease of reality," says the stranger. Continuing to employ sexual imagery, he comments, upon seeing the transience occurring at the edge of things, that such an impending change turns to "curiosa all I know."

Such an imminence, moreover, "changes light to rainbow darkness wherein God waylays us and empowers." The oxymoron "rainbow darkness" is strikingly similar to the "golden darkness" found in the poem "The Ballad of Nat Turner" and the "auroral darkness" of the poem "Baha'u'llah in the Garden of Ridwan." The use of the word *rainbow*, however, adds a note of promise to this image, as Noah was given the rainbow as a sign of God's avowal not to destroy the earth again by water. In such a darkness God waylays and empowers. Reminiscent of the sexual imagery used by Donne and Crashaw, Hayden here depicts God as one who ambushes, *ambush* being synonymous with the word *waylay*, but also suggestive of a sexual overpowering.

Hayden also makes additional use of paradox in his frequent treatment of the theme of struggle, often associated with metamorphosis. Thus the energies of a paradox, resting in tension as they do in the stars, serve to inform much of Hayden's poetry. In "Richard Hunt's 'Arachne'" (23), for example, Hayden focuses on the precise moment when Arachne is changed from a woman into a spider. Arachne, according to Greek myth, had challenged Athena to a weaving contest and was subsequently metamorphosed by her into a spider for her temerity.

Hayden stresses the tension of the moment structurally in at least two ways. First, by using present participles throughout the poem, as well as gerunds, he rivets the reader's attention on the metamorphosis itself:

> Human face *becoming* locked insect face
> mouth of agony *shaping* a cry it cannot utter
> eyes *bulging* brimming with the horrors
> of her *becoming*
>
> Dazed crazed
> by godly vivisection *husking* her
> *gutting* her
> *cutting* hubris its fat and bones away
> In *goggling* terror *fleeing* powerless to flee
> Arachne not yet arachnid and no longer woman
> in the moment's centrifuge of *dying*
> *becoming*
>
> (Italics mine)

A second device used by Hayden to create structural tension in the poem is variation in the indentation pattern of the lines. The poem, composed of three stanzas of four lines each, is organized in the following manner: stanza one is indented so that each line following the first is indented a few more spaces to the right. The second stanza is indented in just the opposite manner: the first line is indented far to the right and each successive line indented a bit farther to the left side of the page. The third stanza repeats the pattern of the first. A zigzag effect is thereby achieved which graphically outlines the wrenching force of Arachne's metamorphosis.

In "The Night-Blooming Cereus" (24) Hayden again focuses on the moment of metamorphosis. Waiting night after night to see the tropical cactus burst into flower, the onlookers have been partially rewarded already by the growing awareness of the "rigorous design" governing the process to which they bear witness. Even before the flower appears, it prompts the desire "to celebrate the blossom, paint ourselves, dance in honor of archaic mysteries," just as in the poem "Full Moon" Hayden fondly remembers agrarian peoples who worshipped the moon and regulated their lives by it. When the onlookers "beheld at last the achieved flower," they were filled with reverence, recognizing the awful struggle by which so grand a moment had been attained. Thus the cereus, whose name comes from the Latin word for *candle* (because of the similarity in shape), sheds a light which, though ephemeral, stirs man's deepest religious impulses. In so doing it achieves a glory worthy of the struggle.

A glorious struggle is also recorded by Hayden in "The Ballad of Nat Turner"[7] (125) in which he achieves a dramatic tension of the first magnitude. At the beginning of the poem Nat Turner wanders into the Dismal Swamp, sees trees "where Ibo warriors hung shadowless" and wonders if it is the sign promised him by God. The sign he awaits is a go-ahead that the Day of Judgment is at hand which he is to lead. From his confession, we know that he had been identified as a prophet early in his life and that he believed God had ordained him for some great purpose. Such a conviction impelled him, said Turner, to return to his master after a successful escape.

The tension of the poem is heightened considerably through the use of dialogue in the first nine stanzas. When Turner cries in the second stanza, "Speak to me now or let me die," an immediate reply is not forthcoming. In the fifth, the blackness whispers, in response to the same question, "Die." Later on, in the ninth stanza, he cries to the rock and the bramble, "Hide me," and they in turn antiphonally utter the same cry, so dazzling is the vision that Turner beheld.

Of equal if not greater importance in establishing tension throughout the poem is Hayden's use of repetition, particularly of the word *and.* Having already used it eight times by the ninth stanza, he then repeats it an additional twenty times in the last eight stanzas. Seven uses of *and* occur at the beginning of sentences; the other thirteen are used as connectives in phrases and dependent clauses. Hayden thereby heaps image upon image, accelerating the action in such a way that the reader reels from its cumulative force much as Turner reels from his vision of the dazzling combat of the angels.

For Hayden, the struggles of others may also help us in our own. In recalling the deaths of Martin Luther King and Robert Kennedy, he suggests that words in the mourning time may be transformed into a morning time. Through the Dawn-breaker's transilluminating word, these deaths become the "major means whereby, oh dreadfully, our humanness must be achieved." Likewise, in Hayden's celebrated poem, "Middle Passage" (118), Cinquez' "voyage through death to life upon these shores" is the life that now transfigures many lives, serving, as do the lives of King and Kennedy, as the means whereby others may effect their own metamorphoses.

Another example of such a transformation can be observed in the poem "El-Hajj Malik El-Shabazz" (55). There Hayden traces the gradual metamorphosis of Malcolm X from his memory of the racist murder of his father when Malcolm X was quite young to his subsequent rise as a leader in the Black Muslim movement. His metamorphosis was not complete, says Hayden, until Malcolm recognized "Allah the raceless in whose blazing Oneness all were one."

Hayden's concern for the struggles of mankind is not limited to publicly acclaimed figures. In "The Diver" (75), for instance, the speaker in the poem says that he strove against the conflicting desires to live and to die. He did so in "languid frenzy," the phrase itself indicative of his contradictory feelings. Somehow, though, he began the "measured rise," finding in order the means whereby to contain his chaotic, opposing feelings. A similar struggle marks the attempts of the old man to fly again in the poem "For a Young Artist" (8). After many painful attempts, he succeeds: "the angle of ascent achieved." Rising, whether from the bottom of the sea to its surface or from the earth to the sky, depends upon the struggle to establish the proper balance. For the diver, it means gauging the speed of his ascent; for the old man, finding the right angle.

Here Hayden is dealing not just with the struggle of a lone individual but with the struggle of the artist. Such a balancing act is much like walking a tightrope. "Death as on either side, the way of life between," the man in the hospital room in "The Broken Dark" (39) recalls the Rabbi saying. The man is also reminded of Baha'u'llah's words, "I have come to tell thee of struggles in the pit."

Not just a figure of speech, the pit refers to an underground dungeon in Tihran where Baha'u'llah spent four months in heavy chains. Called "The Black Pit," the room had only one opening and was crammed with more than a hundred murderers and thieves. Elsewhere, however, Hayden does refer to the pit in a figurative sense. In the poem on Malcolm X he says that Malcolm's vision of a racist Allah "could not cleanse him of the odors of the pit." Representing the stench and foulness of hatred, the pit symbolizes for Hayden what we must struggle to extricate ourselves from, despite the pain it may cause us.

The consideration of the way Hayden uses struggle in his poetry must finally rest upon his tragicomic view of life. In "'Lear is Gay'" Hayden, recalling Yeats' "Lapis Lazuli," praises that gaiety found in an old man who "can laugh sometimes as at a scarecrow whose hobo shoulders are a-twitch with crows" (70). Dedicated to his friend Betsy Graves Reyneau, the poem expresses admiration for someone whose attitude towards irrevocable defeat is tempered with gaiety. The defeat may be the physical deterioration of the body as one is metamorphosed into a "tattered coat upon a stick," to draw a relevant image from Yeats. Or, generally speaking, it may be anything that is reduced to ineffectuality, which Hayden captures precisely in his image of the scarecrow that can no longer scare a crow.

For Hayden, to be able to laugh at the ravages of time is an achievement of the human spirit secure in the knowledge that everything alters even as we behold it. Thus as the jilted lover and the soul-weary people behold the singer in "Homage to the Empress of the Blues," their sorrow is transformed by the power of her song. She not only "flashed her golden smile," lustrous and radiant, but "shone that smile on us and sang" (104). The light of the stars, their tension in delicate balance, is thereby reflected as she sings the blues. Her song thus embodies Hayden's imagery of the stars, his theme of struggle and his use of paradox, bearing eloquent testimony to Hayden's artistry as well as to her own.

NOTES

1. Robert Hayden, *Angle of Ascent* (New York: Liveright, 1975), p. 47. All subsequent references to his poems will be indicated by the relevant page number of this edition.

2. John O'Brien, ed., *Interviews with Black Writers* (New York: Liveright, 1973), p. 13.

3. Donald Stauffer, *The Golden Nightingale* (New York: Macmillan, 1949).

4. The Baha'i faith was founded in the nineteenth century by Baha'u'llah, a member of the Iranian nobility. His message, first heralded by the Bab in 1844, met with strong opposition from the start. As a result, Baha'u'llah spent much of his life in prison (See Gloria Faizi, *The Baha'i Faith: An Introduction*, 1971). Among the central tenets of this religion are the belief in one God, the unity of mankind, sexual and racial equality, universal compulsory education and a universal auxiliary language. The religion has no formal creed and no ordained clergy. Its sacred writings are the one-hundred volumes written by Baha'u'llah.

5. A.Q. Faizi, *Explanation of the Symbol of the Greatest Name* (New Delhi: Baha'i Publishing Trust, n.d.), p. 18.

6. This interpretation may be justified since each interior side of the temple in Wilmette has inscribed upon it a symbol of one of the nine major world religions.

7. Hayden relied upon two sources for his material in this poem. The first is Nat Turner's reputed confessions, reprinted in Herbert Apteker's *Nat Turner's Slave Rebellion* (New York: Grove, 1966), p. 127 ff. The second is the Book of Ezekiel, attributed to a Hebrew prophet by that name who lived in the sixth century, B.C.E. Living in the exiled Jewish community in Babylon, he had predicted the fall of Jerusalem, just as Nat Turner predicted the fall of Jerusalem, Virginia, against which he led the revolt in 1831.

LEWIS TURCO

Angle of Ascent: *The Poetry of Robert Hayden*

For many years Robert Hayden has been writing a seminal and protean poetry. Of his books, *Heart-Shape in the Dust* appeared in 1940; *The Lion and the Archer*, with Myron O'Higgins, was published eight years later, in 1948. Only one collection appeared during the next decade, *Figures of Time*, in 1955. Two collections were issued during the 1960's—*A Ballad of Remembrance*, London, 1962, and *Selected Poems*, 1966. *Words in the Mourning Time: Poems* was published in 1970, and *The Night-Blooming Cereus*, again in London, in 1972.

Julius Lester, reviewing *Words in the Mourning Time* for *The New York Times Book Review*, wrote that Robert Hayden was "one of the most underrated and unrecognized poets in America." Until the publication of Hayden's most recent volume, *Angle of Ascent: New and Selected Poems* (New York: Liveright, 1975), this was true. Various reasons might be given to account for this fact, among them foreign publication of two volumes and small press publication of others, with the attendant problems of limited distribution.

Robert Hayden has better insight into the situation, however. In a videotaped interview which he made for the "Writers' Forum" series at the State University of New York College at Brockport, Hayden was asked about "Black poetry." His response was that such a term, which has the approval of

From *Michigan Quarterly Review* 16, no. 2 (Spring 1977).

many militant black poets, was useful to white academics who wish to ignore poetry written by blacks. Hayden contended that most "Black poetry" was and still is relegated to courses in "Black Literature" and is not often taught in the standard English literature syllabus. The inference to be made is that somehow there are special standards to be applied, standards that need not be applied to "White Poetry" for one reason or another. Clearly, one of the implications here is that poetry written by blacks is not good enough, or not universal enough to be included in the Anglo-Saxon literary canon.

Hayden's poetry had been ghettoized along with the work of the other "Black poets." For proof that this situation remains true, one need merely look to the magazines that have so far reviewed *Angle of Ascent* and notice that most, if not all of them, have felt that the book had to be reviewed by another black.

But Robert Hayden has always wished to be judged as a poet among poets, not one to whom special rules of criticism ought to be applied in order to make his work acceptable in more than a sociological sense. His stance, reiterated in the Brockport interview, has been well known for a long time both to militant blacks and to "liberal" whites. Thus, if the latter have relegated Hayden to the literary ghetto along with the other Black poets, the former have seen him, if not as an "Uncle Tom," at least as a reluctant resident. Perhaps this situation will best explain why Hayden has been ignored.

Yet Hayden has written as much out of his ethnic background as has anyone else. In order to prove this, I intend to examine his work in the light of Stephen Henderson's codification of what constitutes "Black poetry" as distinguished from "White poetry." At the same time I will refute Henderson's arguments that there are such things as ethnic "techniques." I propose to show that, in fact, Henderson's "techniques" are elements of ethnic black styles, and that Hayden, having written in many of these styles, is a paradigmatic poet of the English language who has been true to his roots and history, though not circumscribed by, or limited to, what is merely racial, ethnic, or personal.

In his long scholarly introduction to the anthology *Understanding the New Black Poetry* (Morrow, 1973), Stephen Henderson goes deeply into, as the publisher's jacket blurb puts it, "what is black technique in the poetry." Henderson believes that large questions about the value of Black poetry "cannot be resolved without considering the ethnic roots of Black poetry, which ... are ultimately understood only by Black people themselves."

I am inclined to agree, as long as it is "ethnic roots" we're talking about. I'd go further: A poem may be so heavily ethnical that most who do not belong to the group could not understand, let alone judge, such a poem.

I am well aware that "language is the main cohesive force within a given ethnic group," as Arthur Koestler has pointed out, "but, at the same time, it creates barriers and acts as a repellent force between groups." It is quite possible for Black writers to use English in such ways as to speak directly to a Black audience while, at the same time, the white audience is held at bay. This is done by manipulation of techniques and development of Black styles, *not* by using particular techniques labeled "Black" as distinguished from others labeled "White."

The language techniques used in such poems would be analyzable, and those same techniques would appear in many other kinds of poetry.

Henderson says,

> Although it is an arbitrary scheme for the purpose of analysis, one may describe or discuss a "Black" poem in terms of the following broad critical categories: (1) Theme, (2) Structure, (3) Saturation.
>
> (1) By *theme* I mean that which is being spoken of, whether the specific subject matter, the emotional response to it, or its intellectual formulation.
>
> (2) By *structure* I mean chiefly some aspect of the poem such as diction, rhythm, figurative language, which goes into the total make-up. (At times, I use the word in an extended sense to include what is usually called genre.)
>
> (3) By *saturation* I mean several things, chiefly the communication of "Blackness" and fidelity to the observed or intuited truth of the Black Experience in the United States. It follows that these categories should also be valid in any critical evaluation of the poem.

I have no quarrel with the first and third of these categories, nor even with the parenthetical material in the second category. There are obviously many specifically Black themes possible—Hayden uses many. But writers of other ethnic groups could, if they wished, write on these themes as well, and many have done so. Certainly, there are genres, or *kinds* of Black writing. With regard to "saturation": It is equally obvious that poetry can be heavily saturated with Black ethnic referents; again, Hayden refers very often to such things, though nearly always in such a way that the general reader of whatever background will understand.

But I call into question many of Henderson's remarks about Black techniques under his heading of "Structure." I'd like to discuss each of his subheadings, the first of which is,

A. "Virtuoso naming and enumerating." Though Henderson doesn't say so in so many words, he implies that this is a specifically Black technique, the roots of which "might conceivably lie in the folk practice of riddling and similar kinds of wordplay." As an example, Henderson recommends Ted Joans' "The Nice Colored Man," a portion of which reads,

> Nice Nigger Educated Nigger Never Nigger Southern Nigger
> Clever Nigger Northern Nigger Nasty Nigger Unforgivable
> Nigger Unforgettable Nigger Unspeakable Nigger Rude &
> Uncouth Nigger Mean & Vicious Nigger Smart Black Nigger
> Smart Black Nigger Smart Black Nigger Smart Black Nigger
> Smart Black Nigger ....

Henderson is correct in his derivation from folk literature, but not in his implication that the folk are Black in particular. Here is #749 from the Baring-Goulds' *The Annotated Mother Goose:*

> There was a man, and his name was Dob,
> And he had a wife, and her name was Mob,
> And he had a dog, and he called it Cob,
> And she had a cat, called Chitterabob,
>   Cob, says Dob,
> Chitterabob, says Mob,
>   Cob was Dob's dog,
> Chitterabob Mob's cat.

This nursery rhyme, however, is of later derivation than the 16th-century English poet John Skelton's "Ware the Hawk," a portion of which reads,

> Of no tyrant I read
> That so far did exceed,
> Neither Diocletian,
> Nor yet Domitian,
> Nor yet crooked Cacus,
> Nor yet drunken Bacchus;
> Neither Olibrius,
> Nor Dionysius,
> Neither Phalary
> Rehearsed in Valery;
> Nor Sardanapall ....,

and so on. One might cite other examples, including Whitman, but my intent is not to do an exhaustive study of such techniques—merely to show that these are techniques of the English language, not of a particular ethnic group. The standard term for this technique is "cataloging," and it is in this particular poem of Joans' also a form of repetition, particularly incremental repetition. Robert Hayden is no stranger to the technique since he begins *Angle of Ascent* with a set of poems titled "Beginnings," the first section of which reads,

> Plowdens, Finns,
> Sheffeys, Haydens,
> Westerfields.
> Pennslyvania gothic,
> Kentucky homespun,
> Virginia baroque.

Hayden uses cataloging to particularly beautiful effect in "Theme and Variation," a poem of two parts and four stanzas, the first of which reads, "Fossil, fuschia, mantis, man,/fire and water, earth and air—/all things alter even as I behold,/all things alter, the stranger said."

B. "Jazzy rhythmic effects." Henderson is vague about this technique. He says, "Compare these lines from LeRoi Jones' 'T. T. Jackson Sings' with the traditional dozens lines which are printed just below them.

> I fucked your mother
> On top of a house
> When I got through
> She thought she was
> Mickey Mouse

> * * * *

> I fucked your mother from house to house
> Out came a baby named Minnie Mouse."

Both verses are written in the prosody called "dipodics," which is a derivation from Anglo-Saxon prosody. It is notably the "folk" prosody of nursery rhymes, ballads, and riddles—both the nursery rhyme and the Skelton piece I quoted earlier are dipodic. Here is a verse whose rhythms are very close to those of the first example:

There was a woman
Got laid in a shoe
She said, "Chillun,
Don't never do
What I do."

The original, of course, was,

There was an old woman who lived in a shoe.
She had so many children, she didn't know what to do.

Hayden modulates podic rhythms in Part V of "Beginnings," "(The Crystal Cave Elegy)"—"Floyd Collins oh/I guess he's a goner,/Pa Hayden sighed,/the Extra trembling/in his hands." If the rhythms are "jazzy," they are as old as the English Language.

Stephen Henderson's other examples are very different, mostly prose poems, some of them rhymed. It's difficult to see what these various techniques have in common; they go by different names in prosodic terminology. One might mention that Poe's "The Bells" has been discussed in the 20th century as a "jazz poem" written before jazz had been invented.

Henderson mentions "blues" as a quality of jazz in the poems he cites. Perhaps we can put off till later the question of Black musical forms as bases for Black "techniques."

C. "Virtuoso free-rhyming." Henderson says in effect that these examples typify a Black tradition:

I don't want nothin' old but some gold;
I don't want nothin' black but a Cadillac!

I can't eat a bite, I can't sleep at night,
'Cause the woman I love don't treat me right.

They call me Rap the dicker the ass kicker
The cherry picker and city slicker the titty licker ....

There may be in these fragments identifiably Black "themes" and "saturations," but no race or ethnic group has a corner on the "free rhyming" or internal rhyme markets—nor, for that matter, on scatology. Here is Skelton again, in "The Tunning of Elinor Rumming":

With a whim-wham
Knit with a trim-tram
Upon her brain-pan
Like an Egyptian . . .

* * * *

But let us turn plain,
There we left again.
For, as ill a patch as that,
The hens run in the mash-vat;
For they go to roost
Straight over the ale-joust,
And dung, when it comes,
In the ale-tunnes.

And here is another nursery rhyme, #751:

I need not your needles, they're needless to me,
  For kneading of needles is needless, you see,
But did my neat trousers but need to be kneed,
  I then should have need of your needles indeed.

Finally, here's a piece from Robert Burns' "The Kirk's Alarm":

Dr. Mac, Dr. Mac, you should stretch on a rack,
  To strike evil-doers wi' terror;
To join faith and sense upon onie pretence,
  Is heretic, damnable error.

Burns' poem is, indeed, ethnic, but ethnic Scots.

Robert Hayden is not in any way scatological, as Burns and Skelton and the Black fragments cited can be, but I am not at all sure that that is a criticism. Neither is he much interested in rhyming, particularly bumptious rhyming. The closest he comes, perhaps, is in "Incense of the Lucky Virgin" where some consonance is used instead of rhyme, and each stanza uses an incremental repetion as a sort of substitute for rhyme.

D. "Hyperbolic imagery." Henderson says, "The breathless virtuoso quality of free-rhyming comes from the utilization of a single rhyme sound, the object being to get in as many rhymes as one can." Though he doesn't intend it, Henderson's is about as good a definition of Skelton's dipodic method as one could wish—a method called after its inventor, *Skeltonics*, or "tumbling verse." "Oratorically," Henderson continues, "this is balanced by a passage in which there is no rhyme at all, and the wit and the energy expend themselves in a series of hyperbolic wisecracks, rooted in the tradition of masculine boasting."

He gives an example from the folk tradition:

> I'm the man who walked the water and tied the whale's
> tail in a knot
> Taught the little fishes how to swim
> Crossed the burning sands and shook the devil's hand
> Rode round the world on the back of a snail carrying
> a sack saying AIR MAIL

There's nothing new about the "brag"—the Anglo-Saxon poets understood it as a basic convention in the Middle Ages. It should go without saying that "hyperbole" is an ancient Greek term, and this type of stylized American hyperbole is called "the backwoods boast" by folklorists. It was a feature of the westward movement of the 19th century. Hayden is acquainted with the tradition and uses it in "Witch Doctor"—"He's/God's dictaphone of all-redeeming truth./Oh he's the holyweight champeen who's come/to give the knockout lick to your bad luck;/say he's the holyweight champeen who's here/to deal a knockout punch to your hard luck."

E. "Metaphysical imagery." In speaking of this category, Henderson mentions its uses in English literature. He does not, evidently, mean to make a case for this technique's being particularly "Black." Hayden often uses the conceit, the extended metaphor. A striking example is his well-known "Zeus Over Redeye" in which the classical names applied to rockets are compared with the gods of mythology who were the weapons' archetypes.

F. Henderson polishes off "understatement" or *litotes* in four lines without making racial claims for it. Used in the proper circumstances, this universal technique can be one of the most effective in the poet's toolbox. Robert Hayden has written one of the most touching contemporary poems utilizing litotes, "Those Winter Sundays," one of his best-known poems also:

> Sundays too my father got up early
> and put his clothes on in the blueblack cold,
> then with cracked hands that ached

from labor in the weekday weather made
banked fires blaze. No one ever thanked him.

I'd wake and hear the cold splintering, breaking.
When the rooms were warm, he'd call,
and slowly I would rise and dress,
feeling the chronic angers of that house,

Speaking indifferently to him,
who had driven out the cold
and polished my good shoes as well.
What did I know, what did I know
of love's austere and lonely offices?

G. "Compressed and cryptic imagery." Henderson here is as cryptic as his sub-heading. The example he gives is a brag from Ellison's *The Invisible Man*. No definition is offered beyond "arcane references to what I have called 'mascon' imagery ..." I will discuss *masconception* later. Meanwhile, Henderson makes no claims that Black poets can be more obscure than other kinds of poets. Hayden, too, has his obscure moments—he has been called by others a "Symbolist," and some of his more recent poems, such as "Stars," Part II, which appears to have a relation to Hayden's Bahá'í theology, can be baffling:

Betelgeuse Aldebaran

Abstract as future yesterdays
   the starlight
crosses eons of meta-space
   to us.

   Algol Arcturus Almaak

How shall the mind keep warm
   save at spectral
fires—how thrive but by the light
   of paradox?

   Altair Vega Polaris Maia

H. "Worrying the line." Henderson says, "This is the folk expression for the device of altering the pitch of a note in a given passage or for other kinds of ornamentation often associated with melismatic singing in the Black tradition. A verbal parallel exists in which a word or phrase is broken in order to allow for affective or didactic comment. Here is an example from Rich Amerson's 'Black Woman':

Say, I feel superstitious, Mamma
'Bout my hoggin' bread, Lord help my hungry time,
I feel superstitious, Baby, 'bout my hoggin' bread!
Ah-hmmm, Baby, I feel superstitious,
I say 'stitious, Black Woman!
Ah-hmmm, ah you hear me cryin'
About I done got hungry, oh Lordy!
Oh, Mamma, I feel superstitious
About my hog Lord God it's my bread."

"Melismatic" means, according to the Oxford dictionary, "The art of florid or ornate vocalization." Henderson makes much, later on, of musical comparisons between Black poetry and Black music. The language techniques illustrated by the Amerson passage Henderson quotes are such things as parallelism, incremental repetition, orthographical schemas—elision and apocopation primarily. That Amerson's poem is written in a Black style and tradition is not open to question, but one can find hundreds of examples of the same *techniques* in English poetry from all periods. Hayden, in the ending of "Runagate Runagate," uses them:

Armed and known to be Dengerous

Wanted Reward Dead or Alive

Tell me, Ezekiel, oh tell me do you see
mailed Jehovah coming to deliver me?

Hoot-owl calling in the ghosted air,
five times calling to the hants in the air.
Shadow of a face in the scary leaves,
shadow of a voice in the talking leaves:

Come ride-a my train

Oh that train, ghost-story train
through swamp and savanna movering movering,
over trestles of dew, through caves of the wish,
Midnight Special on a sabre track movering movering,
first stop Mercy and the last Hallelujah.

Come ride-a my train

Mean mean mean to be free.

At this point in his essay Henderson defines his neologism "mascon": "a massive concentration of Black experiential energy." If we look at the poems just cited, by Amerson and Hayden, we must see that they are clearly Black poems. But it is not the techniques that make them Black—*it is how the techniques are applied.* There is "mascon" in the poems, but the "massive concentration of Black experiential energy" is a function of *style*, not structure.

I don't believe anyone could have faulted Henderson if he had called the second of his three major critical categories "Style" rather than "Structure" or, better, "Styles"—there is more than one Black style of writing, as Henderson recognizes; Hayden is a master of several. But Henderson's insisting on identifying particular English language techniques as being somehow "Black" confuses the issue, as for instance when he speaks about "the Black oratorical technique of repetition."

The oldest prosody in the world—and it is universal—is grammatic parallelism, which includes the device of repetition. It is to be found in prose poetry as well as in verse poetry—the Bible is full of it, and Henderson gives an example from Martin Luther King's "I Have a Dream" speech. Where does Henderson imagine that the Rev. Dr. King got his oratorical style if not from the King James Bible? That King's adaptation of this prosodic system gives rise to an identifiably Black traditional style is also apparent.

Curiously enough, though Hayden uses parallelism often, I can find no poem in *Angle of Ascent*, except possibly "Witch Doctor," previously cited, that imitates the style of the Negro sermon, though there are references to preachers, as to King himself in "Words in the Mourning Time." This poem, though, is about the Kennedys as well. Hayden has written not only about Christianity, but also about Judaism, Bahá'í, and Mohammedanism.

Included in the section on "Structure" in Henderson's essay is a subsection titled "Black Music as Poetic Reference." Henderson says,

> Aside from mascon structure, there are other important ways in which music, Black music, lies at the basis of much Black poetry, either consciously or covertly. I have been able to distinguish at least ten types of usage ...

That poetry and music have always been closely associated in all traditions is a truism. Here Henderson is speaking about Black music and poetry:

"In No. 1, *the casual, generalized reference*, there are mere suggestions of Black song types." In Henderson's examples there are mentions of "everlasting song," "Caroling softly souls of slavery," "blues," "jazz," "slave songs," "jubilees" and more generalized musical references. He makes no claim that general reference is a particularly Black technique. Like many other poets of all nations, languages, and times, Hayden uses such allusions in many poems including "A Ballad of Remembrance," "The Dream," and "Beginnings," Part IV.

"In No. 2, there is a careful allusion to song titles." "For a reader familiar with these songs, the titles evoke a more particularized response, and the effect thus borders on the 'subjective correlative' alluded to in type seven." By "subjective correlative" Henderson evidently means an emotional response cued by, in this case, a Black song title. Particular songs and singers carry loads of cultural and ethnic associations and overtones for American Blacks. Plainly, though, the technique of allusion is not racial. I will discuss the "subjective correlative" when we come to item No. 7.

In No. 3, "*Quotations from a song* are incorporated into the poem." My comments regarding "No. 2," above, apply.

No. 4 is "Adaptations of song forms," which "include blues, ballads, hymns, children's songs, work songs, spirituals, and popular songs." Henderson says that in particular the ballad, the hymn, and the blues are "numerous and easily recognizable...." He continues, "The first two have numerous parallels in other literary traditions. But the blues as a literary form was developed and refined by Langston Hughes and later by Sterling Brown, though Hughes clearly overstated his case for the fixity of the blues form in his preface to *Fine Clothes for the Jew.*"

There is a difference between "technique" and "form." Techniques are universal within a language—often, just plain universal, but specific forms may develop in any culture or social heritage. I am willing to grant Henderson his claim that the blues and jazz are specifically Black American *forms*, despite Poe's "The Bells" and Browning's "A Toccata of Galuppi's."

Henderson mentions the "'classic' twelve-bar, three line form" of the blues, as in Eddie "Son" House's Dry Spell Blues":

The dry spell blues have fallen, drove me from door to door.
Dry spell blues have fallen, drove me from door to door.
The dry spell blues have put everybody on the killing floor.

Now the people down south sure won't have no home.
Now the people down south sure won't have no home
'Cause the dry spell have parched all this cotton and corn.

And so forth. Here is a portion of the Browning poem:

Here you come with your old music, and here's all the
good it brings.
What, they lived once thus at Venice where the merchants
were the kings,
Where Saint Mark's is, where the Doges used to wed the
sea with rings.

The rhythms and rhymes are the same. The only thing missing from the Browning poem is the formal repetition. The main point is that, though the *forms* differ slightly, the *techniques* are the same. The *styles* are completely different.

That Hayden has been influenced by the "song forms" Henderson mentions is quite obvious. It is equally obvious that many other poets have been likewise so influenced. But Hayden is usually not content merely to be influenced by a form, he transforms it into something uniquely his. Though "The Ballad of Nat Turner," for instance, looks typographically like a traditional ballad, and might even fool the casual reader into thinking that it is one, in fact it does not rhyme as most ballads do, it consonates; and, though repetition is sometimes used as a substitute for rhyme, there is no ballad refrain. Some stanzas do not even consonate or have repetition, yet the whole poem has the effect of a unified narrative song. This is a masterful wedding of tradition with personal style.

"Device No. 5 is the practice, with considerable variety, of *forcing the reader to incorporate into the structure of the poem his memory of a specific song or passage of a song, or even of a specific delivery technique.* Without this specific memory the poem cannot be properly realized." Evidently, this particular Black technique depends heavily either on a shared live experience, or on the reader's having a phonograph record of a particular Black musician.

Henderson expends a great deal of energy in elaborating on this "device" of "arcane" allusion (the quoted words are his), ranging from Percy Johnson's "Number Five Cooper Square"

I remember Clifford tossing
Bubbles, Scit! Whoom!, from an
Ante-bellum moon. Scit! And
Killer Joe's golden chain, Scit!
While Ornette gives a lecture on
A Sanscrit theme with Bachian
footnotes, scit.....

—to "Don Lee's famous poem 'Don't Cry, Scream'" which contains "the stylized [n.b.] *visual* representation ... 'sing/loud &/high/with/feeling' and 'sing/loud &/long/with feeling'" to "the *stylized* [my italics] rendition of the Coltrane sound"

i can see my me, it was truth you gave,
like a daily shit
it had to come.

can you scream———brother? very
can you scream———brother? soft

i hear you.
i hear you.

and the Gods will too.

The 20th century British poet Dame Edith Sitwell has done similar things in "Polka" from *Facade:*

'... As they watch me dance the polka,'
Said Mr. Wagg like a bear,
'In my top hat and my whiskers that
Tra la la la, trap the Fair.

Tra la la la la
Tra la la la la
Tra la la la la la la la
La
La
La!'

Henderson speaks about references to Black music forms, performers, and performances, but one can use this technique to refer to any sort of music that may be familiar to an audience, as W. S. Gilbert did in *H. M. S. Pinafore:*

When the foeman bares his steel,
                Tarantara! tarantara!
We uncomfortable feel,
                Tarantara!
And we find the wisest thing,
                Tarantara! tarantara!
Is to slap our chests and sing
                Tarantara!
For when threatened with emeutes,
                Tarantara! tarantara!
And your heart is in your boots,
                Tarantara!
There is nothing brings it round,
                Tarantara! tarantara!
Like the trumpet's martial sound,
                Tarantara! tarantara!
Tarantara-ra-ra-ra-ra!

In the 18th century Christopher Smart wrote a poem that is practically a treatise on this sort of thing, and rather than quote it here I recommend it to the reader as an interesting glimpse into the nature of the language. Its title is "Of the Spiritual Musick,"—lest that turn anyone away, let me add that it is a prose poem. Robert Hayden uses many of these so-called techniques in such poems as "Soledad" and "Homage to the Empress of the Blues," from which I quote the first stanza:

Because there was a man somewhere in a candystripe
                                silk shirt,
gracile and dangerous as a jaguar and because a
                                woman moaned
for him in sixty-watt gloom and mourned him Faithless Love
Twotiming Love Oh Love Oh Careless Aggravating Love,

and so forth. Hayden's intent here, however, is not to appeal to one ethnic minority above another, but to build a context for such allusions which enables any reader to understand the situation and emotion of the narrator.

"In the sixth kind of musical referent," Henderson continues, "*precise musical notation is incorporated into the text of the poem.*" It seems to me that this device goes back as far as the invention of musical notation. Certainly, texts have always been written for music and vice-versa. William Walton wrote music for Sitwell's *Facade*, and there is a recording of her reading the poems to his music—not singing them, *reading* them. Thomas Campion published his first *Book of Ayres* in 1601 and a treatise on *Counter-Point* later on. The connection of music with poetry is ancient and continuing—Sidney Lanier, the poet-musician, had a theory of the "symphonic poem" in the 19th century. At any rate, Robert Hayden does not use this device, evidently preferring his language music to stand on its own on the printed page.

"In device number seven, the reader's *emotional response to a well-known song is incorporated into the poem* in a manner resembling the use of a 'rest' in music or an assumed 'obbligato.'" I shall let Henderson's use of traditional musical terms speak for itself. This is merely an elaboration of devices nos. 2-5, with the addition that a cue-word or phrase is used as a refrain, as in the example he gives from Robert Terrell's "Asian Stew," with its play on the word "jelly."

> Wit rice-n-mud-n-bamboo shoots
> Wit sizzled hairs-n-human eclairs
> Wit shrapnel-n-goodwill-n-jelly
> jelly jelly

In "O Daedalus, Fly Away Home" Robert Hayden uses such words as "juba" and "conjo" in similar ways, building a beautiful and, simultaneously, sad song of loss beginning,

> Drifting night in the Georgia pines,
> coonskin drum and jubilee banjo.
>   Pretty Malinda, dance with me.
>
> Night is juba, night is conjo.
>   Pretty Malinda, dance with me.

The poem turns to the thought of "home"—Africa, and of death as a release from longing for rest, ending with

> Night is a mourning juju man

weaving a wish and a weariness together
  to make two wings.

O fly away home fly away

No poet I know of is so capable of couching the American Black's experience and situation, emotion and ambience in language that is accessible to everyone.

Henderson says in this regard, "Since the reference is to a state of mind or feeling instead of to an object or structure, the technique could be called the use of the 'subjective correlative,' in contrast to the 'objective correlative' of the New Criticism."

"Subjective correlative" is an impressive term for "cue" or "cue-word." Such words are intended as automatic triggers for a culturally conditioned emotional response. The technique is no different in kind from the use of the words "apple pie," "motherhood," or "Old Glory" in a political speech. It is not particularly a poetic device but a rhetorical one. It is, in fact, rather anti-poetic in that it requires little skill on the part of the writer—all he needs is to be tapped into the ethos of his audience in order to find the particular word that will set off the response he wants. The question, then, is whether the poet will settle for the effect of the word alone or, like Hayden, build a context for it which provides the alien reader with points of reference which will allow him to understand some of the overtones with which the cues are laden. Hayden does the latter in poem after poem—he cares about the reader, whoever he may be, for Hayden knows that, though there are many forms of humanity, they are all, finally, human and capable of communication. It is the writer's job to help people to understand one another.

In the eighth of Henderson's "devices," "The musician himself functions as subject, poem, history, or myth...." This technique is the same in all cultures: reference to a culture hero of some sort. That in this case the referent is a musician is a very slight reason for the critic's listing it here.

Device No. 9 is "Language from the jazz life or associated with it, commonly called 'hip' speech." There is nothing new about dialect poetry, nor even slang poetry. One of Hayden's finest poems is full of 19th-century Negro southern dialect: "The Dream" alternates narration regarding a character named Sinda with Black letters from the Civil War front. It is the most effective dialect poem I have ever read, though Hayden claims that many people have misinterpreted it. This puzzles me, and the only reason I can think of for it is that the unexpected person dies.

I cannot think why Henderson lists this "device," for the only excuse conceivable seems to be that "hip" talk uses a number of jazz musical terms, and Henderson seems intent upon distinguishing jazz, for cultural reasons, from other forms of music. But where does that leave the other Black musical forms he listed earlier—the spirituals and so forth?

Henderson writes, "In the tenth category, *the poem as 'score' or 'chart,'* we move to the most challenging aspect of Black poetic structure [n.b.: He is still saying "structure," not "style" or "tradition"]—the question of limit, or performance of the text...." Later Henderson writes,

> A poem may thus differ from performance to performance just as jazz performances of "My Favorite Things" would. Moreover, it implies that there is a Black poetic mechanism, much like the musical ones, which can transform even a Shakespearian sonnet into a jazz poem, the basic conceptual model of contemporary Black poetry. The technique, the fundamental device, would be improvisation, lying as it does at the very heart of jazz music.

Neither in music nor in poetry is improvisation in any way linked merely to jazz or to a specific ethnic group. The Anglo-Saxon knights were expected to be able to compose extemporaneous verse brags in the mead-hall after a battle, and the official bards had to be ready on command to compose in public a poem on any subject, with musical accompaniment. None of these compositions was written down until much later, if ever. The "scores" existed only in the oral tradition.

The Arabic *qasida* is a form dating from prehistoric times, and its essence is improvisation. The technique as it is described in Preminger's *Encyclopedia of Poetry and Poetics* (Princeton, 1965, p. 43) is a model for the composition of poetry in many ancient societies, including that of the English:

> Only by considering how poetry is composed in Arabic can the evolution of the qasidah be reconstructed. It its simplest form, verse is composed extempore, sung to some traditional tune, in one *bait* at a time; it is then taken up by the company, sung to rhythmical movement and hand clapping. Until the poet warms to his work he casts about among the many traditional themes in his conscious and subconscious memory—which doubtless explains the qasidah sequence and the recurrent clichés of both classical and colloquial versification, for in Arabia mere originality for its own sake is not sought. When visited by

> Inspiration—which the Arabs conceive as supernatural, a species of demon—the poet now turns to the theme he wishes to treat.

One of the purposes of Henderson's book, evidently, is to provide young Black poets with an arsenal of weapons to use in writing poetry that is acceptably ethnic. But I am sure that Robert Hayden would feel that it is important also that young poets understand the differences between "styles" and "techniques." A style is something that develops with skill, experience, and personality; technique, on the other hand, can be studied and learned. To confuse the two things, as Henderson does and as Hayden obviously does not, is to do a disservice to developing poets by making something racial of the elements—I should say *some* of the elements—of the English language.

If young Black poets believe there are "Black" techniques and "white" techniques, it is likely that they will turn away from the conscious development of skills in the language they must use and turn instead to imitations of approved styles already developed and patented by their predecessors and elders. If such a situation develops, the danger exists that there will be a generation of Black writers who are imitators rather than poets. Hayden, being a teacher, is well aware of this, and he argues against the ghettoizing of poetry in the classroom and, by superb example, in his poetry.

Blake said in the first "Preface" to his *Jerusalem*,

> Poetry fettered, fetters the human race. Nations are destroyed or flourish in proportion as their poetry, painting, and music are destroyed or flourish. The primeval state of man was wisdom, art, and science.

There are wisdom, art, and the science of language in the poetry of Robert Hayden. His work is unfettered in many ways, not the least of which is in the range of technique available to him. It gives his imagination wings, allows him to travel throughout human nature. Yet he is in no way untrue to his personal heritage, nor to the heritage of American blacks. His style is Protean, capable of change and growth as he develops from book to book, poem to poem. If his work has been overlooked in the past, it has been for the smallest of reasons; it is because he has been willing to be neither a propagandist nor a dweller in a literary ghetto. He has preferred to be a poet.

FRED M. FETROW

"Middle Passage": Robert Hayden's Anti-Epic

Now that Robert Hayden's "Middle Passage" has been widely reprinted and included in his recently published *Angle of Ascent* (1975), one would expect the poem to attract more critical attention than it has thus far.[1] Much of the commentary on "Middle Passage" has been limited to passing remarks in discussions of black poetry in general. This kind of "criticism" ranges from mere mention of the title, through lengthy quotations with no analysis, to a brief sentence or paragraph or two in explanation of the poem's chief features.[2] A few scholars have dealt with the poem in ways to illustrate aspects of Hayden's themes or techniques, but to date there exists no sustained analysis of this intriguing montage of narrative voices.[3] Aside from the poem's most striking feature, a virtuoso performance in narrative mode, "Middle Passage" is especially challenging for its resistance to generic classification.

Robert Hayden himself remains rather ambivalent on this point. While he is explicit about his original plan for the poem, he cites a sudden inspiration as the source of his ultimate format. During an interview conducted in 1972, Hayden described in detail the evolution of "Middle Passage."[4] He alluded to Stephen Vincent Benét's *John Brown's Body* (1927) and his own ambition to write an epic poem about slavery and the Civil War from the black man's point of view. Hayden quotes Benét in voicing this aspiration:

From *CLA Journal* 22, no. 4 (June 1979). © 1979 by the College Language Association.

> Well, specifically, I became interested in writing it ["Middle Passage"] largely as a result of reading Stephen Vincent Benet's *John Brown's Body.* There's a passage in which he says, "O, black-skinned epic, epic with the long black spear, I cannot sing you now, having too white a heart." And he goes on to say that someday a poet will rise to sing of the black spear. I dared to hope that I might be that poet.[5]

Hayden began researching the materials for the poem as early as the late 1930s, but did not discover his mode of expression until a few years later:

> I had a great deal of material, I'd taken many notes, I had gathered all the facts I needed, but I couldn't work out a form, a pattern. Actually, I had tried writing the poem in blank verse—unrhymed iambic pentameter—but then, it was too much like Benet, not only in form, but in diction and narrative organization also .... I continued to work intermittently on the slave trade poem during the next year or so, and gradually a form began to suggest itself .... I recall that at four o'clock one morning I suddenly saw how I could fit all the pieces together. I became aware of the fact that there were different voices in the poem, and this helped me to divide it into sections and achieve design and dramatic progression.[6]

These remarks shed considerable light on the narrative structure of "Middle Passage," and certainly its content locates the work in an historical category, but Hayden's poem is clearly much more than diversely narrated history.

The poet's oblique reference to an epic intention warrants scrutiny in view of the poem's content, structure, tone, and theme, because in these aspects Hayden certainly seems in pursuit of an epic mode. "Middle Passage" bears all the tracings of an epic in miniature, but a close reading shows that it is an epic of a decidedly different sort. While the poem has practically all of the "standard" epic characteristics because the poet employs most of the epic conventions and devices, Hayden consistently and ironically inverts or alters these features. Through this inversion technique, he creates what could be called an "anti-epic," a form with which he achieves a coherent merger of formal technique and poetic theme.

The typical epic or heroic poem in the classical sense manifests several characteristics: the invocation of a muse or muses, the formal statement of theme, a narrative structure which begins *in medias res*, and characters of high position in a series of quest-like adventures which stress the historical or legendary importance of a central heroic figure to a particular nation or race.[7] The epic, as a classical genre, also frequently includes extended formal speeches by important characters, catalogues of warriors, ships or armies, epic or "Homeric" similes, an interest in mortal activities and sometimes direct intervention in these activities by supernatural deities or forces, and as part of the quest motif, an archetypal journey to the underworld or descent into hell.

Epic poets use these conventions and devices variously to glorify the heroes and subjects of their poems. Obviously, Robert Hayden does not intend to glorify his ostensible subject, the slave trade he depicts through the mixed narrative voices of "Middle Passage." Rather, his "anti-epic" approach enobles Cinquez, an "anti-hero" who represents his race, and is thus used by Hayden to celebrate the real subject of his poem—the heroic struggle for freedom by the black victims of "Middle Passage."[8]

Some of Hayden's ironic inversions of epic elements are rather direct and apparent; others are more subtle and have profound thematic implications, especially when contrasted with their "straight" counterparts. In the former vein, the poet does not open with a direct statement of the "surface" theme, but instead with a brief but appalling catalogue of ships: "*Jesus*, *Estrella*, *Esperanza*, *Mercy*."[9] These pleasant names and those that follow in line fourteen ("*Desire*, *Adventure*, *Tartar*, *Ann*") initiate the tone of cosmic irony which permeates the entire poem. Hayden deliberately selects historically factual Spanish and English names of real slave ships; since these names are typical, their use (not creation) by the poet emphasizes a situational irony that is as real as it is literary.[10] The poet / narrator, in subsequently describing these symbolic ships, points up this irony: "Their bright ironical names / like jests of kindness on a murderer's mouth" (96-97).

While the narrator opens the poem with an ironic catalogue rather than with a direct indication of theme, that formal statement follows shortly:

> Middle Passage:
> voyage through death
> to life upon these shores. (5–7)

The classic epic premise of a quest-journey is thus established, but in terms that are uniquely Hayden's. The poet uses "death" in a literal sense to counterpoint ironically the figurative use of "life." As his narrative account makes clear, "death" as part of the journey is no more horrible a prospect than the life to be "lived" after arrival. The transit through the Middle

Passage is a "voyage through death," but the life of slavery to be experienced by the survivors will be a living death, a death in life.

Hayden reinforces this thematic concept later in the poem through repetition of phrasing and by using imagery which fuses appearance and reality. In Part III, after the reference to the irony of the ships' names, the narrator describes their arrival. "These shores," mentioned in the formal statement of theme, are "seen" as the ships

> plough through thrashing glister toward
> fata morgana's lucent melting shore,
> weave toward New World littorals that are
> mirage and myth and actual shore. (98–101)

The poet captures with absolute accuracy of visual perspective the appearance of a distant shore to those aboard a ship approaching landfall, and uses that vision to extend the implications of the terse statement of theme. The shore, paradoxically perceived as both lucent and melting, is presented in terms of a sea mirage, the meteorological phenomenon known as "fata morgana." Through connotation and illusion, Hayden retrospectively suggests how largely mythical has been the notion of America as a "melting shore" where diverse races mix with mutual benefit. The allusion to Morgan le Fay compounds this idea as a mirage of evil source; perhaps the poet even intentionally includes the suggestion of "morganatic" as a reference to a royal marriage to one of unequal rank, where no share of regal wealth goes to the partner of lower rank.[11] Certainly, "life upon these shores" completes the coupling of master and slave, to the benefit of the former and the detriment of the latter. So this lucid descriptive imagery, like the catalogue of ships, elaborates the central theme with a counter-balancing of beauty and tragedy.

Just as Hayden uses attractive images to extend the grim aspects of his theme, so he transforms the epic simile, a device of aesthetic beauty in "true" epics, into something opposite in both form and function. Virtually every simile in "Middle Passage" is curt and brutal; here we have no extended, lavish comparisons where a secondary object is developed into an independent aesthetic image. Quite the contrary, these similes are as grotesque as they are brief, and are thus "anti-epic" in both senses. The sails of ships are "like weapons" (2); misfortune follows "like sharks" (32); ships' names are "like jests of kindness on a murderer's mouth" (97); hatred is "like a leper's claw" (114); slave rebellion is "swift as the puma's leap" (125); butchered bodies are thrown overboard "like so much jetsam" (146); men rove the sea "like phantoms" (150). Aside from the appropriateness of these comparisons in their respective contexts, aside from the cumulative effect of such imagery throughout the poem, the character and function of these similes indicate that Hayden consciously avoids extensive comparisons for the purpose of inverting the Homeric patterns.

Thus the poet includes, but inverts, denies or uses ironic substitutes for the typical epic conventions and devices. His treatment of the supernatural element further exemplifies his technique. The "gods" are present in the poem, but neither as fickle pagan deities with vested interests in human endeavor, nor as providential protectors in a "Christian" epic. Instead, Hayden confronts the reader with two alternate pseudo-supernatural influences: indifferent brute nature or pious, hypocritical Puritanism. The sharks who hungrily await the suicidal leaps of crazed slaves are also identified as the "tutelary gods" of the harassed or endangered slavers (12–13, 31–33). These gods "intervene" in that they provide a quick death to the suffering victims of the Middle Passage, and in that they ironically serve as guardians and instructors to those responsible for that suffering. These "grinning" gods accompany the ships in mockery of both slaves and slavers, and with their pointed presence in the poem, Hayden mocks the supernatural role in ordinary epics.

The Christian element in the poem also seethes with irony. The poet is quite clear about his intent here:

> Irony is a constant element through the poem. The reference to Christianity in this section, [Section I] the lines from the hymn, emphasize the irony of the Christian acceptance and justification of the slave trade as a means of bringing "heathen souls" to Christ.[12]

Hayden refers to a hymn entitled "Jesus, Savior, Pilot Me," parts of which he weaves between the narrative segments of Part I as an ironic refrain.[13] For example, lines from that hymn bracket the brief stanza which represents a prayer for God's blessing upon slave ships departing from New England for the west coast of Africa:

> Jesus Savior Pilot Me
> Over Life's Tempestuous Sea
> We pray that Thou wilt grant, O Lord,
> safe passage to our vessels bringing
> heathen souls unto Thy chastening.
> Jesus Savior (20–25)

By enclosing this three-line stanza with lines and phrases from the hymn, Hayden evokes an atmosphere where slave trading was rationalized as a missionary rather than as a commercial venture. The poet also sets off subsequent narrative passages with more phrases from the hymn ("Thou Who Walked on Galilee" [46], "Pilot Oh Pilot Me" [69]), thereby juxtaposing religious sentiments with details of horrible events and immoral carnage aboard slave ships, in order to emphasize the perverted application of Christian doctrine to human inhumanity. God exists neither as a source of hope for the enslaved nor as a divine "pilot" for seagoing Christians, but merely as an excuse to justify cruel exploitation of one group of human beings by another.[14]

Robert Hayden, while denying the presence of Christian love through his treatment of the supernatural, characteristically provides a thematic alternative with a metaphoric basis. The slave ships negotiate the Middle Passage with navigational aids quite in contrast to God's blessing. The "voyage through death" is a "voyage whose chartings are unlove" (102–103) where "horror is the corposant and compass rose" (4).[15] Hayden's term "unlove" is even stronger than "hatred" since "unlove" denotes a total absence of love or compassion. The narrator calls the slave ships "Shuttles in the rocking loom of history" (94), and as these "dark ships move" to weave the fabric of history, their courses are governed not by divine providence, but by inhumanity and horror.

Thus, in effect, God does not exist in "Middle Passage." In comparison with other epic structures, this omission is notable because the presence of God or gods in such poems often verifies the favored status of the central character or epic hero.[16] Indeed, only relatively late in Hayden's poem is the reader introduced to the central character, and then the poet presents the hero both belatedly and indirectly. Hayden's treatment of the conventional epic concern for the fate and accomplishments of a prominent national or racial hero is probably the most thematically significant of his "epic inversions." Cinquez, as an epic hero, demands special attention because with this character Robert Hayden posits the primary message of the poem. Although the manner of Cinquez's presentation and his social stature as an epic hero are unorthodox, this character emerges as the spiritual symbol of the suffering and aspirations of his race. Cinquez becomes a "deathless primaveral image"; his is a "life that trans-figures many lives"; his characterization one of epic dimension achieved through an anti-epic mode. Since the narrative premise of the epic as a distinct genre involves the telling of a story which accounts the exploits of a prominent and noble warrior, such stories usually introduce the hero early in the telling.[17] The "epic hero" of

"Middle Passage" is not introduced until line 138 of a poem 179 lines in length. In the remaining forty-two lines Hayden provides an account of Cinquez's "adventures," establishes the character as central to the narrative structure and theme of the poem, and climaxes the heroic portrayal by identifying Cinquez as the ultimate symbol of the timeless human desire for freedom, a theme of epic proportion. Equally striking are the techniques with which the poet indirectly, even ironically, asserts that theme.

As previously mentioned, epic structures frequently include extended formal speeches by the main characters. Cinquez has no speech at all. As an ironic substitute, one of the two Spanish survivors of the *Amistad* rebellion, in the context of a formal speech as a prosecution witness, characterizes Cinquez by condemning his actions in leading the uprising.[18] Totally the opposite of a typical epic narrator who recounts heroic deeds with objectivity, the Spaniard passionately damns the hero, yet unknowingly indicts himself and his kind. Because Hayden loads with situational irony practically every word the witness utters, the net result of his testimony is the edification of Cinquez. For example, the Spaniard's description of how the mutinous slaves "threw overboard the butchered bodies of / our men, true Christians all, like so much jetsam" (145–146), ironically echoes similar but reversed instances in earlier narrative passages. Compare his accusation with the language of the log entry in Section I, "Lost three this morning leaped with crazy laughter / to the waiting sharks, sang as they went under" (12-13), and with the diary-like account of an officer aboard a disease-stricken slave ship:

> A plague among
> our blacks—Ophthalmia: blindness—& we
> have jettisoned the blind to no avail. (34-36)

The "unspeakable misery" of the two Spanish captives, recalled by one of them (156), only recalls the "spoken" misery endured by thousands of slaves and detailed earlier by the narrator:

> A charnel stench, effluvium of living death
> spreads outward from the hold,
> where the living and the dead, the horribly dying,
> lie interlocked, lie foul with blood and excrement. (105-108)

The preceding passage implies that slavery is a form of moral contamination which spreads like a vapor to engulf the slavers. The Spanish witness unwittingly makes the same point as he perceives the paradox of American ideals of liberty being fostered by an economy based on slave labor:

> We find it paradoxical indeed
> that you whose wealth, whose tree of liberty
> are rooted in the labor of your slaves
> should suffer the august John Quincy Adams
> to speak with so much passion of the right
> of chattel slaves to kill their lawful masters
> and with his Roman rhetoric weave a hero's
> garland for Cinquez. (162-169)

Through the indignation of this "hostile" witness, Hayden reminds (or informs) the reader that the *Amistad* case was a cause worthy of the "august" John Quincy Adams, and that Adams argued for liberty by praising Cinquez for fighting for his freedom.[19] In historical perspective, Cinquez is probably still an obscure figure when compared to Adams. But by indirectly documenting the association of Adams, a prominent figure with Cinquez, a slave whom Hayden wishes to present as a racial hero, the poet partially elevates Cinquez to a stature befitting such a role.

This prominence stems also from the ironic implications of the section representing the Spaniard's testimony. In this passage Hayden uses several techniques to translate Cinquez into a symbolic, representative hero. First, consider the emphasis the poet causes the Spanish speaker to put on the weather conditions before and during the *Amistad* rebellion. The witness, in rationalizing the slavers' defeat, repeatedly attributes the success of the uprising to adverse weather. He begins,

> "But for the storm that flung up barriers
> of wind and wave, *The Amistad*, señores,
> would have reached the port of Príncipe in two
> three days at most; but for the storm we should
> have been prepared for what befell ...." (121-125)

Then, "Swift as a puma's leap" (126), the attack came during an "interval of moonless calm" (127). In the Spaniard's words, the attack "was as though the very / air, the night itself were striking us" (131-134). Thus the storm, the calm, the air, the night itself all seem combined against the slavers.[20]

The witness only reports and rationalizes; he is, of course, blind to the possible moral and thematic implications of this seeming conspiracy. Hayden here suggests that the forces of nature take a sort of elemental vengeance against those supposedly civilized men who pervert nature by enslaving others. Showing nature in active support of the struggle for freedom helps raise that struggle to a cosmic level. Hayden, through this account, indirectly links Cinquez with the instinctive desire for freedom, the eternal struggle for personal liberty, and the aid of elemental nature in the quest. This correlation certainly transcends the historical antecedents of the incident itself and subtly amplifies the name-dropping association of Adams as known hero and Cinquez as emerging hero.

Hayden carefully prepares earlier in the poem for this thematic merger of human will and natural order. He "leads" the reader through allusion and subtle irony. In Section I, a voice which seems to speak directly to, and indirectly for, the slaves as a spiritual narrator, apparently addresses those victimized by the Middle Passage experience:

> *Deep in the festering hold thy father lies,*
> *of his bones New England pews are made,*
> *those are altar lights that were his eyes.* (17-19)

The poet alludes to the song Ariel sings to Ferdinand in Shakespeare's *The Tempest:*

> Full fadom five thy father lies,
> Of his bones are coral made:
> Those are pearls that were his eyes:
> Nothing of him that doth fade,
> But doth suffer a sea-change
> Into something rich and strange.[21]

But note how he completely alters the effect of the images. Hayden's description echoes the song ironically; the passage in his treatment becomes a "land-change" rather than a "sea-change"; a lament rather than a consolation. The language suggests the myriad uses the New England whaling industry found for its prey, and in the context of a spiritual narrator speaking for the slaves, the whale becomes leviathan, as a symbol of primordial nature, of that which is quintessentially natural. Thus the choral narration implicitly asserts that nature and the natural have been exploited by civilized man, distorted to accommodate his cultural convenience. The black slave, as natural man, has been dehumanized and almost destroyed by this perverse "sea-change." Yet that same imaginary voice later in the poem again inversely paraphrases Ariel's song (109-111), warns the captors of the risks they incur (112-115), and emphasizes the human instinctive drive for freedom which is subsequently personified in Cinquez:

You cannot stare that hatred down
or chain the fear that stalks the watches
and breathes on you its fetid scorching breath;
cannot kill the deep immortal human wish,
the timeless will. (116-120)

Hayden attributes personal nobility to Cinquez by again combining history with art. Incorporating and recasting contemporary accounts which refer to Cinquez's princely countenance and demeanor, he makes the Spanish witness echo such references in a sarcastic fashion:

we are determined to return to Cuba
with out slaves and there see justice done.
Cinquez—
or let us say "the price"—Cinquez shall die. (170-173)

Although Cinquez clearly was the leader of the *Amistad* mutiny and was put on trial in that role (in the case of the United States, Appellants, vs. Cinque, and Others, Africans), he was a rice planter, not a chieftain or a prince. As a leader of slaves in rebellion against their captivity, he gave his followers hope and direction, but contemporary events, curiosity, and sympathy elevated him to "regal" status. Public curiosity was abetted by an idealized portrait done by Nathaniel Jocelyn,[22] a phrenological profile,[23] and several sympathetic newspaper editorials in praise of Cinquez, e. g., "The more we learn of the man's character ... the more are we impressed with a sense of his possessing the true elements of heroism."[24] The abolitionists who took up the cause of the "Amistaders" regarded Cinquez as a "noble savage" and saw his situation as an opportunity to set a legal precedent which would forward the abolition movement. Hayden retains these historical perspectives and then transcends them by portraying Cinquez in symbolic terms of epic scope. Cinquez's desire and struggle for freedom become the "deep immortal human wish, / the timeless will" (174-175). Ultimately, then, "Middle Passage" creates a hero who represents his race in a quest for personal liberty—something in which all men have a real shared interest.

Thus Hayden portrays an epic hero in the context of an epic quest, but in terms of a representative struggle rather than as a personal adventure. Usually, epic heroes travel in search of a goal; the journey frequently is a means to an end, both of which are voluntarily sought by the quester. Hayden's journey-quest motif is, of course, inverted, since Cinquez and all other slaves in transit eastward were on travels contradictory to the desire-quest for freedom. Again inversely, Cinquez fights to change the direction of his travel to accomplish his immediate and ultimate goals—personal freedom and the return to Africa. Cinquez's imposed "odyssey" realistically and symbolically duplicates the quest by all slaves striving for liberty.[25]

This symbolic quest, unlike most epic quests, is not augmented by a journey to the underworld where the hero gains assistance or guidance. Quite the contrary, the sea crossing, the Middle Passage in itself, is a descent into hell, a "voyage through death" which Cinquez and all transported slaves must endure even as they yearn for freedom. The variously narrated segments of the poem stress again and again the agony and horror of the crossing, "Where the living and the dead, the horribly dying, / lie interlocked" (107-108). Perhaps in view of the history he recounts, Hayden had little choice but to "include" the quest and descent motifs in his unique epic, but by modifying these conventional formulae, the poet makes certain that the laboring of his hero remains central to the narrative. This centrality rests with Cinquez's symbolic personification of the primary theme of the poem. Hayden makes the hero appear larger than life because his "life transfigures many lives" (177). Cinquez's rebellion against enslavement thus stands for the physical and spiritual struggle for freedom by all blacks then and since.

Therefore "Middle Passage" is epic in theme and import although "anti-epic" in formal structure and technique. Because of Hayden's manner of contrasting his style with epic characteristics, the poem fairly reverberates with thematic implications throughout its length. If "unlove" provides the direction for imposed travel through the Middle Passage, irony is the thematic gloss for reader progress toward an understanding and appreciation of Hayden's pean to his kind—human-kind. The indirect and muted treatment of a horrible chapter in human history at once demonstrates the poet's craftsmanship, verifies his compassionate objectivity (his "negative capability," one might say), and substantiates Robert Hayden's own humanity.

Professor Fetrow acknowledges with gratitude the receipt of United States Naval Academy Research Council funding which allowed him the time to research and write the preceding article.

NOTES

1. Hayden finished an initial version of "Middle Passage" in 1943; it appeared in *Phylon* in 1945 (VI, No. 3, 247-253). A revised version was published in *Cross Section: 1945*. After more revision, Hayden included the poem in his *A Ballad of Remembrance* (London: Paul Breman. 1962). The poem appeared again in *Selected Poems* (New York: October House, 1966), and has since been included in numerous anthologies of poetry.

2. Among those broad surveys of black literature which include some reference to "Middle Passage" are Bernard W. Bell, *The Folk Roots of Contemporary Afro-American Poetry* (Detroit: Broadside Press, 1974); Arthur P. Davis, *From the Dark Tower: Afro-American Writers 1900 to 1960* (Washington, D.C.: Howard University Press, 1974); Addison Gayle, Jr., ed., *Black Expression* (New York: Weybright and Talley, 1969); David Littlejohn, *Black on White: A Critical Survey of Writing by American Negroes* (New York: Grossman Publishers, 1966); Clarence Major, *The Dark and the Feeling: Black Writers and Their Work* (New York: Joseph Okpaku, 1974).

3. For recent articles which touch on "Middle Passage," see Charles T. Davis, "Robert Hayden's Use of History" in *Modern Black Poets*, ed. Donald B. Gibson (Englewood Cliffs, N.J.,: Prentice-Hall, 1973), pp. 96-111; Howard Faulkner, "'Transformed by Steeps of Flight': The Poetry of Robert Hayden," *College Language Association Journal*, XXII, No. 3 (March, 1978), 282-291; Michael Paul Novak, "Meditative, Ironic, Richly Human: The Poetry of Robert Hayden," *Midwest Quarterly*, XV, No. 3 (Spring, 1974), 276-285; Constance J. Post, "Image and Idea in the Poetry of Robert Hayden," *CLA Journal*, XX, No. 2 (December, 1976), 164-175; Lewis Turco, "*Angle of Ascent:* The Poetry of Robert Hayden," *Michigan Quarterly Review*, XVI, No. 2 (Spring, 1977), 199-219.

4. For the full context of Hayden's remarks, see *How I Write / 1* (New York: Harcourt Brace Jovanovich, 1972), pp. 169-176.

5. *Ibid.*, pp. 169-170.

6. *Ibid.*, pp. 175-176.

7. Here are, of course, several literary handbooks and glossaries which list these epic characteristics and those which follow. My list is taken primarily from William Flint Thrall and Addison Hibbard, *A Handbook to Literature*, rev. C. Hugh Holman (New York: Odyssey Press, 1960), pp. 174-176.

8. In the interview previously quoted, Hayden mentions "the motifs, the themes, of the poem—man's cruelty to man, the Negro's heroic struggle to be free." See *How I Write / 1*, p. 176.

9. Robert Hayden, "Middle Passage," in *Angle of Ascent: New and Selected Poems* (New York: Liveright, 1975), p. 118. Subsequent quotation of the poem is from this volume and will be documented by line number(s) within my text.

10. "Ordinary" ships converted to use in the slave trade customarily retained their original names. For the authenticity of those names Hayden uses (*Desire*, *Ann* and *Tartar*, for example) and some names he could have used (*Friendship*, *Brothers*, *Rainbow*, *St. Augustin*, *St. Leon*, or even *Othello*), see, among others, George F. Dow, *Slave Ships and Slaving* (Salem, Mass.: Marine Research Society, 1927), pp. 267, 270, 202, 203, 102, 109, xxxiv, 186. Additionally, *The Amistad*, which figures significantly in the poem, bears a Spanish name which is a translation of "friendship."

11. *The Compact Edition of the Oxford English Dictionary, I* (New York: Oxford University Press, 1971), 1851.

12. *How I Write /*, p. 176.

13. "Jesus Savior, Pilot Me" was originally a six-stanza poem written by Edward Hopper, who first published the poem in *The Sailors' Magazine* in 1871. Hopper then selected the first, fifth and sixth stanzas to be set to music by John Edgar Gould, and the resultant hymn was published in the *Baptist Praise Book* in the same year, and presently appears in the hymnals of several denominations.

14. For a complete history of the role (and culpability) of organized Christianity in the slavery question, see Lester B. Scherere, *Slavery and the Churches in Early America 1619-1819* (Grand Rapids, Mich.: Wm. B. Eerdmans, 1975), Albert Barnes, *The Church and Slavery* (Philadelphia: Parry and McMillan, 1857), reprinted (New York: Negro Universities Press, 1969), and James Gillespie Birney, *The American Churches: The Bulwarks of American Slavery*, reprint edition (New York: Arno Press, 1969).

15. "Corposant" denotes "St. Elmo's fire," a luminous electrical glow caused by corona discharge on masts of ships. See "corposant" in *The American Heritage Dictionary*, ed. William Morris (Boston: Houghton Mifflin, 1976), p. 298. Since this phenomenon was identified by sailors with Saint Elmo (the patron saint of sailors), and since the term "corposant" derives from the latin *corpus sanctum* (holy body), quite likely Hayden uses the term to pose further ironic religious implications.

16. Direct communication between gods and heroes recurs frequently in epic poems. The consistency of this pattern has prompted one modern scholar to give comprehensive treatment to the convention of the "celestial messenger" in heroic poetry. Consult Thomas M. Greene, *The Descent from Heaven* (New Haven, Conn.: Yale University Press, 1963).

17. For examples, Achilles in Homer's *The Iliad*, Odysseus *in The Odyssey*, Aeneas in Virgil's *The Aeneid.*

18. In the spring of 1839, Joseph Cinquez (a Spanish name assigned him in place of his African name, Singbe or Singbe-pieh) led a slave revolt aboard *The Amistad* while being transported with 52 other slaves from Havana to Port Principe. After the slaves killed two of their captors and gained control of the ship, they forced the two spared Spanish slavers to navigate eastward for Africa. For 63 days the ship zigzagged up the Atlantic coast as the Spaniards sailed east by day and reversed course by night. Finally Cinquez and the others were taken into custody near Long Island. The subsequent trial, here represented in part by the poet, concluded with former President John Quincy Adams arguing the case before the Supreme Court, claiming that Cinquez and the surviving 34 Africans were neither slaves nor criminals but "self emancipated" free persons. The Africans were released and returned to Sierra Leone in 1841. For detailed accounts of *The Amistad* incident, see John Warner Barber, *A History of the Amistad Captives* (New Haven, Conn.: E.L. and J.W. Barber, 1840), reprint edition (New York: Arno Press, 1969); Mary Cable, *Black Odyssey* (New York: Vicking Press, 1971); Christopher Martin, *The Amistad Affair* (New York: Abelard-Schuman, 1970); William A. Owens, *Black Mutiny* (Philadelphia: Pilgrim Press, 1968); and Muriel Rukeyser, *Willard Gibbs* (New York: Doubleday, Doran & Co., 1942), pp. 16-46.

19. Hayden employs poetic license here; Adams' arguments were essentially legalistic and nationalistic, and only once did he single out Cinquez for special personal praise: Cinque and Grabeau are uncouth and barbarous names. Call them Harmodius and Aristogiton, and go back for moral principle three thousand years to the fierce and glorious democracy of Athens. They too resorted to *lawless violence*, and slew the tyrant to

redeem the freedom of their country. For this heroic action they paid the forfeit of their lives: but within three years the Athenians expelled their tyrants themselves, and in gratitude to their self-devoted deliverers decreed, that thenceforth no slave should ever bear either of their names. Cinque and Grabeau are not slaves. Let them bear in future history the names of Harmodius and Aristogiton. Note that Hayden omits Grabeau (the co-leader of the revolt) and suggests that Adams defended Cinquez on a personal basis. For the context of the above quotation and the complete record of Adams' argument, see John Quincy Adams, *Argument in the Case of United States vs. Cinque* (New York: S.W. Benedict, 1841), reprint edition (New York: Arno Press, 1969), pp. 86-87.

20. Hayden's witness is a composite of the two slavers, since he appears to be an intelligent, articulate eye-witness. Don José Ruiz testified eloquently in English but he did not actually see the events described by Hayden's speaker. It was Pedro Montes, an older man testifying in Spanish, who described the slayings he saw and mentioned the weather. Significantly, neither "real" witness attributed their defeat to adverse weather. See the source listed in note number 18 above for the testimony of these two witnesses.

21. William Shakespeare, *The Tempest*, Act I, Scene ii, lines 397-405, from *The Riverside Shakespeare*, ed. G. Blakemore Evans, *et al.* (Boston: Houghton Mifflin, 1974), p. 1617.

22. A reproduction of this portrait appears in Muriel Rukeyser's *Willard Gibbs*, facing page 26.

23. The phrenological description, composed by a Mr. Fletcher after he had examined Cinquez, appears as a footnote in the context of "biographical sketches" compiled by John Warner Barber. Fletcher's description concludes, "In fact, such as African head is seldom to be seen, and doubtless in other circumstances would have been an honor to his race." See Warner's *History*, pp. 9-10.

24. Quoted from the New London *Gazette* in Mary Cable's *Black Odyssey*, p. 39.

25. Obviously, Mary Cable, like Robert Hayden, saw the epic significance of historic events when she chose the title of her account of the *Amistad* story.

ROBERT B. STEPTO

After Modernism, After Hibernation: Michael Harper, Robert Hayden, and Jay Wright

> To become aware of our history is to become aware of our singularity. It is a moment of reflective repose before we devote ourselves to action again.
> —OCTAVIO PAZ

> Please, a definition: A hibernation is a covert preparation for a more overt action.
> —RALPH ELLISON

> *Anochecí enfermo Amanecí bueno*
> (I went to bed sick. I woke up well.)
> —JAY WRIGHT

"After modernism"—what does it mean, to what does it refer? As Paul de Man has written,

> The term "modernity" ... designates more generally the problematical possibility of all literature's existing in the present, of being considered, or read, from a point of view that claims to share with it its own sense of a temporal present. In theory, the question of modernity could therefore be asked of any literature at any time, contemporaneous or not. In practice, however, the question has to be put somewhat more pragmatically....[1]

From *Chant of Saints: A Gathering of Afro-American Literature, Art, and Scholarship*, eds. Michael S. Harper and Robert B. Stepto.

With de Man's "pragmatically" in mind, I would suggest that "after modernism" may yet have its day in the hermeneutical sweepstakes, provided that it is properly groomed and well ridden. Literary modernism may never end, but there exist in modern literature certain aesthetic as well as historical moments when the modern writer appears to call for a new order. Because it is his call, and because the new set of images demanded is to be in some sense a natural outgrowth of his own figurative language, we may say that the modern writer is prefiguring his epilogue, or at the very least inaugurating a rather specific type of post-modernist expression even though, as we know, modernism has not run its course. "After modernism" may therefore be discussed as a series of incidents in recent literary history wherein a literary exchange (call and response?) between modern writers and would-be post-modern writers yields epilogues (or epilogues to epilogues, as we will soon see) to the modernist's work. This is only a "working" definition of the phrase, but at least it works—and for the right reasons: it makes no effort to predict the death of one era and the genesis of a new one, or to plump up certain artists before others as avant-garde, and its goal is the correct one of trying to tell us something about literary history and literary process.

In Afro-American literature, the modernist/post-modernist exchanges that interest me most are those which evolve from the post-textual "call" of Ralph Ellison's novel, *Invisible Man.* Readers of the novel will remember that at the end (which is, of course, the beginning), Ellison's protagonist is marked by two extraordinary features: one, that he has lived through a series of hair-raising experiences and yet has come to control that personal history through the act of art-making; and two, despite his control of his history (symbolized rhetorically by the frame created in the novel's prologue and epilogue), he lives in a hole—a "clean, well-lighted place" to be sure, but a hole nonetheless. The Invisible Man is, as he says, "in a state of hibernation," and later he defines a hibernation as "a covert preparation for a more overt action."

In the prologue and epilogue, we are given many fascinating and often bizarre details about the hero's self-confinement, but those which further develop the idea of hibernation as a metaphor for an artist's apprenticeship—the "covert preparation" that the novel is really all about—demand our greatest attention. *Invisible Man*'s call, its prefigurement of epilogues to its epilogue (and prologue), is a clarion cry for multiple images and voicings of the Afro-American articulate hero's post-apprenticeship/post-hibernation condition. Recent literary texts which offer such images and voicings, and attempt as well to resolve the primary dilemmas of artistic apprenticeship which the novel identifies, are texts which create, in response to a specific modern text, a post-modern art.

In the following pages I take the liberty of discussing several recent poems by Michael Harper, Robert Hayden, and Jay Wright as responses to the prefiguring call of Mr. Ellison's novel and hence, in light of my definition, as post-modernist expressions. Each poem or sequence of poems displays a "post-apprenticeship" voice, and each situates that voice upon a rather specific "post-hibernation" terrain. The order of my presentation of the poems is almost chronological, but chronology is not the organizing principle of the discussion. My purpose is rather to begin with images of smaller physical landscapes and to end with depictions of larger ones, and in that way to impose a modest narrative order on the articulate hero's "overt activities" upon the landscape—and within the reader.

Michael Harper's "Photographs/*Negatives*," section IV of his third book of poems, *Song: I Want a Witness* (1972), is a sequence of nine poems that intersplice two variations upon the same basic photographic metaphor. One variation, stated and restated in five poems, "The Negatives," "Photographs," "Utility Room," "The Borning Room," and "Trays: A Portfolio," studies the process of printmaking—of negative becoming photograph—and in so doing orders a husband and wife's nightmare of child loss by presenting their activities in a cellar darkroom as a ritualistic search for the presence and images of children "torn away." In each of the five poems, printmaking initiates image-making of a different order:

> A simple enlarger
> a bulb with a shade,
> images born through her lens
> packed on the contact sheet;
> fatted negatives under thick
> condenser glass,
> prints from her uterus,
> cramps from her developing tank....[2]

"Negative," above and beyond its obvious literal meaning, is both a referent to the children who might have lived and a description of an indelible yet skewed image of child loss repeated mercilessly upon the proof sheet of memory:

> The hypo fix
> fastens the images
> hardening against light
> on her film and papers.
> I imagine her movement

at night as her teeth grind:
I know she dreams the negatives. (*S*, 45)

The other metaphoric variation, generated within the lines of the four remaining poems, "The Night of Frost," "At the Cemetery," "The Families Album," and "History as Apple Tree," also studies the process of image-making, but in different terms. In these poems, the narrative situation to be invested with metaphorical properties is always that of the solitary poet, as articulate or self-conscious (as opposed to "double-conscious") hero, traversing what Octavio Paz would term a labyrinth of solitude. This labyrinth is simultaneously a literal landscape rich in lore and history (here, a south-of-Boston terrain including both Massachusetts and Rhode Island land) and a figurative landscape of racial memory. In each poem, the landscapes link and appear as concentrated images of a graveyard; and it is upon this land, this ritual ground as negative plate, that the poet as a potential human image—

I walk as negative
image over white crusted
gravestones as my dark feet
stamp their footprints ... (*S*, 47)

—searches for the process by which he will "imagine" himself.

While we may identify certain poems in the series as "darkroom" poems or "cemetery" poems, we mustn't lose sight of how each type of poem feeds on the other and thus contributes to the series as a whole. The cemeteries, graves, and apple tree in one sub-series are of a piece with the darkroom, developing pans, and blossoming images of the dead in the other. Furthermore, the implicit fear pervading the entire sequence, that "human photographs" may remain "negative images" if process is not found and enacted, is conveyed both by the poet's quest—in all its racial involvements—upon the "white crusted" land, and by the parents' search for lost children who will only "develop" in "black and white eyes." Of course, the poet himself also binds the exterior and interior landscapes of the series: he is a negative image to be imagined, a shadow to be cast on ritual ground, as well as a seeker for images in negatives of

two sons stoppered
from isolette
to incinerator.... (*S*, 55)

But the unity of the sequence is perhaps best demonstrated by the manner in which the "cemetery" and "darkroom" poems share the burden of response to *Invisible Man*'s call. Whereas the former poems—especially "The Night of Frost" and "History as Apple Tree"—return the articulate hero to an above-ground labyrinth in which he must unravel the mysteries of personal history bound to public history, the latter sub-series, especially in lines like these from "Trays: A Portfolio":

> *contact: print:*
> *blacken our negatives with light* ... (*S*, 56)

provides a photographic metaphor through which we may comprehend what the Invisible Man sought through his underground writing (and lighting!). They also explain why he must end his hibernation and return, while at least self-imagined (or self-"developed"), to a world where, as an outwardly Invisible Man, he is, in varying degrees of exposure, a negative.

These many figurative threads come together in the sequence's concluding poem, "History as Apple Tree." The landscape of the poem is a historical field, a culture's magic circle—

> Cocumscussoc is my village,
> the western arm of Narragansett
> Bay; Canonicus chief sachem;
> black men escape into his tribe ... (*S*, 58)

—upon which the poet, aware of the private as well as public dimensions of this ritual ground, may complete his self-willed metamorphosis from "negative image" to "human photograph." Historically, the landscape has been assaulted by certain European preoccupations:

> How does patent not breed heresy?
> Williams came to my chief
> for his tract of land,
> hunted by mad Puritans,
> founded Providence Plantation ... (*S*, 58)

Yet to some degree the effects of assault have been assuaged by the powerful workings of nature in its course:

In your apple orchard
legend conjures Williams' name;
he was an apple tree.
Buried on his own lot
off Benefit Street
a giant apple tree grew;
two hundred years later,
when the grave was opened,
dust and root grew
in his human skeleton;
bones became apple tree. (*S*, 59)

In the poem's final stanza, the poet's immersion and positioning within this landscape, for which we are partially prepared by such earlier lines as "black men escape into the tribe" and "Williams came to my chief," unfolds as he becomes history—an orchestrated image of past and present—instead of remaining outside of it:

As black man I steal away
in the night to the apple tree,
place my arm in the rich grave,
black sachem on a family plot,
take up a chunk of apple root,
let it become my skeleton,
become my own myth:
my arm the historical branch,
my name the bruised fruit,
black human photograph: apple tree. (*S*, 59)

This portrait of a primal image-in-process is rich and exquisitely layered, but I admire even more its subtle humor. The joke, like those which keep the Invisible Man in stitches, depends for its effect upon the inability of people to *see* one another. Therefore, by employing a phrase from the spirituals ("steal away"), a phrase which plays wonderfully upon the theory that slaves had no rights to self-initiated mobility, Harper suggests that his poet's ritual act of claiming a place in history, a piece of the ground, is a self-configuration of his humanity. Clearly, just as the line "black sachem on a family plot" sustains the essential serio-comic quality of the poet's actions ("essential" because it is rooted in a culture's traditional modes of expression), the poem's final line, "black human photograph: apple tree," restates what is, in effect, a culture's right to be imagined.

Still, we must ask, especially since we are interested in how "History as Apple Tree" responds to the prefiguring call of *Invisible Man*, whether it is a "hibernation" or "post-hibernation" poem. I would argue that it is a "post-hibernation" (or "post-apprenticeship") poem, partly because, as the final line tells us, it is a "tree" poem and not a "root" poem, and because the poet's achieved state is, in the language of Harper's conceit, not so much print as image. "Black human photograph" and "apple tree" as printed image and emblem emblaze each other through the lens which is at least one configuration of the line's colon; but this is only a fleeting parity, since the phrases are most certainly not interchangeable. As the emblematic manifestation of public and private history as well as racial memory converging upon ritual ground, the "apple tree," not the "black human photograph," is the poet's final destination; and yet it is, of course, through the photo or print that we *gain* the emblem. This passage through printed image to emblem transports the poet to a post-hibernation/post-apprenticeship state: in hibernation, the human photograph is processed or imagined; after hibernation, it is contextualized within a culture's figurative landscape and thereby made an initial manifestation of grander trope.

Once the articulate voice returns to the upper landscape or historical field, we are interested not only in his movements as a solitary seeker but also in how he reassumes the posture of kinsman. Of course, Harper's "Photographs/*Negatives*" poems study this matter: the "black human photograph" in organic relation to the "apple tree" is the "stoppered" children, as well as the poet blood-bound to the private *and* public family that might have been. Kinship is, in short, another term for the process envisioned and hopefully gained through immersion in the sequence's photographic metaphor. But kinsmen also have ties (Harper would say "responsibilities") to their extended tree. After hibernation, what is our voice's posture toward bloodline kin? Will he speak to adopted family? In what ways will the upper landscape be re-peopled once it assumes the proportions of a historical field larger, if not always more accoutred, than the Invisible Man's hole or Harper's poet's burial and birthing ground? Where are—in the language of Ellison's signbook—Supercargo and Tod Clifton? Where are Mary Rambo, Louis Armstrong, Buckeye the Rabbit, and the Lenox Avenue Yam Man? These questions are expressions of the prefiguring call of Ellison's text; and while Robert Hayden's recent series of poems, "Elegies for Paradise Valley,"[3] does not answer all of these questions directly, it does provide a splendid example of a mature (that is, post-hibernation) voice re-embracing both bloodline and adopted kin, and in that way re-ordering a landscape experienced previously before hibernation.

The "Elegies for Paradise Valley" are presently eight in number, and while each poem may be said to be "set" in Paradise Valley—Hayden's name for his boyhood neighborhood in Detroit—the "Elegies" do not limn a place as much as they illuminate the ties between kinfolk who are bound as well to place. In this way, Hayden's "Paradise Valley" is a historical field—a culture's magic circle—much like the one established in Harper's "Photographs/ *Negatives.*" And, just as Harper (like Ellison, in some measure) deliberately orchestrates his images so that both birth and burial are contextual properties of photograph and negative, darkroom and graveyard, human image and apple tree, the antipodes of Hayden's field are similarly conjoined and disparate because "Paradise Valley" is also a birthing and burial zone, a vision of the Garden as well as of the Pit of the Fall.

Indeed, it is with images of the Pit that the series of Elegies begins, forcing us to wonder if the series' narrative vector will chart upward and, if so, in what form the incremental stops will appear. The first poem is short and taut, a window on a wasteland infested with race rituals including those cultural carcinogens which, as Ellison's Invisible Man observed, promote certain phases of blindness:

> My shared bedroom's window
> opened on alley stench.
> A junkie died in maggots there.
> I saw his body shoved into a van.
> I saw the hatred for our kind
> glistening like tears
> in the policeman's eyes.

The second elegy, shorter still and possibly even more taut, offers through its negative definitions and images of time, place, and shelter (and hence, of historical field) another portrait of the pit:

> No place for Pestalozzi's
> fiorelli. No time of starched
> and ironed innocence. Godfearing
> elders, even Godless grifters, tried
> as best they could to shelter
> us. Rats gnawing in their walls.

It is in the third poem, however, that Hayden's landscape is peopled not just with neighbors and other adopted kin but most especially with the voices that inhabit the poet's memory. The poem opens with spare images of life (floral pieces, Christmas tree, Chinese lantern, freesias) stippled in such a way that they both veil and center the beautiful wooden coffin in which "Waxwork Uncle Henry / (murdered Uncle Crip)" lies. As it closes, however, the chill is (in memory) upon the poet as he learns amid Uncle Crip's warm laughter of a "wicked" song and dance of which they will partake together:

> Mahogany—I'd heard
> the victrola voice of
>
> dead Bert Williams
> talk-sing that word as macabre
> music played, chilling
> me. Uncle Crip
> had laughed and laughed.

The fourth poem introduces Madam Artelia, the fortune-teller who attempts to "find" Crip's voice-in-death and is, with Aunt Jemina of the Ocean Waves among others, one of the great women in Hayden's canon. But it is in the lyrical fifth elegy that Paradise Valley is transformed into a busy place full of the miscellaneous visages so conspicuously absent from the Invisible Man's underground hole. In that poem, in two chiseled yet plaintive ten-line catalogs of questions answered by a single declarative refraining line (based on Villon's *ballade)*, the poet does not merely list his adopted kin, he *calls* their names:

> And Belle the classy dresser, where is she,
> who changed her frocks three times a day?
> Where's Nora, with her laugh, her comic flair,
> stagestruck Nora waiting for her chance?
> Where's fast Iola, who so loved to dance
> she left her sickbed one last time to whirl
> in silver at The Palace till she fell?
> Where's mad Miss Alice, who ate from garbage cans?
> Where's snuffdipping Lucy, who played us 'chunes'
> on her guitar? Where's Hattie? Where's Melissabelle?
> Let vanished rooms, let dead streets tell.

In this catalog, so full of melody, and in the one following it calling the names of menfolk including "Jim, Watusi prince and Good Old Boy," "Tump the defeated artist," "Les the Huntsman," "Tough Kid Chocolate," and "dapper Jess," we receive—in language Hayden may share with Harper—an orchestration of "negative images" becoming "human photographs." Hayden's fifth elegy very nearly completes the family album which is one of the sequence's responses to the prefiguring call of Ellison's novel.

Another response—quite possibly *the* other response—is stated through the poet's resolution of his relationship with his Uncle Crip. In the first few elegies we sense that Crip was both a boon and a bane to his young nephew because he generated complex situations and hence emotional confusion by mischievously pitting and even blending the sacred and the profane. Crip, in brief, was one of the ones—probably *the* one—who taught Hayden's artist-as-a-young-man by gesture, word, and deed that the world in all its complexity is as much "both/and" as it is "either/or." The artist's search for Crip within a reincarnated Paradise Valley is, then, an effort not only to rediscover those singular moments when Crip's teachings took hold, but also to explore how Crip offered his knowledge (and himself) to his nephew—and how his gifts were received and embraced.

Knowledge and pedagogy, dilemma and resolution, elder and youth are fused in the poetic sequence by a simple, marvelous image and metaphor of dance. In the sixth elegy, for example, are the lines:

> I scrounged for crumbs:
> I yearned to touch
> the choirlady's hair,
> I wanted Uncle Crip
>
> to kiss me, but he danced
> with me instead;
> we Balled-the-Jack
> to Jellyroll
>
> Morton's brimstone
> piano on the phonograph,
> laughing, shaking the gasolier
> a later stillness dimmed.

And in the eighth elegy, after opening lines which speak both of inner tuggings to be resolved ("Of death, of loving, / of sin and hellfire too ...") and of Crip's death (" ... pitched / from the gamblingtable—/ Lord have mercy on / his wicked soul—/ face foremost into hell ..."), we witness the poet's dance with mentor and kin which comes when inherited gifts yield self-knowledge:

> We'd dance there, Uncle
> Crip and I,
> for though I spoke
> my pieces well in Sunday School,
>
> I knew myself (precocious
> in the ways of guilt
> and secret pain)
> the devil's own rag babydoll.

We appreciate the expression of affection that warms these final lines, as well as the manner in which youthful confusions are finally resolved. Crip is a devil, and the artist his rag babydoll, but like their richly peopled landscape they are self-defined and, as their dance suggests, triumphantly mobile. Hayden's revision of Paradise Valley is an answer to *Invisible Man*'s prefiguring call, not only because it re-peoples an exterior landscape and fashions an artist who "calls the names," but also because Paradise Valley is a landscape outside those definitions of history—and, hence, of historical fields—created by others. In his epilogue the Invisible Man declares, "Step outside the narrow borders of what men call reality and you step into chaos ... or imagination." Paradise Valley, like the Harlem vibrating above Ellison's hero's head, is unreal because it is for the most part unseen. After hibernation, as Ellison and Hayden tell us, the unseen must be not only seen but also imagined.

But let's pursue these matters on yet a larger scale: after hibernation—after apprenticeship—how does the articulate figure view the universe (which I will define quite simply as *all he can see*)? What happens when his culture's magic circle of myth, rite, and landscape—its literal and figurative birthing and burial ground—*becomes* the world? What ordering of the universe—and fashioning of poetic voice—is prefigured by the Invisible Man's final question, "Who knows but that, on the lower frequencies, I speak for you?" Clearly, these questions constitute a call for field and voice of fantastic scale, and among Afro-American poets Jay Wright has made the most ambitious attempt to respond with images of macrocosmic proportions. His poet is a dyēli, another namer of the names,

> ... a dark and dutiful dyēli,
> searching for the understanding of his deeds ...[4]

whose song, "The Second Eye of the World," is part three of the first part of Wright's long poem, *Dimensions of History.* In Mande culture, a dyēli is, like the dyāru and gyeserē in Soninke and Songhay cultures, a professional archivist, a member of the caste responsible for the family histories of nobles. Thus, even though the kinship he studies binds the rites and fields of the world far more than it re-peoples a given field, Wright's dyēli is kin to Harper's and Hayden's questing artists. Like the passage from negative to print to emblem, and the circumchange of epilogue as prologue, the dyēli's journey upon and within a world as large as vision is a return to a primal world (Apple Tree, Paradise Valley) occasioned by the exhaustion of an increasingly sophisticated, and hence temporal, world's domain. Through Wright's dyēli, even more than through Harper's printed voice becoming metaphor, we hear a response to what may be the most baffling yet essential command of Ellison's text—the call for images of the return to hibernation (even Jack-the-Bear would admit to life's endless cycle) or at very least of hibernation's pulsing, clouded presence as a precursor rite birthing those other rites and fields which are the stuff of history, art, and vocation in this world.

"The Second Eye of the World" begins with selections from texts which, as incantatory rites, are fragments of the "one sentence" to be realized through vocation and the art that is the poem. "Anocheci enfermo / Amaneci bueno" is sung at the beginning to suggest, as Wright informs us, not simply the Arabic influence on the Spanish but also the essential oneness of the world and the one, the voice, who experiences it. The lines sketch the moral as well as linguistic geography of the poetic unit while providing a concentrated image of hibernation and its aftermath: "I went to bed sick. I woke up well." All of these energies are sustained by the second fragment, which is from *The Egyptian Book of the Dead:*

> 'I am the bennu bird in annu,
> I am the keeper of the book of things which are
> and things which shall be.
> Who then is this ... ?
> The things which are the things which shall be
> are his dead body.' (*D*, 31)

To this is appended:

> My breath leaves my body in dreams.

Who is mounted here?
Who returned? (*D*, 31)

Like the artists in the Harper and Hayden poems, Wright's dyēli seeks images of personal history; but the dyēli pursues these images through a new kind of question, suggesting both the mobility and the stasis that accompany "the understanding of his deeds." "Who is mounted here?"—the kinetic image of the dyēli upon his mount initiated by "My breath leaves my body in dreams" is reversed soon thereafter in the lines:

Under the white moon
The gods will straddle you.
Santiago on a white horse,
twin bolts, or a lance,
brother of Christ,
give us a nation. (*D*, 31)

The ambiguity of "mounted" prepares us to see that the "nation" is—for the dyēli as much as for the voices of Ellison, Harper, and Hayden—a false capital, a center that cannot hold. "Nation" initiates fragments:

'We must MAKE an ISSUE, CREATE an EVENT,
and ESTABLISH a NATIONAL POSITION FOR OURSELVES ...' (*D*, 31)

But since it does not circumscribe a spirited center, its verbal manifestations must be glossed:

Muhammad to Mecca again
for the weavers of souls,
clothiers of a body gone fat with stillness. (*D*, 32)

What must be understood here is the fundamental incongruence between the idea of nation and that of historical field (and, hence, the distinction between static and perpetually evolving centers of spirit) which informs the dyēli's song of self-discovery much as it influences the Harper and Hayden poems. *Invisible Man* calls for certain very particular universal, as opposed to national, images ("Whence all this passion toward conformity anyway? ... Life is to be lived, not controlled.... Our fate is to become one, and yet many—This is not prophecy, but description"), images which live and enliven the living principally because they are not constrained by national or generic boundaries. Harper's emblem of the apple tree (blossom *and* root) and Hayden's portrait of kin (in death *and* dance) are such images; they are evolving centers of spirit. In "The Second Eye of the World," there is a greater sense of dual, errant energy; both knight and grail are set in motion, both center and circumference seek an understanding of their deeds:

> Who chooses me?
> In Cuba,
> Black Melchior caresses the cobra.
> Dahomey dance Havana Boa
> This Python, sacred serpent of Delphi,
> this Pythia, stretching the dark corners,
> dark herself, caught in darkness,
> sees the fat sin burned on the island.
>
> Upon a Day of Kings,
> these women dressed in white
> group themselves and pirouette,
> and become my dawn,
> my sun,
> my earth,
> my lamb,
> my buzzard,
> my butterfly.
> I live this day through them,
> counting no clock time
> but the blood's time,
> the gentle rise and fall
> of a donu bird's wings.
> I assert that I am twinned to your light within.
> Will we get these symbols right?
>
> In Lima,
> Thirsting for the waters of worship,
> the lost tribes keep our Lady of the Rosary
> in the Monastery of Santo Domingo.
> There in our brotherhood,
> we awake with breath in place.
> So many waters crossed,
> yet crossing is no journey.

And will we get these symbols right?

Gold of Guinea, gold of Gao,
Morocco rides Gao under Judar Pasha.
Under the flat flags,
there is left a cannon
        with the arms of Portugal,
a statue of the Holy Virgin,
        a crucifix,
all these powers lying dead,
with no one to transform them.
Still, anochecimos enfermo amanecimos bueno,
learning the dwelling-place of the act,
the spirit holding the understanding
of one life among ourselves. (*D*, 32, 33)

The map is full of symbol, dance, rite, and the melodic exchange of names; the persistent questions—pauses, signposts, catapults announcing pulsing energy—express both the stasis and mobility characterizing the dyēli's act of self-discovery. That act of self-discovery upon the map of rites and acts forces transgeographic compressions (South American Day of Kings rites restated, for example, by "the gentle rise and fall" of an African riverbird's wings) which pre-vision "the dwelling-place of the act" as much as they delineate metaphorically the dyēli's deeds and hence substantiate the dyēli himself. This marvelous conjoining of voice and place connotes a new space, a vital rhythm ("... anochecimos enfermo amanecimos bueno ...") beyond stasis ("all these powers lying dead, / with no one to transform them"), and we cannot help but wonder whether this geography is to be understood as a vision of hibernation or as a pre- or post-hibernation state. My feeling is that it is a vision of all three, prefacing and epiloging each other, but that the *return* to hibernation—the furthest reach of Ellison's circumference *and* its contraction—is the phase imagined with greatest intensity and attention to language.

In the lines just cited above are powerful images of the necessity of regeneration and of hibernation as a precursor rite ("we awake with breath in place ..."). But as the dyēli's song continues, the dominant images are of re-entry and descent—of the end which is the beginning:

        Hawk-headed,
with a disk upon my head,

> and the ankh upon my knees,
> I sit in this sun bark.
> Your speech is the speech of hands upraised,
> your eyes give as much light as mine.
> I have heard the timid call
> The lord of the hidden world, great god,
> lord of the underworld.
> Shrine-clad,
> White feather crowned,
> he holds the emblems of dominion.
>
> Who is the greater teacher?
> What is the first act
> if not the body rising from itself,
> becoming itself again,
> spirit, shadow, spirit,
> heart of its own bones,
> the name of the wise one?
>
> Can this be hidden from the hidden one? (*D*, 34, 35)

The glory of these lines is Wright's synthesis of process, vocation, myth, and language. By and large, the other landscapes in "The Second Eye" are horizontal—we travel *upon* circumference from Cuba to Brazil (or Colombia) to African cities, from "Havana Boa" to "lamb," "buzzard," "butterfly," "donu bird," and crucifix. But in this passage travel is vertical, circumference is crossed, the world is defined on high by the realm of Ra, the sun god, and in its nether regions by the domain of Osiris, "lord of the hidden world." One imagines, then, that the "X" formed by these two powerful vectors of symbolic geography denotes "the dwelling-place of the act" or, in the language of this essay, the site (sight) of hibernation, and that it is precisely this intense conjunction of seen and unseen as well as of exterior and interior language ("... sun bark ... speech of hands upraised ... emblems of dominion ... the body rising from itself, / becoming itself again ...") which occasions the pattern of return to "the hidden one":

> I am always approaching my end,
> looking for the hidden one.
> Tongue-tied in time for my nani's deeds,
> I have done my trembling,

but the soul must be an All in All,
laid out in one sentence,
over the Pool, over the absolute intention,
Even the knowledge of death. (*D*, 35)

In his notes, Jay Wright reminds us that "Nommo of the Pool, among the Dogon, is sacrificed for the purification and reorganization of the universe"; this suggests that we are to understand the archivist's return to the hidden realm to be at the very least a rite of self-discovery through self-sacrifice. I would add the thought that the "one sentence" or "All in All" which the soul must become above and beyond the "speech" of the dyēli's trembling—and beyond the perpetuating circumferences of epilogues birthing prologues—is a fertile mantle *and* a lid: a supreme emblem beyond image of hibernation's dominion. Osiris—lord of hibernation, custodian of root, amanuensis of root tongue, alchemist of the nether side of the colon and, hence, of image before emblem—is both confined by the lid and renewed by the act of nurturing the fertile mantle. This is his distinction from Ra, the voyager within seen tongues whose "sun bark" is both vessel and tongue; this is why the dyēli seeks him out—Osiris knows the way out as well as the way in.

And so the song ends:

We are born to trade upon and build
the heads intent
    in the river's seed,
    the seed's irruption,
    the milk of a lamb,
    the star's sudden fall,
    the rock's mountain breaking shape,
    the saint bickering with the birds,
    the sceptre, flail and crook,
    the coffin at the neck of things,
    the joker in the soul's bequest,
    the eye,
    the key,
    the second eye.
This, before you,
    is the life
of a dark and dutiful dyēli,
searching for the understanding of his deeds.

Let my words wound you
into the love of the emblems
of the soul's intent. (*D*, 35, 36)

With these lines, the "dwelling-place of the act" or site of hibernation is located upon yet another axis of language and ritual energy—that which fills the space between the intent of the head and that of the soul. Thus, the "X" created by the travels of speech and rite along and across geographies of circumference becomes a "*"—a star that is not so much the Southern Cross of our literal heavens, which the Dogon call "The Second Eye of the World," as it is the source of light in darkness which, for Wright's dyēli as well as for Ellison's Invisible Man, is the light by which one's form is finally seen.

Notes

1. Paul de Man, *Blindness and Insight: Essays in the Rhetoric of Contemporary Criticism* (New York: Oxford University Press, 1971), p. 166.

2. Michael S. Harper, *Song: I Want a Witness* (Pittsburgh: University of Pittsburgh Press, 1972), p. 50. 3. These poems appear elsewhere in this volume and in *American Journal* (Taunton, Mass.: Effendi, 1978).

4. Jay Wright, *Dimensions of History* (Santa Cruz, Calif.: Kayak, 1976), p. 36.

WILBURN WILLIAMS, JR.

Covenant of Timelessness and Time: Symbolism and History in Robert Hayden's Angle of Ascent

I

The appearance of Robert Hayden's *Angle of Ascent* is something of a problematic event for students of the Afro-American tradition in poetry, for while it gives us occasion to review and pay homage to the best work of one of our finest poets, it insistently calls to mind the appalling tardiness of our recognition of his achievement. A meticulous craftsman whose exacting standards severely limit the amount of his published verse, Robert Hayden has steadily accumulated over the course of three decades a body of poetry so distinctive in character and harmonious in development that its very existence seems more fated than willed, the organic issue of a natural principle rather than the deliberate artifice of a human imagination.[1] But in spite of official honors—Hayden is now the poetry consultant at the Library of Congress and a Fellow of the Academy of American Poets—and a formidable reputation among critics, Hayden has received surprisingly little notice in print. Unless we suffer another of those sad fits of inattention that have so far limited Hayden's readership, *Angle of Ascent* should win for him the regard he has long deserved. With the exception of *Heart-Shape in the Dust*, the apprenticeship collection of 1940, poetry from every previous work of Hayden's is represented here, and we can see clearly the remarkable fertility of the symbolist's union with the historian, the bipolar extremes of Hayden's singular poetic genius.

From , *Chant of Saints: A Gathering of Afro-American Literature, Art, and Scholarship*, eds. Michael S. Harper and Robert B. Stepto.

Robert Hayden is a poet whose symbolistic imagination is intent on divining the shape of a transcendent order of spirit and grace that might redeem a world bent on its own destruction. His memory, assailed by the discontinuities created by its own fallibility, is equally determined to catch and preserve every shadow and echo of the actual human experience in which our terribleness stands revealed. In poem after poem Hayden deftly balances the conflicting claims of the ideal and the actual. Spiritual enlightenment in his poetry is never the reward of evasion of material fact. The realities of imagination and the actualities of history are bound together in an alliance that makes neither thinkable without the other. Robert Hayden's poetry proposes that if it is in the higher order of spirit that the gross actualities of life find their true meaning, it is also true that that transcendent realm is meaningful to man only as it is visibly incarnate on the plane of his experience.

Viewed as a theory of poetics, Hayden's characteristic method of composition will hardly strike anyone as unique. His preoccupation with the relationship between natural and spiritual facts puts him squarely in the American tradition emanating from Emerson; we are not at all amazed, therefore, when we find correspondences between his work and that of figures like Dickinson and Melville. The brief lyric "Snow," for instance (all page references in this essay are to *Angle of Ascent*, New York, 1975):

> Smooths and burdens,
> endangers, hardens.
>
> Erases, revises.
> Extemporizes
>
> Vistas of lunar solitude.
> Builds, embellishes a mood. (p. 84)

recalls the Dickinson of "It sifts from Leaden Sieves—."[2] But the brooding presence of death lurking behind the brave outward show of a playful wit that is common in Dickinson is uncharacteristic of Hayden, and a comparison with Melville casts more light on his habitual concerns. In "El-Hajj Malik El-Shabazz" Malcolm X is likened to Ahab—"Rejecting Ahab, he was of Ahab's tribe. / 'Strike through the mask!'" (p. 57)—and "The Diver" (pp. 75–76) closely parallels Chapter 92 of Melville's *White-Jacket*. To be sure, Hayden's speaker and Melville's narrator are impelled by distinctly different motives. The former's descent is a conscious act, a matter of deliberate choice, whereas White-Jacket's one-hundred-foot fall into a nighttime sea cannot be ascribed to his sensible will, however strong his subconscious longing for death might be. Yet the underlying pattern of each man's ordeal is the same. The approach to death is paradoxically felt as a profound intensification of life. Death takes, or at least seems to promise to take, both men to the very core of life. Thus White-Jacket in his precipitous drop "toward the infallible center of the terraqueous globe" finds all he has seen, read, heard, thought, and felt seemingly "intensified in one fixed idea in [his] soul." Yielding to the soft embrace of the sea, he is shocked into revulsion of death almost purely by chance—"of a sudden some fashionless form" brushes his side, tingling his nerves with the thrill of being alive.[3] In like manner, Hayden's diver's longing to be united with "those hidden ones" in a kind of well-being that lies so deep as to be beyond the reach of articulate speech, his passion to "have / done with self and / every dinning / vain complexity," can be satisfied only if he tears away the mask that sustains his life. The intricate contrapuntal development of the poem brings an overwhelming extremity of feeling to the critical moment that finds the diver poised between life and death. His going down is both easeful and swift, a plunge into water and a flight through air. The flower creatures of the deep flash and shimmer yet are at the same time mere "lost images / fadingly remembered." The dead ship, a lifeless hulk deceptively encrusted with the animate "moss of bryozoans," swarms with forms of life that are themselves voracious instruments of death. And what liberates the diver from this labyrinthine and potentially annihilating swirl of contradictory instincts and perceptions is never clear. As is the case with White-Jacket, he "somehow" begins the "measured rise," no nearer to winning the object of his quest but presumably possessed of a deeper, more disciplined capacity for experience. ("Measured" is decidedly meant to make us think of the poet's subordination to the rules of his craft.)

The most fruitful area of comparison between Hayden and Melville is to be found in their tellingly different attitudes toward the symbolistic enterprise itself. Committed to reconciling within the ambiguous flux of poetic language the warring oppositions created by the divisiveness of discursive logic, the symbolist finds himself necessarily presupposing the very terms of order—subject and object, mind and matter, spirit and nature—his method seeks to erase.[4] Because the symbolist's stance is such a difficult posture to keep, the idea of the artist as acrobat and the conception of his craft as a dance of language are conventional figures in modern literature and criticism. In Hayden, however, the drama of the symbolist's tightrope walk is objectified infrequently. The symbolist's striving for balance is not seen in what Hayden's speakers do but is heard in how they talk: tone assumes the burden that topic might bear. Hayden's characteristically soft-spoken and fluid voice derives much of its power from the evident contrast between the maelstrom of anguish out of which it originates and the quiet reflecting pool of talk into which it is inevitably channeled. Interestingly enough, when Hayden does write poetry in which the action is clearly analogous to the symbolist's task of wizarding a track through a jungle of contraries, the prevailing tone is not his customary seriousness. In "The Performers," the modesty of two high-rise window cleaners subtly mocks the speaker's misuse of their daring as a pretext for a kind of absurd metaphysical strutting that his own desk-bound timidity will not allow (p. 27). In "The Lions" an animal trainer whose mentality is a peculiar blend of Schopenhauerian wilfulness and transcendentalist vision breaks out into an ebullient speech that is at once divinely rapturous and somehow wildly funny:

> And in the kingdom-cage
> as I make my lions leap,
> through nimbus-fire leap,
> oh, as I see them leap
> unsparing beauty that
> creates and serves my will,
> the savage real that clues
> my vision of the real
> my soul exults and Holy cries
> and Holy Holy cries, he said. (p. 64)

Yet whenever Robert Hayden loses his artistic balance, his fall is not likely to be in Melville's direction. The enormous gulf between the unified paradise of the symbolistic imagination and the outright hellishness of a world rife with division, the gulf which drew Ahab and Pierre to their deaths and drowned Melville the writer in silence, poses no threat to Hayden. Hayden's peril comes from a different quarter, and it comes disguised as his salvation. It is precisely Hayden's faith in the ultimate redemptiveness of the universal and timeless order of spirit that threatens to kill the life of his art. Insofar as his poetry is concerned, Hayden's God and Devil are one. The blinding light of faith can shrivel up the sensuous specificity of poetry just as surely as it can enkindle the life of the world of inert fact. Hayden's divergence from Melville here is nowhere more apparent than in "Theme and Variation." Readers of Hayden will recognize the voice of the Heraclitus-like stranger who delivers the poem's wisdom as the poet's own:

> I sense, he said, the lurking rush, the sly
> transcience flickering at the edge of things.
> I've spied from the corner of my eye
> upon the striptease of reality.
>
> There is, there is, he said, an imminence
> that turns to curiosa all I know;
> that changes light to rainbow darkness
> wherein God waylays and empowers. (p. 115)

Set the above lines against this sentence from the famous last paragraph of "The Whiteness of the Whale" in *Moby Dick:*

> And when we consider that other theory of the natural philosophers, that all other earthly hues—every stately or lovely emblazoning—the sweet tinges of sunset skies and woods; yea, and the gilded velvets of butterflies, and the butterfly cheeks of young girls; all these are but subtle deceits, not actually inherent in substances, but only laid on from without; so that all deified Nature absolutely paints like the harlot, whose allurements cover nothing but the charnel-house within; and when we proceed further, and consider that the mystical cosmetic which produces every one of her hues, the great principle of light, forever remains white or colourless in itself, and if operating without medium upon matter, would touch all objects, evaj tulips and roses, with its own blank tinge—pondering all this, the palsied universe lies before us a leper; and like wilful travellers in Lapland, who refuse to wear coloured and colouring glasses upon their eyes, so the wretched infidel gazes himself blind at the monumental white shroud that wraps all the prospect around him.

Hayden's stranger reverses Ishmael on every point. His perceptions nourish belief; Ishmael's skepticism and doubt. He is pious and Ishmael is blasphemous. Melville's Nature dresses while Hayden's disrobes. The former's adornment is emblematic of a diabolical deceitfulness; the latter's nudity points to a sanctuary of grace. Where Melville's eye strips away delusory hues to gaze in horror upon the "blank tinge" of a "palsied" and leprous universe, Hayden's eye spies out an indwelling spirit that transforms an undifferentiated light into a sacredly tinged darkness wherein man discovers his hope and his blessing. But here Hayden can no more be accused of a naive optimism than Melville can be charged with blind cynicism. The ironic intimation of violent assault reverberating in "waylays" checks the stranger's rush into the plenitude of divine imminence, maintaining the poem's complexity and integrity.

Nevertheless, the point remains that the beneficent banditry of Hayden's divinity has far more in common with the onslaughts of Donne's Three-Personed God than with anything ever done by the maddeningly elusive Jehovah of Melville. Hayden's supreme high-wayman is more apt to strip the poet of his facts than to rob him of his faith, which might be heaven for religion but certainly hell for poetry. As much is evident in the increasingly sparing detail and more cryptic utterance that marks the poet's recent work. At his best Hayden composes poetry that is paradoxically both rich in statement and ascetic in temperament. In "Stars" and the Akhenaten section of "Two Egyptian Portrait Masks," however, an abstract and unconvincing expression of acute religious belief shows only a marginal relation to the concrete particularities of human experience. The latter verse segment plainly suffers in contrast to the paean to Nefert-iti that precedes it. Meditating on the carving of a woman

> whose burntout
> loveliness alive in stone
> is like the fire of precious stones
>
> dynastic
> death (gold mask and vulture wings)
> charmed her with so she would never die (p. 16)

the poet tersely harmonizes a succession of discordant sensations. But in the Akhenaten companion piece, the poet's contemplativeness has no equivalent object on which it can focus—admittedly, it would take an extraordinary imagination to bridge the gap between the majesty of Akenaten's dream of human oneness and the fat hips and bloated abdomens of the Pharaoh's Karnak colossi—and consequently the poetry lacks force:

> Aten
> multi-single like the sun
> reflecting Him by Him
>
> reflected.
> Anubis howled. The royal prophet reeled
> under the dazzling weight

> of vision,
> exalted—maddened?—the spirit moving
> in his heart: Aten Jahveh Allah God. (p. 17)

Certainly there is nothing in this like the faultless description of death as "dynastic," a brilliant conceit whereby Hayden associates the idea of the unbroken hereditary transfer of power from generation to generation with the eternal dominion of death, thus finding death's very indomitability dependent upon the principle of generation, or life. What Emerson, the one indispensable figure in any discussion of American symbolism, once said about the poet's duty is patently applicable to Robert Hayden, and it can serve both as an accurate representation of what Hayden does in his best work and as a necessary corrective to the etherealizing proclivities of Hayden's symbolist genius:

> The poet, like the electric rod, must reach from a point nearer the sky than all surrounding objects, down to the earth, and into the dark wet soil, or neither is of use. The poet must not only converse with pure thought, but he must demonstrate it almost to the senses. His words must be pictures, his verses must be spheres and cubes, to be seen and smelled and handled.[5]

II

However much we might like to dwell on the manifold possibilities of Hayden's symbolism, particularly in relation to the practices of Yeats and Eliot (to whom he sometimes alludes) and to Auden (whom he has said was a key factor in his growth as a poet[6]), no discussion of his poetry can avoid the question of the place a sense of history occupies in his work. Every reader is quick to detect a pervasive sense of the past and a powerful elegiac strain in his work. In the most thorough examination of Hayden's poetry we have, Charles T. Davis has recounted the crucial contribution of Hayden's extensive research in the slave trade to "Middle Passage," and he has called attention to the importance of Hayden's grasp of the Afro-American folk tradition to "O Daedalus, Fly Away Home," "The Ballad of Nat Turner," and "Runagate Runagate."[7] Aware of the paradox, Hayden has referred to himself as a "romantic realist," a symbolist compelled to be realistic, and Michael Harper has called him a "symbolist poet struggling with the facts of history."[8] Now, nothing is perhaps more tempting or more mistaken than to infer from all this that the historian in Hayden is at odds with the symbolist.

A close reading of the poetry will not support such a conclusion. Because of the popularity of "Middle Passage" and "Runagate Runagate"—poems unmistakably black in subject matter and sometimes identifiably black in use of language—the historical impulse in Hayden is understandably allied in the minds of many readers with the poet's pride in his own blackness. Since Hayden's recognition of his blackness is widely (and, we think, most aberrantly) perceived as a grudging one, the symbolist in Hayden is often viewed as the enemy of his essentially historical, and black, muse. If that Bob Hayden only knew better, the argument (it is hardly reasoning) goes, he would leave that symbolism stuff alone (the poetry of *The Night-Blooming Cereus*, for example) and get back to his roots. Certainly Hayden's insistence that he be judged as a poet and not as a Negro poet only exacerbates this misapprehension, and no appeal to the extensive exploitation of symbolism in the spirituals and the blues is likely to quiet the suspicion that Hayden's symbolist clings parasitically to the creativity of his black historian.[9]

But while it is easy to see that the symbolistic method is operative in poems as disparate as "Middle Passage" and "The Night-Blooming Cereus," it is not so evident that Hayden's historical sensibility is also at work in poems that have no obvious connection with historical incidents. To apprehend the unity of Hayden's entire body of work, it is necessary to understand that his fascination with history is but one part of a more comprehensive entrancement in the mystery of time. Robert Hayden is clearly more intrigued by the process of change, the paradoxes of permanence and evanescence, than the particular substances that undergo change. Here we are interested in the psychological and artistic implications of his dramatic re-creations of historical events, and not just in the nature of the events themselves. Throughout the poetry of Hayden we encounter a memory and an imagination pitted against the losses time's passage inevitably entails. We meet a consciousness struggling to retain the finest nuances of its own experience and seeking to enter into the experience of others from whom it is alienated by time and space. The fundamental source of Hayden's productivity, the wellspring of his poetic activity, lies in the ability of the human memory to negotiate the distance between time past and time present and the capacity of a profoundly sympathetic imagination to transcend the space between self and other. The complex interactions generated by the life of memory and imagination define the basic unity of Hayden's work.

But while we think that Hayden's obsession with time is, in a sense, larger than his deep involvement in the Afro-American past, it would be foolish to deny the special place black American history occupies in his development as a poet. The 1940s, the years in which Hayden patiently studied the annals of his black past, are also the years in which he matured as artist.[10] To simply live in a culture with a sense of the past as notoriously shallow as this one's is burden enough. A black like Hayden, the fierceness of whose need to know his history is matched only by the ponderousness of the mass of distortion and fabrication under which his past lies buried, finds that even the truthful accounts of the black American experience, which cannot really take him farther back than the eighteenth century anyway, give him the composite picture of a collectivity, rather than detailed portraits of individuals. It can hardly seem an accident to him that historians have until recently slighted the value of the slave narratives, documents that shake him with a revelation more awesome than any truth contained in the most complete compilation of data seen even in the wildest dreams of the maddest cliometrician. When he looks at his mental picture of Representative Afro-American Man, he sees that it is a mosaic formed of bits of the lives of many men, and there are moments when he wonders whether the portrait typifies the truth of art or the deceit of artifice. The face is formed of fragments themselves faceless; the sacred text of his people's experience an accretion of footnotes culled from the profane texts of another's. His past is pregnant with a significance that it is incapable of giving birth to. It is a speechless past peopled with renowned personalities who are ironically impersonal:

> Name in a footnote. Faceless name.
> Moot hero shrouded in Betsy Ross
> and Garvey flags—propped up
> by bayonets, forever falling. ("Crispus Attucks," p. 20)

Viewed in this somber light, the primary significance of Hayden's famous poems of Cinquez, Turner, Tubman, and Douglass resides in the poet's imaginative attempt to reforge his present's broken links with the past. The past, Hayden says, need not be past at all. His speakers confront their history as active participants in its making, and not as distant onlookers bemoaning their isolation; the past is carried into the present. Although the poet's mind ventures backward in time, the poems themselves invariably close with a statement or action that points forward to the reader's present. The progress of "Middle Passage" is through death "to life upon these shores," and the reader leaves the poem with his attention riveted to *this* life on *these* shores just as much as it is fixed on the historical reality of the slave trade. The man we leave at the conclusion of "The Ballad of Nat Turner" has his revolution still before him. "Runagate Runagate" ends with an invitation, "Come ride-a my train," whose rhythm subtly anticipates the action to be undertaken, and the powerful assertion of yet another intention to act—"Mean mean mean to be free" (p. 130). The accentual sonnet to Frederick Douglass is poetry that moves like the beating of a living heart. The poet emphasizes that the dead hero is still a vital force. The first long periodic sentence seems to resist coming to an end. The poem celebrates not a man who has been, but a man still coming into being. Although commemorative in nature, it does not so much elegize a past as prophesy a future. Frederick Douglass, the poet, and all enslaved humanity are united in one generative process:

> When it is finally ours, this freedom, this liberty, this beautiful
> and terrible thing, needful to man as air,
> usable as earth; when it belongs at last to all,
> when it is truly instinct, brain matter, diastole, systole,
> reflex action; when it is finally won; when it is more
> than the gaudy mumbo jumbo of politicians:
> this man, this Douglass, this former slave, this Negro
> beaten to his knees, exiled, visioning a world
> where none is lonely, none hunted, alien,
> this man, superb in love and logic, this man
> shall be remembered. Oh, not with statues' rhetoric,
> not with legends and poems and wreaths of bronze alone,
> but with the lives grown out of his life, the lives
> fleshing his dream of the beautiful, needful thing. (p. 131)

A great deal of Hayden's success in undoing the dislocations of time and space can be attributed to his poet-speakers' uncanny ability to give themselves over to the actuality they contemplate. They become what they behold; known object and knowing subject unite. Like psychic mediums, his speakers obliterate distinctions between self and other; the dead and distant take possession of their voices. Take for example these lines from "The Dream (1863)":

> That evening Sinda thought she heard the drums
> and hobbled from her cabin to the yard.
> The quarters now were lonely-still in willow dusk
> after the morning's ragged jubilo,
> when laughing crying singing the folks went off
> with Marse Lincum's soldier boys.
> But Sinda hiding would not follow them: those
> Buckras with their ornery

funning, cussed commands, oh they were not were not
the hosts the dream had promised her. (p. 36)

The poem is obviously a third-person narrative, but the space separating narrator and actor is frequently violated. The speaker's voice modulates effortlessly into the cadences of the slaves. "Marse Lincum," "Buckra," and "ornery" are words heard in the accents of the slaves. The pathos of the cry "oh they were not were not" is so extraordinary because, syntax notwithstanding, it is Sinda's own voice we hear, and not the poet's. In six lines in "The Rabbi" Hayden gives a virtuoso demonstration of the resources of his voice:

And I learned schwartze too

And schnapps, which schwartzes bought
on credit from "Jew Baby."
Tippling ironists laughed and said
he'd soon be rich as Rothschild

From their swinish Saturdays. (p. 81)

In the first two lines the poet's retrospective view of the blacks of his youth is clearly refracted through the cultural lens of the Jews he knew. By the end of the third line, however, his perspective has shifted, and it is now the Jews who are being looked upon from a black point of view. "Credit" is the pivotal term in this transition, for it not only allows the speaker to describe objectively the economic relationship of black to Jew but also lets him draw on the powerful connotations this word has in the Afro-American speech community. The last three lines of indirect quotation, framed by two jocularly incongruous phrases that are clearly of the poet's own making, indicate that the speaker finally assumes an amused posture independent of the viewpoint of either black or Jew, but remarkably sensitive to both. And there is a social morality implicit in this display of Hayden's multivocal talents. What might at first seem to be merely a technical device has enormous ethical implications. When the poet says in the last stanza,

But the synagogue became
New Calvary.
The rabbi bore my friends off
in his prayer shawl (p. 81)

he means for us to see that the loss of his childhood friends Hirschel and Molly is part of a wholesale separation of black and Jew, a separation that will brook no opposition from considerations as flimsy as one human being's love for another. "New Calvary," tellingly isolated in a single line, is not only the name of the black church that succeeds the synagogue. It represents too a place and an action. It is the hill where Christianity and Jewry part ways, the site where Hayden's ideal of human oneness is sacrificed, a modern reenactment of that old attempt at redemption that ironically, bitterly, only sped man in his fall out of unity into division.

But there is a sinister dimension to this intercourse between self and other, present and past. Robert Hayden knows, and this is a sign of his strength, that openness is also vulnerability, that the past in which one finds possibilities of inspiration and renewal can exert a malignant influence on the present. In "A Ballad of Remembrance" the poet is besieged by specters pressing upon him the value of their individual adaptations to American racism. The Zulu King urges accommodation, the gunmetal priestess preaches hate, and a motley contingent of saints, angels, and mermaids, blind to the realities of evil, chime out a song of naive love. These competing voices drive the poet to the brink of madness. In "Tour 5" an autumn ride into the country becomes a frightening excursion into a surreal world alive with ancient conflicts between black, white, and red men. In "Locus" the Southland lies wasted under the blight of its own history. The present abdicates to the superior force of the past. The redbuds are "like momentary trees / of an illusionist"; there is a "violent metamorphosis, / with every blossom turning / deadly and memorial soldiers." Life here is stunted, reality the bondsman of a dream of disaster. The past forecloses its mortgage on the future:

> Here spareness, rankness, harsh
> brilliances; beauty of what's hardbitten,
> knotted, stinted, flourishing
> in despite, on thorny meagerness
> thriving, twisting into grace.
> Here symbol houses
> where the brutal dream lives out its lengthy
> dying. Here the past, adored and
> unforgiven. Here the past
> soulscape, Old Testament battleground
> of warring shades whose weapons kill. (p. 45)

Closely related to Hayden's interest in the cunning ironies of history is his anxiety for the fate of myth and religion in the modern world. This concern provides the motivation of some of his best poetry. Take "Full Moon," for example, which we quote in full:

No longer throne of a goddess to whom we pray,
no longer the bubble house of childhood's
tumbling Mother Goose man,

The emphatic moon ascends
the brilliant challenger of rocket experts,
the white hope of communications men.

Some I love who are dead
were watchers of the moon and knew its lore;
planted seeds, trimmed their hair,

Pierced their ears for gold hoop earrings
as it waxed or waned.
It shines tonight upon their graves.

And burned in the garden of Gethsemane,
its light made holy by the dazzling tears
with which it mingled.

And spread its radiance on the exile's path
of Him who was the Glorious One,
its light made holy by His holiness.

Already a mooted goal and tomorrow perhaps
an arms base, a livid sector,
the full moon dominates the dark. (p. 79)

The world we encounter here is radically impoverished. The slow process by which the rise of positivistic science has emptied Nature of all religious significance is recapitulated in the fall of childhood's illusions before the advance of adult skepticism. For contemporary man, the moon exists only as a means of flaunting the triumphs of his technological vanity. But the poet sees in this diminished moon an analogue to the deprivations death has exacted from him, and with this crucial recognition of a mutuality of fates begins the movement toward recovery. Like the breathtaking expansion of meaning we witness in Eliot's "Sweeney Among the Nightingales" when we leap from the nightingales "singing near / The Convent of the Sacred Heart" to those that "sang within the bloody wood / When Agamemnon cried aloud,"[11] there is a startling intensification of feeling in the transition from a light that "shines tonight upon their graves" to the light that "burned in the garden of Gethsemane." But Hayden knows that this age looks upon Jesus Christ and the prophet Baha'u'llah (The Glorious One of the penultimate stanza and the founder of Hayden's Baha'i faith) with a cynical regard, and that any appeal to them to restore the significance of a degraded Nature would sound highly artificial and entirely unconvincing. Like Flannery O'Connor, who frequently discerns in overt denials of faith ironic avowals of the existence of God, Hayden subverts the materialism of technology to make a claim for the reality of spirit. The moon that is now meaningless will once again become all-meaningful, he says, not as the throne of a benign deity or as an object of harmless childish fancies, but as an arms base that can end all life. The meaning that has been lost to the achievement of science reasserts itself with a vengeance by means of that very same achievement. This ironic turn of events is itself fully in keeping with the traditional view of the moon as the symbol of eternal recurrence. The full weight of this paradox is felt in the critical word "livid," on which a whole world of ambiguities turns. As meaning ashen or pallid, livid is both a forthright description of a full moon and suggestive of the moon's fearful retreat before the press of technology. As meaning black and blue, livid, in conjunction with the reference to the moon as "the white hope of communications men," suggests a moon bruised and discolored by the assaults of the Jack Johnsons of science. As a synonym for enraged or angry, livid further elaborates upon the implied meanings of this prize-fighting metaphor, and, by connecting it to the ominous possibilities of the moon's use as an arms base, subtly transforms the earlier reference to the moon as victim into an image of the moon as aggressor. And when we finally consider livid as meaning red, that satellite's consequence as an object of martial reverence is fully revealed, for the red moon is the moon foreseen by John of Patmos, and its appearance announces the coming of God in His wrath, the destruction of nations and the end of time.

III

When we review the entire course of Hayden's development, the importance of the poet as historian seems to lessen drastically over time. In his last two volumes of verse, only "Beginnings" immediately strikes us as aspiring to the largeness of historical vision of a "Full Moon" or the early explorations of the Afro-American past for which Hayden is chiefly known. What we feel is responsible for this change is not something so simple as the symbolist's displacement of the historian, but a growing preoccupation in the historian with ever smaller units of time. Having exhausted his examination of the problematic interactions of present and past, Hayden's historian is free to chronicle the mystery of change itself. Instead of feeling obliged to overcome the effects of change, he is more and more fascinated by single moments of metamorphosis. This is clearly the case in the poetry of *The Night-Blooming Cereus.* Standing before the "Arachne" of the black sculptor Richard Hunt, the poet is transfixed by the impenetrable mystery of the total change of essence he witnesses. At the same time his language manages to evoke Arachne's terror, it confesses, by the violent juxtaposition of concepts of motion and stasis, the human and the animal, birth and death, the singular incapacity of rational terms to represent adequately such an event:

> In goggling terror fleeing powerless to flee
>   Arachne not yet arachnid and no longer woman
>   in the moment's centrifuge of dying
>   becoming (p. 23)

The capacity of short-lived and seemingly trivial events to manifest truths of exceptional import is shown in "The Night-Blooming Cereus." The speaker initially anticipates the blooming of that flower with a casual disregard for the miracle it will actually be. He and his companion are, in effect, two decadent intellectuals whose interest in the "primitive" is really just a shallow trafficking in the exotic. For them the blossoming sanctions hedonistic indulgence: they will paint themselves and "dance / in honor of archaic mysteries." Yet so much more than they can possibly imagine depends on the appearance of that blossom. When the bud unfolds, the phenomenon of its transformation enlarges into the enigma of eternal recurrence, the riddle of the cyclical alternation of life and death. And the blasphemous are reduced to near speechlessness:

>   Lunar presence
> foredoomed, already dying,
> it charged the room
>   with plangency

older than human
cries, ancient as prayers
invoking Osiris, Krishna,
Tezcatlipoca.

We spoke
in whispers when
we spoke
at all ... (p. 26)

Just as Hayden's historian's engrossment with the epochal modulates into an absorption with the momentary, there is a parallel shift of his focus away from the history of a people to the biographies of individuals, away from the public figures of the past to persons who are the poet's contemporaries. The boxer Tiger Flowers and the artist Betsy Graves Reyneau take the place of Nat Turner and Harriet Tubman. If the personages that engage him impress us as having little relation to the main currents of our history, they clearly arouse anxieties in him that nothing less than a total reconsideration of the nature of history itself can assuage. Just as Hayden's early historian is compelled to personalize the past he confronts, his later one is compelled to objectivize his own subjectivity. His private anguish never locks him into the sterile deadend of solipsism; it impels him outward into the world. "The Peacock Room," Hayden tells us, grew out of an intense emotional experience. A visit to that room designed by Whistler excited painful recollections of his dead friend Betsy Graves Reyneau, who had been given a party in the same room on her twelfth birthday.[12] Contemplating the rival claims of art and life,

Ars Longa	Which is crueller
Vita Brevis	life or art?

the poet seeks shelter in Whistler's "lyric space," as he once did in the glow "of the lamp shaped like a rose" his "mother would light / ... some nights to keep / Raw-Head-And-Bloody-Bones away." But he knows that the dreadful facts of the nightmare that is our history—"Hiroshima Watts My Lai"—scorn "the vision chambered in gold." The very title of the poem, however, has already hinted that his meditations will not issue into a simplistic espousal of art's advantages over life. The peacock is an ambiguous figure. The legendary incorruptibility of the bird's flesh has led to its adoption as a type of immortality and an image of the Resurrected Christ; but as the emblem of Pride, the root of all evil, the bird has always had ominous connotations in Christian culture. These intimations of evil remind the poet of the artist driven mad by Whistler's triumph, and the Peacock Room is transformed in his mind from sanctuary to chamber of horrors. The echoes of Stevens's "Domination of Black" and Poe's "Raven" heighten the poet's fears:

> With shadow cries
>
> the peacocks flutter down,
> their spread tails concealing her,
> then folding, drooping to reveal
> her eyeless, old—Med School
> cadaver, flesh-object
> pickled in formaldehyde,
> who was artist, compassionate,
> clear-eyed. Who was beloved friend.
> No more. No more.

The paradox of a lasting art that mocks man's fragility at the same time that it realizes his dream of immortality is resolved in the beatific, enigmatic smile of the Bodhisattva ("one whose being—sattva—is enlightenment—bodhi"):

> ... What is art?
> What is life?
> What the Peacock Room?
> Rose-leaves and ashes drift
> its portals, gently spinning toward
> a bronze Bodhisattva's ancient smile. (pp. 28-29)

In a remarkable way, "Beginning," the first poem of *Angle of Ascent*, reenacts the course of the fruitful collaboration of Hayden's historian and symbolist. The historian summons up the essential facts of the poet's ancestry, and the symbolist immediately translates them into the terms of art:

> Plowdens, Finns,
> Sheffeys, Haydens,
> Westerfields.

Pennsylvania gothic,
Kentucky homespun,
Virginia baroque.

As the poem moves forward in time, the ancestors are particularized. Joe Finn appears "to join Abe Lincoln's men" and "disappears into his name." Great-grandma Easter lingers longer before the poet's gaze, and she is remembered not for the role she took in an historic conflict, but for her individual qualities: "She was more than six feet tall. At ninety could / still chop and tote firewood." The progression toward individuation that accompanies the poem's movement to the present—the sharpness of focus of the portrait of an ancestor is a direct function of that ancestor's nearness to the poet's own present—is paralleled by a growth in the poet's awareness of the figurative possibilities of language. As the historian's field of view contracts, the symbolist's artfulness becomes increasingly apparent. As we move from summaries of the entire lives of Joe Finn and Great-grandma Easter to select moments in the lives of the poet's aunts, the symbolist's reveling in words for the beauty of their sound and rhythm becomes more evident:

Melissabelle and Sarah Jane
oh they took all the prizes one Hallowe'en.
And we'll let the calico curtain fall
on Pocahontas and the Corncob Queen
dancing the figures the callers call
Sashay, ladies, promenade, all.

But when the poet himself finally appears, a curious—but, for Robert Hayden, characteristic—change occurs. The historian reasserts his centrality (the concluding piece is called "The Crystal Cave Elegy"), and the poem's steady flow toward life and the present is momentarily reversed in commemoration of the death of the miner Floyd Collins. The symbolist's increasing involvement in the resources of his art does not end in an autistic preoccupation with the poet's inner life but finally turns outward in prayer for the liberation of Collins. The timeless paradise of the imagination is invoked to release humanity from the limitations of time:

Poor game loner
trapped in the rock
of Crystal Cave, as

once in Kentucky coalmine
dark (I taste the
darkness yet)
my greenhorn dream of
life. Alive down there
in his grave. Open
for him, blue door. (p. 5)

The province of the poet is neither the realist's moonscape of inert matter nor the romantic's starfire of pure spirit, but the middle kingdom of actual earth that unites the two. Robert Hayden's symbolist and historian long ago joined hands to seize this fertile territory as their own. Together they have kept it up very well.

NOTES

1. This meticulousness poses problems for the critic. Robert Hayden frequently revises his work, and a poem in one collection can appear in considerably altered form in a later collection. In general, Hayden's revisions involve deletions; he characteristically seeks greater economy of expression. His revisions could form the topic of a separate essay. To avoid confusion among variants, all our references are to poems as they appear in *Angle of Ascent* (New York, 1975). Page numbers after quotations pertain to this volume.

2. Thomas H. Johnson, ed., *Final Harvest: Emily Dickinson's Poems* (Boston, 1962), p. 59. The Dickinson influence here might not be direct. It is quite possible, given the extraordinary likeness Hayden's "Witch Doctor" bears to Gwendolyn Brooks's well-known "The Sundays of Satin-Legs Smith," that the Dickinson influence is filtered through Brooks, particularly the Brooks of *Annie Allen* where one finds poems ("A light and diplomatic bird," for example) that are virtually indistinguishable from the work of Dickinson's own hand.

3. Herman Melville, *White-Jacket: The World in a Man-of-War* (New York, 1952), p. 370.

4. Charles Feidelson, Jr., *Symbolism and American Literature* (Chicago, 1953), p. 71.

5. Quoted in F.O. Matthiessen, *American Renaissance* (New York, 1941), p. 54.

6. John O'Brien, ed., *Interviews with Black Writers* (New York, 1973), p. 114.

7. Charles T. Davis, "Robert Hayden's Use of History," in Donald Gibson, ed., *Modern Black Poets* (Englewood Cliffs, N.J., 1973), pp. 96-111.

8. *New York Times Book Review*, February 22, 1976, p. 34.

9. Hayden's insistence that he is a poet who happens to be Negro, made most dramatically at the Fisk University Centennial Writers' Conference in 1966, inevitably calls to mind the stance taken by Countee Cullen in the Foreword to *Caroling Dusk* (New York, 1927). Hayden was enamored of Cullen as an undergraduate, and the careful reader can detect significant correspondences between "The Ballad of Nat Turner" and "The Shroud of Color." Yet when Cullen rejected the idea of a black poetry in favor of a poetry written by blacks, his equation of a black movement in poetry with disease clearly indicated how much he underestimated the possibilities for poetry in black American culture and

how much he was intimidated by the richness of the Anglo-American poetic tradition: "to say that the pulse beat of their [i.e., the blacks'] verse shows generally such a fever, or the symptoms of such an ague, will prove on closer examination merely the moment's exaggeration of a physician anxious to establish a new literary ailment." Hayden throughout his career has prized his independence, but he has never hesitated to exploit the possibilities for poetry in Afro-American culture. At any rate, Melvin B. Tolson, the magnificent and neglected black poet who rose in opposition to Hayden at Fisk to say that blackness is prior to poetry, has himself been accused of denying his own blackness. No issue in Afro-American letters has to date generated more heat or less light than the question of what "black poet" means.

10. For the assertion that Hayden was especially concerned with Afro-American history during the 1940s, we refer the reader to Davis, "Hayden's Use of History," p. 97. Proof that Hayden reached his maturity during these years is to be found in the difference between the stiff poetry of *Heart-Shape in the Dust* and the elastic verse of *The Lion and the Archer* (New York, 1948).

11. T.S. Eliot, *The Waste Land and Other Poems* (1922; rpt. New York: 1962), p. 26.

12. O'Brien, *Interviews*, pp. 120–22.

CHARLES T. DAVIS

Robert Hayden's Use of History

History has haunted Robert Hayden from the beginning of his career as a poet. In 1941, when a graduate student at the University of Michigan, he worked on a series of poems dealing with slavery and the Civil War called *The Black Spear*, the manuscript of which was to win for him a second Hopwood Award.[1] This effort was no juvenile excursion, to be forgotten in the years of maturity. Though some of the poems have not been reprinted in *Selected Poems* (1966),[2] *The Black Spear* survives in a severely altered form in Section Five of that volume. What remains is not simply "O Daedalus, Fly Away Home" and "Frederick Douglass," but a preoccupation with a continuing historical ambition. This was the desire to record accurately the yearnings, the frustrations, and the achievement of an enslaved but undestroyed people. "Middle Passage," "The Ballad of Nat Turner," and "Runagate, Runagate," all written later, share this concern. In these poems noble blacks, Cinquez, Nat Turner, and Harriet Tubman, rise from oppression and obscurity.

An extended period of study and research, as well as correspondence in theme, links these later poems with *The Black Spear*. Hayden had intended "Middle Passage" to be the opening work of *The Black Spear*, but the poems in 1941 would not assume a shape that would satisfy a meticulous craftsman.[3] "The Ballad of Nat Turner" and "Runagate, Runagate" come from poring over journals, notebooks, narratives, and histories dealing with the slave trade, plantation life, slave revolts, and the Underground Railroad, reading begun about 1940 and continued for perhaps a decade, judging from his recollection of the activity of composition.[4]

A generation later Hayden displays an attachment somewhat less strong to historical themes. In 1966 "Frederick Douglass" closed Section Five of *Selected Poems* and the book, a sign of a surviving commitment. "El-Hajj Malik El-Shabazz (Malcolm X)" opens Section Three, "Words in the Mourning Time," of Hayden's most recent book of poems, bearing the title of the section and published in 1970.[5] Though the commitment to interpreting history is still present, the emphasis has changed. The poems of *The Black Spear* emerge from the suffering of black people before Emancipation and record their assertion of manhood, more than the simple ability to survive, but those in "Words in the Mourning Time" describe the agony undergone by Malcolm and others to achieve spiritual liberation in our own day and the search for meaning in history upon which that liberation depends. What has endured through the years is the central importance of history in Hayden's poetry—not history as the poet would like it to be, but history as he has discovered it.

The birth of the historical impulse in Hayden is not easily described. He seems to have nourished always a sense of the past. Hayden said in conversation with Paul McCluskey, his editor at Harcourt Brace Jovanovich: "For some reason, I don't know why, I seemed to have a need to recall my past and to rid myself of the pain of so much of it."[6] The poet, then, was discussing poems written in the 1950s, but the statement applies with equal force to his work at any stage in his career. The activity of truth-telling from memory, of reconstructing the past, is purgative—at least in part, and it is intimately connected with the necessity to write poems.

Hayden's predisposition acquired quite early a formal reinforcement. The record of this is bound up with the writing of the poems in *The Black Spear.* Though W.H. Auden, his mentor at Michigan, looked on when Hayden received a prize for *The Black Spear*, the British poet was not the dominant influence shaping the work. That, rather, was Stephen Vincent Benét, whose long historical narrative *John Brown's Body* (1927) moved Hayden to think of approaching slavery and the Civil War "from the black man's point of view."[7] Indeed, Hayden has acknowledged that the title of his sequence of historical poems, *The Black Spear*, comes from Benét and has pointed to a passage appearing late in *John Brown's Body*,[8] in which the reaction of the newly emancipated slaves to Sherman's march through Georgia is described. Benét, in this passage, commented upon his failure to register in verse the full range and depth of the black response to the trauma of freedom:

> Oh, black skinned epic, epic with the black spear,
> I cannot sing you, having too white a heart,
> And yet, some day, a poet will rise to sing you
> And sing you with such truth and mellowness,
>
> That you will be a match for any song
> Sung by old, populous nations in the past, ... (p. 308)

Hayden aspired to become the poet called for by Benét, one with a heart sufficiently black. Indeed, he told Benét, several years after reading *John Brown's Body* and a year or so before the commencement of serious work on *The Black Spear*, that he intended to write a poem on the materials pointed to by the white poet,[9] though possibly not the "black skinned epic" so solemnly predicted.

Benét was a hindrance as well as a help, as every major influence must be for a poet struggling to find his own voice. The story of the writing of "Middle Passage" documents the point. This poem, in many ways the most impressive achievement of Hayden's early career, was completed in some form by the time that *The Black Spear* was submitted to the Hopwood judges. But Hayden refused to include it in his volume, even though he had planned it as the inaugural piece of the whole sequence. And his reasons for delay are good ones: "Actually I had tried writing the poem in blank vers—unrhymed iambic pentamete—but, then, it was too much like Benét, not only in form, but in diction and narrative organization also."[10] The statement prepares us for differences in the final form of the poem, published originally in *Phylon* in 1945,[11] but it also requires us to look for correspondences with *John Brown's Body*, because Benét's influence has been so powerful and pervasive.

The section of *John Brown's Body* which is closest to Hayden's "Middle Passage" is the one that appears immediately after the "invocation," "Prelude—the Slaver."[12] Benét presents here the captain of a slave ship who is moved to comment on a profession in which he is skilled, while actually transporting a cargo of black ivory from Africa to America. The impulse toward self-revelation is aroused by the questions, often not stated but implied, posed by a young mate, who is inexperienced and innocent. The bulk of the narrative consists of exchanges between the two. The Captain is firm in his piety: he reads his Bible regularly and sees no contradiction between practicing Christianity and ferrying blacks for profit to a life of enforced and unending servitude. The Mate is less certain; he recoils from what he sees—the blacks in chains, the threat of the plague, the hatred of the enslaved—and he yearns for his and the Captain's native New England. Most of all, he is upset by what he calls the Blackness, the stench that is everywhere, the stain that will not wash out. His own emotions approach a mystical terror that seems to deny the Captain's pieties, a terror more appropriate for the sinning than for those who take comfort in the fact that they are adding heathen black souls to Christ's kingdom.

Hayden takes over the problem of reconciling Christianity and slavetrading in "Middle Passage,"[13] though the machinery of his narrative is much more complicated. The first of three parts offers the log entries, the prayers, and the ruminations of a pious member of the crew of a slaver. The conflict, however, is internal rather than external. The spur toward self-revelation is not an innocent youth on a maiden voyage, but the consciousness of the speaker, as he feels the threat to body and soul in the hazards and the emotional excesses that come from participation in the slave trade. Once again we find black resistance, rebellion and implacable hatred, and the threat of the plague. To these familiar difficulties, Hayden adds a new trial—the temptation to lust with black wenches, the giving up wholly to sex and alcohol so that ship, slaves, and self are all lost.

Hayden's addition points to one of the differences separating Benét's poem from his own—the richness of his documentation. The accurate touches that come from Hayden's wide reading are impressive. His wealth of information is to be seen in Part One in the names of the slave ships, the form of the ship's log, the description of the creeping blindness (Ophthalmia), and the graphic account of the drunken orgy aboard *The Bella J*. Parts Two and Three, almost untouched by the example of Benét's poem, display evidences of extensive research in the slave trade in the library of the University of Michigan.[14] The recollections of the bluff slave trader, undistorted by qualms of conscience, describe the slave factories, the collection methods, the corruption of black kings, and the good times on the West African coast. Following this straightforward statement, we hear in Part Three the testimony of a Spanish slaver, who supplies from his own point of view the details of the *Amistad* Mutiny in 1839. Now, the sources of Hayden's knowledge are many, but he recalls two as being especially rewarding, *Adventures of an African Slaver*[15] and Muriel Rukeyser's biography *Willard Gibbs*,[16] which presents an accurate description of the *Amistad* Mutiny and the trial that followed.

Though Benét's poem might have suggested to Hayden the technique of handling the poetic problems of "Middle Passage" through the use of voices, it could not provide a model for the subtle use of the technique which Hayden's poem displays. Benét's "Prelude" has three voices—the skipper's, the mate's, and the poet's. Actually the poet intrudes very little, only to utter prophecy in a brief section toward the end of the poem. According to the poet, the black seeds "robbed from a black king's storehouse" (p. 12) would fall on American earth, "lie silent, quicken" (p. 12) and then grow. A seed would become "A black shadow-sapling, a tree of shadow," and the tree, the poet promises, would ultimately blot out "all the seamen's stars" (p. 12). An ominous prediction, then, is offered, one that identifies the shaking of the leaves of the shadow tree with the trampling of the "horses of anger," the "Beat of the heavy hooves like metal on metal" (p. 12), the signs of war. The poet of the "Prelude" engages, then, in the necessary prefiguration of the Civil War that he will describe in later books.

The poet of "Middle Passage" has a good deal more to do. His is the central consciousness of the poem, providing a frame in Part One for the description of the painful voyage from Africa to America and, at the beginning of the poem, extracting meaning for the journey: "voyage through death to life upon these shores" (p. 65). A crew member of a slave ship provides the actual description of the middle passage itself. His narration is not simple because it is made complex by the fact of his piety. On the one hand, there is the sailor's prosaic voice, instructing us in entries in ship's logs and, finally, in a legal deposition, of the hazards of a rebellious cargo, disease, and lust. On the other hand, there is the voice praying for "safe passage" to bring "heathen souls" to God's "chastening" (p. 65). What the sailor tells has so much cruelty and depravity that it seems finally to overwhelm the teller of the tale. The secure sense of accomplishing God's design departs, and there is only the cry, despairing, now, rather than confident: "Pilot Oh Pilot Me" (p. 67).

The poet echoes, clearly, the cry of the sailor. He has been moved deeply by the prosaic account in rather different ways. For one thing, he is aware of the irony present in the crewman's piety, and he comments, in the language of Shakespeare's Ariel and with a precedent provided by *The Waste Land:*[17]

> Deep in the festering hold thy father lies,
> of his bones New England pews are made,
> those are altar lights that were his eyes. (p. 65)

The allusion to Shakespeare's sea-change mocks a less spiritual transformation, though Hayden's too has a claim to religious motivation.

The "altar lights" in a church in New England are vulgar consequences of an investment in black gold. Moreover, the poet speculates quite openly on the destiny of the Yankee slave ship, with the benefit of a greater perspective and more knowledge than the sailor:

> What port awaits us, Davy Jones'
> or home? I've heard of slavers drifting, drifting,
> playthings of wind and storm and chance, their crews
> gone blind, the jungle hatred
> crawling up on deck. (p. 66)

The poet's historical perspective appears more clearly in subsequent parts. In Part Two the poet becomes the "lad," who listens to the recollections of a hardened and unrepentant slaver, reconstructing the beginnings of the wretched trade in Africa in greed, vanity, war, deception, devastation, and disease. In Part Three the historical perspective acquires an important spiritual dimension. Here the slave ships become "shuttles in the rocking loom of history" (p. 68) and the pattern from the loom itself emerges. The ships, though they may bear "bright ironical names like 'Jesus,' 'Estrella,' 'Esperanza,' 'Mercy'" (p. 65), contribute to "New World littorals that are/ mirage and myth and actual shore" (p. 68). The poet promises the "actual shore," and the journey to it, the middle passage, becomes a descent into death resembling the dark night of the soul. The "shore" is life at the end of death, but first blacks must experience death, a "voyage whose chartings are unlove" (p. 68).

Cinquez, the leader of the *Amistad* Mutiny, assumes especial prominence in the poet-speaker's vision of "Middle Passage." The Spanish slaver considers Cinquez "that surly brute who calls himself a prince,/ directing, urging on the ghastly work" (p. 69). But in the enlightened historical perspective of the poet, Cinquez is an expression of "The deep immortal human wish,/ the timeless will" (p. 70). He is seen as an early sign of "life upon these shores," a "deathless primaveral image,/ life that transfigures many lives" (p. 70). Hayden describes, then, a second sea-change, one more genuine than the transformation of the "festering hold" into pews and altar lights in New England because this change transfigures blacks. Cinquez, on the bloody deck of the *Amistad* and beyond the "butchered bodies" (p. 69) of the slave crew, points to the discovery of manhood and human dignity, even to recognition by law (thanks to "the august John Quincy Adams," p. 70).

Nothing resembling this historical vision appears in *John Brown's Body*.

Benét sees the Civil War as the "pastoral rebellion of the earth/ Against machines, against the Age of Steam" (p. 334), and out of John Brown's body grows "the new, mechanic birth,/ ... the great, metallic Beast/ Expanding West and East" (p. 335). Hayden is not concerned with these problems, but rather with the transformation of slave to man, a transfiguration frequently touched with mystical overtones in his poems.

All of the poems of Section Five of *Selected Poems* have this preoccupation of Hayden's. Nat Turner in the darkness of the Dismal Swamp has a vision of bright angels in fiery combat, and he rises from his dream "at last free/ And purified, ..." (p. 74), and committed to holy war. He knows, then, that the "conqueror faces" (p. 73) of his dream were like his. Harriet Tubman, in "Runagate, Runagate," rises above the impulsive, headlong flight of slaves to the North to insert steel in the spines of the timid, to provide light and direction to the bewildered, and threaten death to the faltering and craven. She is "woman of earth, whipscarred,/ a summoning, a shining" (p. 76), asserting a single objective, "Mean to be free" (p. 76). Indeed, only she, "alias The General/ alias Moses Stealer of Slaves" (p. 76), knows that one must be "mean" to be free. The spiritual justification of her purpose comes in lines echoing the language of a Negro spiritual toward the conclusion of the poem:

> Midnight Special on a sabre track movering movering,
> first stop Mercy and the last Hallelujah

Though the mystical transformation of the desire to be free, to assert manhood, links all of Hayden's historical poems of this period, "The Ballad of Nat Turner" and "Runagate, Runagate" point to the importance for Hayden of another kind of source material. Behind these poems, indeed, lies the research of the 1940s that supported "Middle Passage" as well, an accumulation of materials so rich that Hayden was moved to write a play about Harriet Tubman, *Go Down, Moses.*[18] He recalls, in reviewing formal sources, that *The Negro in Virginia*, a study completed in 1940 by the Writer's Program of the Works Projects Administration and supervised by Roscoe E. Lewis of Hampton Institute,[19] had especial value for him as he prepared to write "The Ballad of Nat Turner." But this familiar pattern of research and rumination received support from a knowledge of a type of source material not found in "Middle Passage." This was the Negro folk tradition.

Nat Turner is struck by the cessation in the turning of the wheel within a wheel, an image that recalls the spiritual celebrating Ezekiel's illumination. The details of the celestial combat have the vividness and the primitive power of a folk sermon. Nat's account in a moment of intense excitement tends to employ the repetition found so frequently in the words of a folk preacher, suggesting with its incantatory rhythms the chant that accompanies traditionally God's direct influence upon his mortal instrument:

> But I saw I saw oh many of
> those mighty beings waver.
> Waver and fall, go streaking down
> into swamp water, and the water
> hissed and steamed and bubbled and locked
> shuddering shuddering over. (p. 73)

There is a folk basis too for the references to Africa, for those intimations of the mother land that come to blacks frequently in darkness and in the forest:

> where Ibo warriors
> hung shadowless, turning in wind
> that moaned like Africa. (p. 72)

"Runagate, Runagate" has linguistic touches that suggest a strong folk inspiration, with "jack-muh-lanterns" (p. 75), "patterollers" (p. 76), an "a-murbling" (p. 76) fear, a "movering" (p. 77) train, "jaybird-talk" (p. 76), and "oh Susyanna" (p. 76). The invitation to get aboard the coach to the North is extended to enslaved blacks in accents that show dialect roots:

> Come ride-a my train
> Mean mean mean to be free. (p. 77)

The language is just a sign of the rich reliance upon the materials that come ultimately from the folk imagination. We have the vision of the free North as the "star-shaped yonder Bible city" (p. 75), the association of the journey to freedom with the "North star and bonanza gold" (p. 76), the identification of the flight itself as "crossing over" (p. 75) or as the freedom train, and the assumed connection between the calling of the hoot-owl and the "hants in the air" (p. 77). Not the least of these evidences of the pressure of folk culture intimately known are the snatches from the spirituals. Though these are mostly echoes rather than direct quotations, there are two lines, indeed, that come without change from the great spiritual that begins with the phrase "Oh-h freedom":

And before I'll be a slave
I'll be buried in my grave.

Hayden relies upon folk materials almost exclusively in only one poem in Section V of *Selected Poems*—"O Daedalus, Fly Away Home." Like the others, this poem transforms mystically the desire for freedom. In the interview with Paul McCluskey, Hayden has identified the source of the poem as "a legend common among the Georgia Sea Island Negroe—the legend of the Flying African."[20] He adds that it was their belief that certain slaves had the magical power to fly to freedom in Africa. The poetic machinery that supports this central idea uses other elements in a folk culture. The metrics of the poem suggest the rhythm of a folk dance called "juba," widely performed by slaves in the antebellum South. The instruments providing the musical background are a "coonskin drum" and a "jubilee banjo" (p. 71). The only touch in the poem that does not show the influence of Negro folk history is the reference to Daedalus in the title and the resonance that is achieved throughout from the comparison with an earlier and better-known historical flight.

History, formal and folk, serves Hayden's purpose, and that purpose in the early historical poems is to describe the mystical emergence of freedom from circumstances that appall and degrade, and the making of a man, a black man in America. No better description of the poet's objective exists than the first lines of the justly famous tribute to Frederick Douglass:

When it is finally ours, this freedom, this liberty, this beautiful
and terrible thing, needful to man as air, usable as earth; .... (p. 78)

Contributing to Douglass's eminence is his own "middle passage," his painful exposure to death in various form—physical violence, humiliation, and ostracism:

this man, this Douglass, this former slave, this Negro
beaten to his knees, exiled, visioning a world
where none is lonely, none hunted, alien, ... (p. 78)

Following death comes life, not simply for Douglass, whose image survives in our memories, but for us all. In a voice touched with awe at the transformation, the poet concludes his tribute in this way:

Oh, not with statues' rhetoric,
not with legends and poems and wreaths of bronze alone,
but with the lives grown out of his life, the lives
fleshing his dream of the beautiful, needful thing. (p. 78)

The end of the Douglass sonnet echoes, then, the theme of "Middle Passage":

Voyage through death
to life upon these shores

and offers again the great theme of the historical poems of Hayden's early period.

Hayden's poems published in 1970, *Words in the Mourning Time*, reveal a persistence of an interest in historical materials, but they do not have the focus or the concentration which the ideal of *The Black Spear* provided. No doubt, the poet's own soul has yielded to "migratory habits" (p. 64),[21] which the poet represents as being the theme of Socrates at his "hemlock hour." Like Socrates, Hayden faces a world not entirely reassuring to the firmness of his early vision. The startling carcasses, "death's black droppings" (p. 64), strewn about the Fisk University lawns are bad enough, but they suggest, with their troublesome presence, the existence of more serious challenges elsewhere.

The consequences of "middle passage" are not all good, nor all life. The poet travels to Lookout Mountain,[22] the site of a great Civil War battle, where the agony of suffering, struggle, and death was most acute, and finds himself among "Sunday alpinists" who "pick views and souvenirs" (p. 26). The Union victory seems "dubious," to say the least, when from the perspective of "A world away" the poet is moved to say:

... the scions of that fighting climb
endless hills of war, amid war's peaks
and valleys broken, scattered fall. (p. 26)

The Roman rhetoric heard at the *Amistad* trial in "Middle Passage" has become the song of the "stuffed gold eagle" (p. 26).

Confusion comes from something other than the failure of the time to live up to its brightest vision; it occurs in the minds of those who stand to benefit most from the realization of the dream—he oppressed blacks. Hayden's dramatic poem "The Dream" deals with this problem. Old Sinda remains behind in the slave quarters after "Marse Lincum's soldier boys" (p. 12) have brought freedom to the plantation. This "ragged jubilo" (p. 12) does not accord with Sinda's expectations, and she hides in the quarters rather than follow, rejoicing, in the wake of the army. Her dream of emancipation is infinitely more attractive, and Sinda sees the faces of her sons Cal and Joe, and that of Charlie, possibly their father, who was sold to the ricefields many years before, on "the great big soldiers marching out of gunburst," and she will not accept "those Buckcras with their ornery/ funning cussed commands" (p. 12). These are not "the hosts the dream had promised her" (p. 12). Sinda fails to understand that war is prose, recorded in Cal's letters to her about the "Kernul" and the "contrybans," the rain, the hardtack and the bullybeef, the "ficety gals," and the constant worry about the "Bullit" with his name "rote on it." And liberation is prose too. But Sinda will cling to her vision until she dies, until the very end of her waning, "brittle strength" (p. 13).

"On Lookout Mountain" and "The Dream" are comments on history that have especial value in light of *The Black Spear*, since they deal with the pain and the expectation attached to the Civil War, but they do not confront directly the problems of recent history. "El-Hajj Malik El-Shabazz (Malcolm X)" does this. Certain prefigurations come from "On Lookout Mountain" and "The Dream" that prepare us for Hayden's approach to the career of Malcolm X. One is the poet's objection to the vulgar and materialistic limitations in contemporary American culture; another is the poet's sense of the possibility of distortion, even corruption, in the mind of the holder of the dream. Both are related to the epigraph of "El-Hajj Malik El-Shabazz": "O masks and metamorphoses of Ahab, Native Son" (p. 37).

Malcolm, like Douglass, is a folk hero. What is required to measure the man is an understanding of the folk milieu out of which he came as well as his position in history as a charismatic leader of black people. The two kinds of historical knowledge which Hayden displayed in "The Ballad of Nat Turner" and in "Runagate, Runagate" are present here as well. The folk mores that rest behind Malcolm's emergence are urban, however, not rural. No doubt, the poet's memory of his own childhood in black Detroit gives especial poignancy to the reconstruction of Malcolm's early years. There is no question about the authority of his description of "Dee-troit Red" on the street:

> He conked his hair and Lindy-hopped,
> zoot-suited jiver, swinging those chicks
> in the hot rose and reefer glow. (p. 37)

Hayden is equally prepared to face the thorny problem of Malcolm's place in history. His consideration must begin with Malcolm's sense of his role, with the facts of the *Autobiography*.[23] The reliance seems to be especially clear when the poet refers to the tragic end of Malcolm's father and mother, to his reputation in prison ("'Satan' in The Hole" [p. 38]), and to his intimations of his own violent death. But Hayden moves beyond the *Autobiography* to comment on Malcolm's Black Muslim faith. What stirs the poet is something other than a casual interest in Islam; it is the concern of a man deeply touched by the power of an Eastern religion, a devoted Bahaist who can sympathize with a conversion to a faith that many think exotic. Personal factors as well as the passion for accuracy combine to describe the historical phenomenon that is Malcolm.

The documentation of Malcolm's commitment to Islam has impressive economy. Important to his faith is the narrative attributed to Elijah Muhammad, the leader of the Nation of Islam among black Americans, about the creation of the white man. "Yacub's white-faced treachery" (p. 38) refers to the original mistake in genetic experimentation that led to the ultimate suppression of blacks by upstart and diabolical whites. In this version of creation there is no doubt about the color, rather the lack of it, of Ahab, the unholy king. Arabic phrases in Hayden's poem are fortunate and functional additions. Something of the evangelical character of the faith and of the excitement that thrills the faithful is conveyed through these exclamations. The poet describes with precision Malcolm's role in the movement:

> He X'd his name, became his people's anger,
> exhorted them to vengeance for their past;
> rebuked, admonished them,
>
> their scourger who
> would shame them, drive them from
> the lush ice gardens of their servitude. (p. 59)

Malcolm becomes Christ in this passage, angrily driving the money changers from the temple. There is accuracy in this comparison, and there is irony, too, if we consider Christ something other than Calvin's creation, with the "hellward-thrusting hands" (p. 38) that so repelled Malcolm. The irony becomes explicit rather than potential when the poet adds: "Rejecting Ahab, he was of Ahab's tribe" (p. 39).

The presence of ironies ties "El-Hajj Malik El-Shabazz" to "Middle

Passage." In the earlier poem the play upon "sea-change" adds dimension to Hayden's statement; in the poem about Malcolm the "dawn" functions in much the same way. A "false dawn of vision" precedes a true awakening. Malcolm is first converted, through the offices of Elijah Muhammad to a faith in a "racist Allah," one whose "adulterate attars could not cleanse/ him of the odors of the pit" (p. 38). His pilgrimage to Mecca sparks a "final metamorphosis," a truer revelation that eliminates hate as a necessary component of faith. Malcolm moves from neo-Islam to orthodox Islam, and Hayden celebrates the second conversion:

He fell upon his face before
Allah the raceless in whose blazing Oneness all
were one. He rose renewed renamed, became
much more than there was time for him to be. (p. 40)

Hayden's tribute to El-Hajj Malik El-Shabazz, formerly Malcolm X, renamed after the Hajj rituals or the rites of the pilgrimage to Mecca, expresses a view of what the movement in history should be. The early poems record Hayden's vision of a black man who has acquired freedom and humanity. The later poems, dealing with history after Emancipation, describe the confused wanderings and the tormenting frustrations of the liberated man, but they still maintain that modern man must become more human. The first part of the long poem "Words in the Mourning Time," a lament for the deaths of Martin Luther King and Robert Kennedy, sketches this necessary development in our culture, upon which our survival depends. The destruction of King and Kenned—and of El-Hajj Malik El-Shabaz—represents for us a "middle passage" to "life upon these shores":

the agonies of our deathbed childbed age
are process, major means whereby,
oh dreadfully, our humanness must be achieved. (p. 41)

The heroes of history in this time of mourning are different from those in *The Black Spear.* They are more fallible, more vulnerable, more confused, and more easily destroyed, but El-Hajj Malik El-Shabazz matures to share a vision that Douglass has seen and which Hayden still enunciates with eloquence:

a human world where godliness
is possible and man

is neither gook nigger honkey wop nor kike
but man
permitted to be man. (p. 49)[24]
1973

NOTES

1. Robert Hayden discusses the genesis of *The Black Spear* in the third section of a series of exchanges with his editor, Paul McCluskey, recorded in New York in January 1971. The whole series was subsequently published in five sections in *How I Write/1* (New York: Harcourt Brace Jovanovich, Inc., 1972). Hayden is one of three literary artists discussed in the book; the others are Judson Philips and Lawson Carter. The third section, "The Black Spear," of "Robert Hayde—The Poet and His Art: A Conversation" is to be found on pp. 169–193.

2. *Selected Poems* (New York: October House Inc., 1966). Subsequent references to *The Black Spear* poems and other early poems will be to this volume.

3. *How I Write/1*, p. 175.

4. Ibid., pp. 175–180.

5. *Words in the Mourning Time* (New York: October House Inc., 1970). Subsequent references to "El-Hajj Malik El-Shabazz" and other late poems will be to this volume.

6. *How I Write/1*, p. 143.

7. Ibid., p. 170.

8. Stephen Vincent Benét, *John Brown's Body* (New York: Farrar and Rinehart, Inc., 1927). Subsequent references to this poem will be to this edition.

9. *How I Write/1*, p. 170.

10. Ibid., p. 176.

11. "Middle Passage," *Phylon*, 6 (Third Quarter 1945), pp. 247–253. The poem was revised and shortened by the omission of an introductory section before republication in *Selected Poems.*

12. *John Brown's Body*, pp. 8–13.

13. *Selected Poems*, pp. 67–70.

14. *How I Write/1*, p. 175.

15. Brantz Mayer, *Adventures of an African Slaver* (New York: A. and C. Boni, 1928).

16. Muriel Rukeyser, *Willard Gibbs* (Garden City, N.Y.: Doubleday, Doran and Co., 1942).

17. Ariel's famous song in *The Tempest* begins:

Full fathom five thy father lies,
Of his bones are coral made,
Those are pearls that were his eyes,
Nothing of him that doth fade
But doth suffer a sea-change
Into something rich and strange. (I.ii.397–402)

One reference in *The Waste Land* (T.S. Eliot, *The Complete Poems and Plays, 1909–1950* [New York: Harcourt, Brace and World, Inc., 1952]) appears in Part II, "A Game of Chess" (p. 41):

I remember
Those are pearls that were his eyes. (II.124–125)

18. *How I Write/1*, p. 188.
19. *The Negro in Virginia* (New York: Hastings House, Publishers, 1940).
20. *How I Write/1*, p. 180.
21. In "A Plague of Starlings." The poem has this final stanza:

And if not careful
I shall tread
upon carcasses
carcasses when I
go morning now
to lecture on
what Socrates,
the hemlock hour nigh,
told sorrowing
Phaedo and the rest
about the migratory
habits of the soul. (p. 64)

22. "On Lookout Mountain" (p. 26).
23. Malcolm X, *The Autobiography of Malcolm X* (New York: Grove Press, Inc., 1966).
24. The final lines of Part IX in "Words in the Mourning Time."

FRITZ OEHLSCHLAEGER

Robert Hayden's Meditation on Art: The Final Sequence of Words in the Mourning Time

Published in 1970, Robert Hayden's *Words in the Mourning Time* responded directly to one of the most violent decades in American history. The violence of the 1960s is at the very center of Hayden's volume, both in the magnificent poem on El-Hajj Malik El-Shabazz (Malcolm X) and the volume's title poem. The first of these concludes with a tragic recognition of time's insufficiency. Malcolm was struck down before he could realize what Hayden considers the promise of his "final metamorphosis,"[1] his vision of the oneness of man under Allah achieved while making the *Hajj* to Mecca:

> He fell upon his face before
> Allah the raceless in whose blazing Oneness all
> were one. He rose renewed renamed, became
> much more than there was time for him to be. (ll. 52–55)

"Words in the Mourning Time" is dedicated to two other American martyrs of the 1960s: "For King, for Robert Kennedy, / destroyed by those they could not save, / for King for Kennedy I mourn" (ll. 1–3). But while the poem begins with this specific dedication to King and Kennedy, it soon becomes a much broader poem of mourning for America itself, a nation "self-destructive, self-betrayed" (1. 4). That self-destruction and betrayal are

From *Black American Literature Forum* 19, no. 3 (Fall 1985).

evident for Hayden in the Vietnam War and in the explosions of violence in America's cities during the 1960s: Watts, Newark, and Hayden's own birthplace, Detroit. The poem emphasizes particularly the double betrayal of Vietnam: Americans destroyed a nation in order to save it and, in doing so, destroyed themselves. For Hayden, who taught throughout the decade at Fisk and at Michigan, the thought of his own students' brutalizing the Vietnamese and being brutalized in turn made of Vietnam a "bloodclotted name" in his consciousness:

> Vietnam and I think of the villages
> mistakenly burning the schoolrooms devouring
> their children and I think of those who
> were my students
> brutalized killing
> wasted by horror
> in ultimate loneliness
> dying
> Vietnam Vietnam (ll. 25–33)

No less indicative of America's self-betrayal were the riots of the central cities, in which blacks responded to racism and continued economic exploitation by turning to violence as a means of affirming identity:

> I hate
> I destroy
> I am I am
> sing hey nonny no
> sing burn baby burn. (ll. 58–62)

Such is the cry, Hayden argues—alluding at once to Richard Wright, James Baldwin, and Ralph Ellison—of the "man who / lives underground whose / name nobody / knows" (ll. 91–94) as he seeks the "soul-country of his/meaning" (ll. 99–100) more than three hundred years after his passage to America.

"El-Hajj Malik El-Shabazz" and the title poem are grouped together in *Words in the Mourning Time* as section three of the books' four sections. Following them is a series of six poems—"Monet's 'Waterlilies,'" "The Lions," "October," "The Return," "'Lear Is Gay,'" and "A Plague of Starlings"—whose devotion to artistic themes might seem at first to indicate a radical shift in the nature of Hayden's volume. But as I will argue, these six poems actually grow out of, and respond to, the bitter realities that dominate the third section of the book. Indeed the six poems can be most richly and revealingly read as a loose sequence in which Hayden makes use of recurrent patterns of allusion and imagery to contemplate the value of art in times of political violence and chaos, the value of words in a mourning time. The poems represent, in short, his coming to terms with his own vocation as a poet in a period of despair.

"Monet's 'Waterlilies'" begins the final sequence by depicting a stark antithesis between the political violence of the 1960s and the serenity of one of Monet's water garden paintings:

> today as the news from Selma and Saigon
> poisons the air like fallout,
>   I come again to see
> the serene great picture that I love. (ll. 1–4)

With some delicate ironies, the rest of the poem accounts for the serenity derived from the painting's being a self-enclosed world. In the waterlily canvases, Monet discarded traditional notions of perspective to emphasize the two-dimensional picture space. The "Waterlilies" do not provide a window onto the world; instead each is a world, a world of light as Monet apprehended its movement on his water garden at a specific instant in time. The paintings deliberately conflate surface and depth, reality and reflection, near and far, water and sky:

> Here space and time exist in light
> the eye like the eye of faith believes.
>   The seen, the known
> dissolve in irridescence, become
> illusive flesh of light
>   that was not, was, forever is. (ll. 5–10)

The analogy introduced here between religious belief and artistic creation—as well as re-creation by those who bring art to life by viewing it—is one that Hayden insists on throughout the sequence of poems. The work of art becomes an incarnation, the "illusive flesh," with a fine pun on *elusive*. What is incarnated is a quality of belief in the artist that is very like that of the religiously faithful. In the "Waterlilies" the conflation of reality and illusion, water and sky, surface and depth creates an effect of joyous wholeness that perhaps approaches the mystic's sense of unity with the cosmos as nearly as it is possible for art to do. The "illusive flesh of light," with its impression of wholeness, is one that "was not" and yet "was." It "was not" part of the objective reality of Monet's water garden or part of the perception of the ordinary observer whose vision is cued by notions of position, depth, and distance. The "illusive flesh of light" "was," however, because Monet perceived it to be or, to adopt Hayden's metaphor, believed it into being. And once it was believed into being, it "forever is" in the work of art.

The final lines of "Monet's 'Waterlilies'" darken the poem significantly, suggesting the ambiguity of our response to Monet's bold attempt to reconstitute the broken world in an image of unity and joy:

> O light beheld as through refracting tears.
> Here is the aura of that world
>   each of us has lost.
> Here is the shadow of its joy. (ll. 11–14)

The visual accuracy of the lines deserves comment: The shimmering irridescence of Monet's waterlily paintings is very much like what one beholds through squinted eyes full of tears. What precisely is lost here is difficult to define. When asked in an interview whether the poem referred to a world of childhood innocence, Hayden responded that he was "absolutely cold to the voguish and over-used theme of 'lost innocence,'" adding wryly that he was perhaps "just too pseudo-Freudian." Instead Hayden argued for a broader interpretation of the loss: "Each of us has lost something that once gave the world a dimension it will never have again for us, except in memory."[2]

Hayden called this a "botched" explanation, but perhaps it was not so "botched" after all, for clearly it is less important to determine exactly what is lost than it is to note the paradoxical relations among subject, artist, and viewer that the poem's final lines imply. Implicit is the suggestion that Monet beheld the light on his water garden as "through refracting tears," for he understood that the best he could create was but the "aura" of a lost world, a "shadow of its joy." Hayden, too, recognizes the limits of art. Standing before Monet's canvas, he rejoices in the artist's approximation of a world of joy but remains fully aware that the painting is but an approximation, the "shadow" of a moment forever lost. Both Monet and Hayden attempt to fix time, to create or participate in a reality that, while not transcendent, is yet impervious to time. Both know, however, that the attempt must fail, but both also know that this failure paradoxically ensures the attempt—that it is the world's turning that moves Monet to capture what is lost, the impression of light as it appears in a single instant of time among his waterlilies at Giverny. "Death is the mother of beauty" for Monet and Robert Hayden no less than for Wallace Stevens.

One final point needs to be made about Hayden's revision of "Monet's 'Waterlilies.'" When it appeared in *Words in the Mourning Time*, Hayden described the painting in the first stanza as one "flames disfigured once/and efficient evil may yet destroy" (ll. 5–6). These lines, dropped entirely when the poem reappeared in *Angle of Ascent* (1975), may refer to the fact that some of Monet's late water landscapes were damaged by tank and artillery fire during the Nazi retreat from France.[3] If so, the allusion would reinforce the antithesis of political violence and Monet's serenity. By indicating the fragility of the work of art itself, the lines also suggest that the value of art must lie primarily in the process of creation rather than in the product alone. What can stand finally against the violence of political systems is not the work of art itself but the quality of imagination that creates the world anew in images of unity, connection, and joy.

Hayden's concern with artistic making is especially evident in "The Lions," the next poem of the sequence. The poem focuses on a circus lion tamer, who as both the servant and master of "unsparing beauty" (1. 11) exults in almost religious fashion as he makes his lions leap "through nimbus-fire" (1. 9). Here the art is of the most transitory nature; indeed there is properly no art object at all that is separable from the creative process. We cannot distinguish the lion leaping through the fire from the lion itself any more than Yeats could know his "dancer from the dance." Indeed the poem may well be indebted to Yeats, who was clearly on Hayden's mind during the writing of *Words in the Mourning Time*, as is indicated by "Kodachromes of the Island," in which Hayden compares himself specifically to the Yeats of "The Circus Animals' Desertion." Feeling "Alien, at home—as always / everywhere," Hayden is caught in a moment of poetic indecision, a wrestling with poetic subject matter and direction:

> I roamed
> the cobbled island,
> and thought of Yeats,
> his passionate search for
> a theme. Sought mine. (ll. 31–36)

"The Lions" can be seen as a response to the dilemma that leads Yeats to question his vocation in "The Circus Animals' Desertion." The lions have not become purely "masterful images" isolated from "those things that they were emblems of."[4] Their tamer understands what Yeats comes round to at the end of his poem: that the ideal and the real are interdependent, that the image must paradoxically draw its beauty or strength from the beauty and strength of the flesh:

> And in the kingdom-cage
> as I make my lions leap,
> through nimbus-fire leap
> oh, as I see them leap
> unsparing beauty that
> creates and serves my will,
> the savage real that clues
> my vision of the real
> my soul exults and Holy cries
> and Holy Holy cries, he said. ("The Lions," ll. 7–16)

The lion tamer's "vision of the real" is clued by the "savage real"; the lion's physical glory, its "unsparing beauty," is the servant of art, but also its source.

The beginning section of "October," the third poem in Hayden's sequence, extends the analogy of physical, artistic, and spiritual beauty suggested by "The Lions." Hayden likens October's "plangency" and "glow" to those "of words in / the poet's mind" or "of God in/ the saint's" (ll. 2–6). The second section of the poem brings what seems a rather abrupt shift. Hayden remembers the birth of his daughter, born on an "October morning" and named "for a star," Maia, one of the Pleiades (ll. 12–14). For Hayden the day of Maia's birth was one of tears, much like those tears through which he sees Monet's "Waterlilies." Here too was an occasion of simultaneous joy and suffering:

> I wept for your mother
> in her pain, wept in
> my joy when you were
> born,
> Maia,
> that October morning. (ll. 7–12)

The name "Maia" needs particular attention here, for its allusions are central to the poem's meaning. In Greek mythology, Maia is the oldest and most beautiful of the Pleiades, the seven daughters of Atlas and Pleione, whom Zeus placed among the stars, where they form part of the constellation

Taurus. In some accounts, Zeus transformed the Pleiades into stars in order to save them from the lust of the hunter Orion, who pursues them now across the sky. Maia is also known as a prominent maternal figure, for she is the mother of Hermes. Indeed in Roman mythology, Maia, sometimes associated with the Greek Maia, appears as an earth goddess, the name itself becoming specifically associated with "mother." For this figure the month of May is named.[5]

Both Maia's role as one of the Pleiades and as an important figure for motherhood are central to Hayden's poem, but I believe that in the second section the maternal associations are more pertinent. The child's name stresses first her role as mother, as regenerative force, but because it associates her with her own mother, seen in the pains of labor, it also suggests her own mortality, which is, along with beauty and joy, what one inherits from one's parents in this world of generation. Because she too will endure the pains of labor, going almost to death's door to bring new life into the world, "October / like the phoenix sings" her (ll. 19–20). In this world in time, the world of "those dying generations at their song," to use another Yeatsian phrase that seems remarkably apt here, death and birth are inseparable parts of the process of life. One gives life because one dies; like the phoenix, the race rises from its own burning, a burning that in this context connotes both sexuality and destruction. Moreover, because man has the ability to transmute experience into myth, he is able to see October, with its burning color, not simply as the year's death but as the phoenix singing the birth of May, the resurrection of spring from the ashes of winter.

In the third section of the poem, the ancient sexual suggestions of burning and dying come specifically into play. Hayden begins the section by elaborating the musical metaphor of October's "plangency": The season resounds with a "chiming / and tolling / of lion / and phoenix / and chimera / colors" (ll. 21–26). October becomes a "huntsman's / horn":

> sounding
>   mort for
> quarry fleeing
> through mirrors
>   of burning
> into deathless
>   dying. (ll. 27–34)

The references here to "mirrors / of burning" and "deathless / dying" seem to suggest that the quarry pursued are the Pleiades, followed in carnal chase by the huntsman Orion across a sky that serves, to use a phrase by Galway Kinnell, as "pattern and mirror to the acts of earth."[6] The chase of the Pleiades by Orion "mirrors" the "burning" of earth, the sexual "burning" of this world of dying generations. For the Pleiades, however, there can only be a "deathless dying." In their transformation into stars, they have been removed by Zeus from this world of time and generation. They die out of life into a deathless life among the heavens, but it is a life that is deathless in the sexual sense as well. They will never "die" in the Donnean sense, but will instead remain as chaste as the maidens on Keats'urn. Orion's chase of the Pleiades remains an image and paradox of immortal unfulfillment to "tease us out of thought." As such it reminds us of the price of transcendence: The Pleiades will remain forever fair, but they will not bring new life into the world or shed the double tears with which we greet beauty and birth.

The final section of "October" returns us abruptly to the world of time and death; a "Rockweight / of surprising snow" crashes through "the October trees," breaking branches and plunging the blazing leaves to the ground (ll. 35–38). The final image is of "branches that / crashing set / the snow on fire" (ll. 40–42). Clearly the snow signals the death of the year, but the poem has prepared us to see a promise of regeneration even in this beginning moment of winter. Associated throughout the poem with the phoenix-like quality of this world in time, the fire promises spring, rebirth, May. Such are the "plangency" and "glow" of "words in / the poet's mind"; by drawing on the resources of myth the poet can himself effect a transmutation worthy of Zeus, converting an image of the year's death to one of regeneration. The fire will melt the snow to life-giving water; Maia is born in October.

The image of snow links "October" to the next poem in the sequence, "The Return," whose revealing subtitle, "(after Pasternak)," supplies an important key to the poem's meaning. The controlling mood of "The Return," however, is in stark contrast with the triumphant affirmation of creative imagination in "October." Here there is no image of snow aflame with regenerative fire. Instead the snow invades a room, producing a bizarre effect of disuse, chaos, and death:

> Rooms are grotesque with furniture of snow,
> ice blisters the hair of portraits;
> spiderwebs of snow and ice
> are skeleton stars in wolf-wind gloom. (ll. 1–4)

Hayden's image of the frozen "skeleton stars" heightens the contrast with "October," in which stars are associated first with the joy of Maia's birth and then with the images of carnal chase ordered into myth in the figures of

Orion and the Pleiades. In "The Return" there is no humanizing of the ice stars; instead they remain part of a mindless nonhuman force that overwhelms humanized space, the ordered enclosure that was once a center of culture, civilized grace, and the more tender feelings:

> Faces, voices, books we loved.
> There were violets in Chinese bowls.
> And, ah, the dancers—(ll. 5–7)

Hayden's suggestion that his poem follows Pasternak indicates a possible reading of the otherwise rather mysterious symbolism. As Paul and Mary Rowland have pointed out, Pasternak uses the snowstorm in *Doctor Zhivago* to foreshadow the Russian Revolution. In fact, the storm was "widely used to represent the Revolution. It was officially adopted by the Bolsheviks, who inscribed upon the former Moscow City Hall: 'Revolution is a storm, sweeping aside everythng in its path.'"[7] In one early scene from *Doctor Zhivago*, the young Yura is waked from sleep by a howling storm that seems to want to invade his room in a monastery, just as the snow invades the room in the first stanza of Hayden's poem.

If Hayden's poem is meant to suggest the kind of mindless obliteration of everything human that Pasternak associates with the Russian Revolution, then the contrast between "The Return" and the previous poem, "October," acquires an additional chilling irony. The Russian Revolution of 1917 is itself often called the "October Revolution" or, perhaps just as frequently, simply "October." Hayden's "October" and "The Return," then, might be thought of as a pair of antithetical versions of October. One stresses the creative human energy that sets the snow on fire and looks forward to May, the kind of creative energy that Pasternak celebrated everywhere in *Doctor Zhivago*, in his poems, and in his two autobiographies. The other freezes an entire nation in the mindless stupor of eternal winter, a death of the spirit that the Pasternak of *Zhivago* considered the true legacy of the Bolshevik Revolution.

The final stanza of "The Return," in fact, presents a macabre image of the dance of death. Death, that of Pasternak or perhaps of the creative energy of the individual that he worshipped, becomes the occasion of celebration (as opposed to Maia's birth in "October") for the Bolsheviks and perhaps by extension for all those devoted to the collectivist, technocratic mentality of the modern state:

> They would hunt us down tonight,
> they would caper on our graves.

> We lived here—when?—under a spell.
> We have awakened. We are here. (ll. 8–11)

The absurd capering of these celebrants of death contrasts specifically with the graceful dancing that once dominated the now snow-filled room. Moreover, the hunting metaphor of this final stanza may well be meant to connect with the "wolf-wind gloom" of the opening lines; like wolves "they would hunt us down," confirming the ancient adage that "man is a wolf to man." We should remember, too, that the wolf has had a particularly terrifying significance in Russian culture and that the animal has long been associated, particularly in the Bible, with the ancient forces of evil and corruption that threaten man's attempts to create anything of spiritual value on earth. In short, the wolf is an appropriate symbol for the Russian statists who have suppressed the ancient religious life of their people and proclaimed socialist realism, with its mechanistic, reductionist view of human behavior, the official version of literary creativity.

"The Return" ends in defeat rather than in triumph. The persona "awakens," a term used ironically here, from the "spell" of civilized existence evoked in stanza two to the snow-dominated room of the poem's opening lines. The next poem in the sequence, however, works to correct the despair of "The Return," for it suggests that the indomitable creative and life-affirming urge of humanity will inevitably be felt. This poem, "'Lear Is Gay,'" had very strong personal associations for Hayden. As he remarked in an interview, Hayden had in mind during the writing of the poem his "old friend Betsy Graves Reyneau" to whom "nothing human was alien" and who had "endured much physical suffering but had a rich and exciting life nonetheless." "Ultimately," however, Hayden added, "this poem is for myself. I've reached old age, and these days I hope the poem will be a sort of talisman for me."[8]

Endurance, affirmation, and "gaiety" in the face of old age are what "'Lear Is Gay'" celebrates. Such "gaiety" "has limbs askew / often as not, / has dimming sight. / Can manage, can / in fevers, rags, / decrepitude" (ll. 5–10). Moreover, Hayden's subject endures with humor born of true humility and pride, humility at recognizing how little she is and pride in knowing that the spirit is nevertheless greater than time:

> And oh can laugh
> sometimes
>
> at time as at
> a scarecrow whose

hobo shoulders are
a-twitch with crows. (ll. 11–16)

"'Lear Is Gay'" is further enriched when read in the contexts provided by its allusions to Yeats and its place within the sequence of poems closing *Words in the Mourning Time*. The poem's title derives of course from "Lapis Lazuli," itself a meditation on the value of art in a time of political crisis. Hayden's poem echoes the word which stands at the center of Yeats's defense of art: "gaiety." Yeats finds gaiety in Hamlet and Lear, in those who rebuild fallen civilizations, and in the Chinamen carved in lapis lazuli who look down "on all the tragic scene" of human life as if from a great height. Hayden's allusions suggest that the figure of his poem, like Yeats's Lear, finds a transfiguring gaiety in discovering and extending the limits of suffering and human experience. He may wish to imply a comparison, too, between his subject and Yeats's Chinamen, for their gaiety involves the similar achievement of a detachment from time. Hayden's figure of the scarecrow is also a particularly Yeatsian one, occurring in "Sailing to Byzantium" and "Among School Children," both meditations on the relationship between art and the suffering of old age. By allying his poem to this whole cluster of Yeatsian ideas, Hayden deepens his theme: that his subject's "gaiety" lies in a creative response to suffering that is akin to the artist's. Such a response produces a *King Lear* or *Words in the Mourning Time*. One can easily see the reason that Hayden liked to think of the poem as a "talisman" for himself.

If "'Lear is Gay'" represents a striking affirmation of creativity, the poem that follows it, "A Plague of Starlings," concludes both the sequence and *Words in the Mourning Time* with a somber meditation of human destructiveness and the value of art. The poem's concern with destructiveness is evident from the beginning, as Hayden hears "workmen" routinely "fire / into the stiff / magnolia leaves, / routing the starlings / gathered noisy and / befouling there" (ll. 2–7). The dead birds seem to "explode / into mica sky" before falling to the ground "raggedly ... in clench of cold" (ll. 11–14). Those that escape the guns take on a larger symbolic reference:

The spared return,
when the guns are through,
to the spoiled trees
like choiceless poor
to a dangerous
dwelling place,

chitter and quarrel
in the piercing dark
above the killed. (ll. 15–23)

It is impossible to read these lines without being reminded of the title poem of Hayden's volume, with its double emphasis on the destruction of America's central cities and the napalming of the Vietnamese.

The fourth stanza brings a turn in the poem, as Hayden describes himself walking across campus in the morning on his way to class. Fastidiously, as if to avoid contamination, he "pick[s]" his "way past death's / black droppings," the "troublesome / starlings" whose bodies still litter the campus (ll. 24–30). "Frost-salted," the starlings are, he writes, "troublesome still" (ll. 31–32), with a pun on both senses of *still* so brilliantly exploited by Keats in "Ode on a Grecian Urn." The body stubbornly persists; the evidence of slaughter remains—on the Fisk campus, in Newark and Detroit, in Saigon and My Lai.[9] Amid the carnage Hayden carries on, but not without the most honest and self-deprecating contemplation of his own vocation as teacher and as artist:

And if not careful
I shall tread
upon carcasses
carcasses when I
go mornings now
to lecture on
what Socrates,
the hemlock hour nigh,
told sorrowing
Phaedo and the rest
about the migratory
habits of the soul. (ll. 33–44)

What Socrates tells his students in the *Phaedo* is that pure wisdom is possible only after death, for it depends on the complete separation of the soul from the body, whose needs and loves and fears are constantly at war with the soul. Thus "those who tackle philosophy aright are simply and solely practising dying, practising death, all the time."[10] The philosopher's task is to free the soul from the prison of the body for its migration to the other world. Moreover, the *Phaedo* justifies the value of words in a mourning time. In an amusing incident early in the dialogue, Criton tells Socrates that the man who is to administer the poison hopes he will not talk too much, for "'people get hotter by talking, and nothing like that ought to accompany the poison; otherwise people who do that often have to take two or three potions'" (p. 466). To this Socrates replies wittily, insisting that he will talk to the end, "'Oh, let him be; he must just be ready to give me two, or three if necessary'" (p. 466). Socrates does talk to the end, even turning aside from his main discourse at one point to remind Phaidon of the value of arguments. With these words amid his already mourning students, Socrates affirms an afterlife, eternal justice, and the immortality of the soul.

The words of Socrates must sound terribly hollow, however, when spoken among the "carcasses" of the 1960s. We should remember that the students to whom Hayden lectures about the *Phaedo* are those whose deaths in Vietnam caused part of the anguish of "Words in the Mourning Time." Hayden's closing his volume with the allusion to the death scene of Socrates is stunningly appropriate. Socrates met death on his home soil, surrounded by friends and confident that his life had been just. We can well believe words of triumph in the mourning time from one so favored. But Hayden's students may die far from home in a cause whose justice is questionable, and he must wonder about the value of Socrates' words, or perhaps any words, to the "choiceless poor" punished into the violent self-betrayal of "burn baby burn." The extraordinary honesty of Hayden's questioning extends of course beyond Socrates to his own concept of the poetic vocation articulated in the final sequence of *Words in the Mourning Time*. While "A Plague of Starlings" does not repudiate the celebration of the artist as life-affirmer that Hayden has stressed from "Monet's 'Waterlilies'" to "'Lear Is Gay,'" it does represent the chastened wisdom of a poet who knows the immense human capacity for destruction as well as for creation.

Notes

1. All quotations are from *Words in the Mourning Time* (New York: October House, 1970). Line numbers will be given parenthetically. For an excellent discussion of "El-Hajj Malik El-Shabazz" and "Words in the Mourning Time," see Charles T. Davis's essay "Robert Hayden's Use of History," in *Modern Black Poets: A Collection of Critical Essays*, ed. Donald Gibson (Englewood Cliffs, NJ: Prentice-Hall, 1973), pp. 108–11.

2. *Interviews with Black Writers*, ed. John O'Brien (New York: Liveright, 1973), pp. 122–23. A similar interpretation of this loss is advanced by William H. Hansell in "The Spiritual Unity of Robert Hayden's *Angle of Ascent*," *Black American Literature Forum*, 13 (1979), 28. Pages 28–29 of this article are especially valuable for their comments on Hayden's ideas about art.

3. See William C. Seitz, *Claude Monet: Seasons and Moments* (New York: The Museum of Modern Art, 1960), p. 50.

4. Lines 32–33 of Yeats' "The Circus Animals' Desertion."

5. For details on Maia, the Pleiades, and the complex myth of Orion, see Robert Graves, *The Greek Myths* (New York: George Braziller, 1955), I, 151–54; *The Oxford Classical Dictionary*, ed. N.G.L. Hammond and H.H. Scullard (Oxford: Clarendon Press, 1970), pp. 640, 757; and *The New Century Classical Handbook*, ed. Catherine B. Avery (New York: Appleton-Century-Crofts, 1962), pp. 668, 792–93, 903.

6. "To Christ Our Lord," in *What a Kingdom It Was* (Boston: Houghton Mifflin, 1960).

7. *Pasternak's* Doctor Zhivago (Carbondale and Edwardsville: Southern Illinois Univ. Press, 1967), p. 20.

8. *Interviews with Black Writers*, pp. 117–18.

9. For a similar suggestion about the starlings, see Davis, p. 107.

10. *Phaedo*, in *Great Dialogues of Plato*, trans. W.H.D. Rouse (New York: New American Library, 1956), p. 466. Future citations are to this edition; they are given parenthetically.

VERA M. KUTZINSKI

Changing Permanences: Historical and Literary Revisionism in Robert Hayden's "Middle Passage"

And if I dared
the agonies
of metamorphosis,
would I not find
you altered then?

—*Robert Hayden*, "The Tattooed Man"

In his poem "American Journal," Robert Hayden, posing as an alien observer in a culture of "charming savages" and "enlightened primitives," describes America as

an organism that changes even as i
examine it   fact and fantasy never twice
the same   so many variables.[1]

The posture Hayden adopts in this poem seems curious until we remember that the figure of the mysterious stranger appears in his poetry with some regularity.[2] This is true particularly of *American Journal*, which is quite a remarkable collection of "alien" presences flaunting their "gaudy otherness" like the gypsies at the end of "Elegies for Paradise Valley": What Phillis Wheatley, John Brown, Paul Laurence Dunbar and Paul Robeson

From *Callaloo* 9, no. 1 (Winter 1986).

share with the Rag Man, the Prisoners, the Tattooed Man, Madam Artelia, Jamaican Cynthia and other characters in Hayden's "journal" is that they are all more or less grotesque outsiders in a society unable (or unwilling?) to comprehend the nature of their difference. As Hayden astutely puts it in "The Tattooed Man":

> Hundreds have paid
> to gawk at me
> grotesque outsider whose
> unnaturalness
> assures them they
> are natural, they indeed
> belong.
>
> (*AJ*, 20)

These lines recall yet another of Hayden's "aliens": the winged old man ("actual angel? carny freak?") of "For a Young Artist."[3] The list could easily be extended to include a host of historical and fictional characters from *Angel of Ascent*—e.g., Nat Turner, Malcom X, Cinquez, Harriet Tubman, and Fredrick Douglass, as well as the "stranger" in "Theme and Varation," who anticipates the words of the alien chronicler in "American Journal":

> all things alter even as I behold
> all things alter, the stranger said.
>
> Alter, become a something more,
> a something less. Are the revelling shadows
> of a changing permanence. Are, are not
> and same and other, the stranger said.
>
> (*AA*, 115)

Both the stranger and the alien observer not only speak for Hayden; even more importantly, they embody in their own peculiar strangeness the poetic posture Hayden assumes both before history as well as before and within language, that is, the perspective or *angle* of perception he brings to bear on his historical and cultural identity and on the language that shapes and textures that identity.

Much has been written about Hayden's fascination with history, and Afro-American history in particular, while relatively little has been said about the links between his historical and his literary revisionism. Always preoccupied with "the sly transience of things" (*AA*, 115), Hayden becomes a chronicler of change, of transformations, of metamorphoses.[4] Writing poetry, for him, is what William Carlos Williams has called "an agony of self-realization,"[5] but the self to be realized in language is so multi-faceted that it seems too reductive to speak of it as a single self. When Hayden writes, in "Names,"

> You don't exist—at least
> not legally, the lawyer said
>
> (*AJ*, 35)

we get a glimpse, not only at the personal anguish caused the poet by the discovery that "Robert Hayden" was not his "real" name, but of the absence of a conventional self and of the tenuous presence of a "ghost, double, alter ego" in the blank space marked by the hyphen. As at the end of the penultimate stanza in "For a Young Artist," this incisive hyphen is a locus of transformation, the place where "self" metamorphoses into "other." That otherness is something that eludes, as in the story on which "For a Young Artist" is based, "legal" definitions.[6] Legal, in this context, signifies constraints imposed upon the poet in the form of social, cultural or literary conventions, which Hayden appropriately figures as a "barbedwire pen" and a "gilt and scarlet cage" in "For a Young Artist" and "The Tattooed Man," respectively. These conventions or "laws" are what delimit Hayden's own identity, on the one hand, by imposing on him the name of Asa Bundy Sheffy, and on the other hand, by labeling him a "black poet." Both, to him, are equally pernicious for very similar reasons: They assign to him fixed institutional identities unable to contain Robert Hayden the poet. These names or labels are representative of the legalistic definitions of self Hayden seeks to undo, of the kinds of societal and cultural strictures he struggles to efface in order to inscribe his "other" self or selves in the form of that "ghost" or "double" that defies and eludes the lawyer. For Hayden, identity or selfhood is a matter of history and of historicity, that is, of change, not of institutional affiliations. He used to say to himself that he was not a "joiner." The implications of that pronouncement for his poetics are of unsuspected complexity.

"Alien, at home—as always / everywhere," Hayden proclaims in "Kodachromes of the Island" (*AA*, 49) and he sets out to explore the dimensions of his otherness. Frequently viewing himself from the double perspective of both native and stranger, which suggests a kind of DuBoisian "double consciousness," he assumes the posture not of a conventional historian chronicling Afro-American history, but of a modern anthropologist studying the language and the myths of an unfamiliar culture, in this case North America:

> disguise myself in order to study them unobserved
> adapting their varied pigmentations   white black
> red brown yellow
>
> (*AJ*, 57)

This posture accounts, at least in part, for Hayden's unrelenting criticism of ethonocentric definitions of poetry despite vehement attacks by Melvin Tolson and proponents of the "Black Aesthetic." Hayden insists on defining poetry as "the art of saying the impossible"[7]—that is, as the art of exercising a freedom of self-definition that effectively penetrates the biases responsible for cultural and intellectual ghettoization. Ultimately, his allegedly apolitical attitude toward poetry emerges not as a weakness but as a strength: rather than making overt political statements and turning his poetry into propaganda, Hayden, in the guise of an inoffensive observer, steadily undermines the ideological foundations of American society to clear a space in which to articulate his own difference. His poetic language does not simply protest or praise; it *transfigures* and, in the process, establishes its own form of self-knowledge.

Hayden's best poems are preoccupied with processes of displacement, both in historical and in literary terms. For example, he displaces traditional concepts of order (unity) and of time (linearity) as they manifest themselves in the form of certain literary and historical (or historiographical) conventions. We may call Hayden's poetry a consistent "experiment in disorder" (to borrow a phrase from Octavio Paz)[8] or incoherence, as long as we do not associate incoherence with unintelligibility. Hayden's incoherence is a strategy to free language from static, fixed meanings. "Middle Passage" is a fine example of this strategy which, as we shall see, effectively links historical with literary revisionism.

The poem's title already refers to a very specific historical process of geographical, social, and cultural dislocation: the Middle Passage. This context is rendered more concrete by references to the transatlantic slave trade throughout the poem, including lists of actual names of slave ships and lengthy "quotations" from logbooks and other seemingly authentic historical documents.[9] A transition from freedom to slavery, the crossing from Africa to the New World is indeed a "Voyage through death," a "voyage whose chartings are unlove" (*AA*, 121). But Hayden is hardly content to enumerate the horrors of the slave trade and to condemn the injustices of slavery. His is a more ambitious goal: to change the very texture of history, to alter the insidious design the dark ships have created:

> Shuttles in the rocking loom of history,
> the dark ships move, the dark ships move,
> their bright ironical names
> like jests of kindness on a murderer's mouth.
>
> (*AA*, 121)

Hayden's use of a metaphor of weaving as a figure for writing is most significant: for him, the pattern of crisscrossing lines connecting Africa with the Americas constitutes the charts or "chartings" of Afro-American history, that is, its official text(s), represented in the poem by the fragmented "quotations" from what at first glance appear to be historical documents. "Middle Passage" as a whole is a careful reading of those official texts, one that unravels the threads of their fabric to weave them together in very different ways. Hayden is indeed a most diligent and skillful weaver of poetic textures, of designs that revise official historical charts and offer correctives or alternatives to historical documentary. Resituated in a new context, the texts Hayden purports to quote lose not their appearance of authenticity but their historical authority. Broken up into textual fragments, they are no longer capable of offering a coherent, unified historical narrative. They become voices among many other, competing voices, or better perhaps, images of language, of the discourse of slavery, without claims to representational authority and historical truth.

This displacement, and in fact effacement, of authority indicated by the conspicuous absence of a central, controlling consciousness or "voice" in the poem, is significantly reinforced by the fact that these "documents" are not just general accounts of the slave trade. They all have to do, directly or indirectly, with slave mutinies:

> "10 April 1800
> Blacks rebellious. Crew uneasy. Our linguist says
> their moaning is a prayer for death,
> ours and their own...."
>
> (*AA*, 118)

Hayden has carefully "selected" passages reporting various "misfortunes" that interfere with the steady course of the slavers: Ophthalmia ("It spreads, the terrifying sickness spreads. / Its claws have scratched sight from the

Capt.'s eyes"; *AA*, 119); suicides; fires, and stormy seas. All these interferences build up to a lengthy narrative of the famous *Amistad* rebellion (1839) in the poem's final section.

On its way from Havana to Puerto Principe (today's Camaguey), the schooner *Amistad*, with fifty-four blacks and two passengers on board, was taken over by the Africans under the leadership of Cinquez (or Cinque). Their intention was to reverse the course of the vessel, using as navigators the two Spaniards they had spared. But instead of returning to the African coast, the *Amistad*, after several months of aimless zigzagging due to the deception of its navigators, finally reached the Connecticut shoreline. The mutineers, seized by the local authorities, were taken first to New Haven and then to Hartford to await the trial that would determine whether they were to be freed or returned to their owners. Due to the involvement of prominent New England abolitionists such as Lewis Tappan, as well as of former President John Quincy Adams, the *Amistad* case became something of an international incident. In short, the Court ruled that the Africans be freed and returned to their native land on the grounds that their enslavement and transport to Cuba had been in violation of international treaties banning the transatlantic slave trade.[10]

I am not offering this brief sketch of the *Amistad* affair in lieu of a reading of Hayden's poem; nor is it simply intended as background material. At least some familiarity with this event is crucial to an understanding of the historical bases of Hayden's literary strategies of displacement in "Middle Passage." It should further be noted that the *Amistad* case not only created considerable publicity for the New England abolitionists; it also generated a substantial body of writing in the form of legal documents and newspaper reports, not to mention the numerous historical studies it has inspired since. Finally, it set a legal precedent that literally reversed the direction of the Middle Passage and the "laws" that continued to sanction, albeit implicitly, the illegal trade in slaves.

Hayden's account of the *Amistad* mutiny and the subsequent trial merits detailed scrutiny and proves particularly revealing when compared to the poem's first version, published in *Phylon* in 1945.[11] Although cast in the form of a citation, presumably from Pedro Montez' court testimony, Hayden's narrative bears little resemblance to contemporary transcripts of that report.[12] One of the most striking deviations from those documents is the emphasis Hayden places on the storm that delayed the vessel's scheduled arrival. While this information was obviously not relevant to the trial, Hayden explores the way in which it served to rationalize the success of the mutiny:

> "But for the storm that flung up barriers
> of wind and wave, *The Amistad*, señores,
> would have reached the port of Principe in two,
> three days at most; but for the storm we should
> have been prepared for what befell.
> Swift as the puma's leap it came. There was
> that interval of moonless calm filled only
> with the water's and the rigging's usual sounds,
> then sudden movement, blows and snarling cries
> and they had fallen on us with machete
> and marlinspike. It was as though the very
> air, the night itself were striking us.
> Exhausted by the rigors of the storm,
> we were no match for them. Our men went down
> before the murderous Africans....
>
> (*AA*, 122)

While the storm probably did facilitate the revolt, the undue and apologetic stress the speaker places on that event invests it with a significance particularly suggestive in connection with Hayden's allusions to Ariel's song in *The Tempest:*

> Full fathom five thy father lies,
> Of his bones are coral made,
> Those are the pearls that were his eyes,
> Nothing of him that doth fade
> But doth suffer a sea-change
> Into something rich and strange.
>
> (I. ii. 397–402)

Charles Davis was certainly correct in stating that "the allusion to Shakespeare's sea-change mocks a less spiritual transformation," that of "black gold, black ivory, black seed" into "New England pews" and "altar lights."[13] Both are no doubt products of a hypocritical religious investment later figured as "the corpse of mercy" and "love's rotten gelid eyes" (*AA*, 121). Similar ironies resound in the names of the slave ships listed at the very beginning of the poem: "*Jesús, Estrella, Esperanza, Mercy.*" Interestingly enough, the second such list ("*Desire, Adventure, Tartar, Ann*") features names completely devoid of religious connotations. This change in language is significant in that it represents the widening chasm between slavery and institutionalized religion during the early eighteenth century. By 1820, the year of the official abolition of the transatlantic slave trade, it had already become evident that the Christian doctrine would hinder economic profits. The increasing secularization of the language of slavery, then, indicates gradual, but profound changes in the ideological make up of American slave societies: Religious values were displaced by economic concerns. The name "Amistad" is, of course, an obvious case.[14] Further ideological transformations surface as we probe even more deeply into the way in which Hayden adapts the concept of sea-change to the historical environment of slavery.

It is worth recalling that the sea-changes in Shakespeare's play are brought about by the tempest which Ariel unleashes at Prospero's command. That tempest signifies a violent upheaval, the disruption of reality through imagination (Ariel's "magic"). In that sense, the storm marks the transition from one state of being, or one mode of perception, to another, which is also a "voyage through death." The references to the storm in "Middle Passage" have a very similar function: They signal and anticipate the kinds of violent changes associated with slave mutinies and revolts. The storm physically throws the *Amistad* off its intended course, an act which prefigures the more drastic and violent change of course that results from the mutiny itself. The reversal of the schooner's voyage, then, stands for a reversal of colonial power structures, those of the master-slave relationship. Put differently, the revolt represents a struggle against and a successful dislocation of illegally assumed authority. This, in turn, suggests further parallels with *The Tempest*, where both Prospero and Antonio, each in his own way, are guilty of such injustices: Prospero with respect to both Ariel and Caliban; Antonio with respect to Prospero.

Insofar as the *Amistad* revolt epitomizes the successful struggle against an unjust institution and thus the achievement of freedom from bondage, it serves Hayden as an historical paradigm for throwing off course conventional notions of history and of time. History, for him, is not a unilinear progression, an orderly procession of events regulated by laws of causality. The *Amistad* case is of particular interest to Hayden, the revisionist, because it successfully disrupts the official design of Afro-American history by reversing the direction of the Middle Passage, not just in geographical terms, but, even more importantly, in conceptual ones: it literally changes the conceptual and ideological structures, the "laws," that define the power relationships upon which the slave trade is predicated: the idea of European racial and cultural supremacy. Within this context, Montez' fictionalized account of the mutiny becomes a self-indictment mainly because of his attempt to rationalize that ideology as "lawful." What Hayden illustrates brilliantly and subtlely in the following passage is a significant discrepancy between "lawful" and just.

> Now we
> demand, good sirs, the *extradition* of
> Cinquez and his *accomplices* to La
> Havana. And it distresses us to know
> there are so many here who seem inclined
> to *justify* the mutiny of these blacks.
> We find it paradoxical indeed
> that those whose wealth, whose tree of liberty
> are rooted in the labor of your slaves
> should suffer the august John Quincy Adams
> to speak with so much passion of the *rights*
> *of chattel slaves* to kill their *lawful masters*
> and with his *Roman rhetoric* weave a hero's
> garland for Cinquez. I tell you that
> we are determined to return to Cuba
> with our slaves and there *see justice done.* Cinquez
> or let us say 'the Prince'—Cinquez shall die."
> (*AA*, 123; my italics)

The legalistic rhetoric of this passage, particularly evident in the words and phrases I have emphasized, is clearly a more aggressive attempt at rationalization than the previously employed references to the storm. A noticeable change in tone announces the shift from the impressionistic description of the revolt and its presumed causes to an interpretation of the legal case; Montez' voice in that latter passage is tellingly conflated with that of the Spanish Minister.[15] An important connection exists, however, between the two rhetorical modes Hayden employs here: On the one hand, the speaker's strategic emphasis on the storm implies that the uprising of the slaves was simply another "misfortune," a lamentable interference in the "natural" course of events; on the other hand, he treats it as a criminal act that requires punishment. The projected expectation is that order will be restored, that justice will be done. The question, is, What order and whose justice? This is not an ethical problem as the speaker seems to imply; it is a legal and a rhetorical one. Neither the Middle Passage as representative of the process of enslavement nor the distinction between master and slave is a "natural" phenomenon. Both are social conventions, and the way in which they define the idea of justice is as paradoxical as the image of the "tree of liberty" rooted in slave labor. These same conventions define the struggle for freedom as a crime (as evidenced by the terms "extradition" and "accomplices") against laws that conceive of slavery and, for that matter, of the proposed murder of Cinquez, as acts of justice.

The exposure of the internal contradictions that characterize the discourse of slavery and result from the confusion and conflation of natural laws with ideological precepts is one of the trademarks of abolitionist rhetoric, which provides a kind of subtext in this passage. But even the language of abolitionism is not free from inconsistencies: what is at issue here for Hayden is clearly not the paradox of defending "the right of chattel slaves to kill their lawful masters," but the contradictions inherent in the very distinction between *chattel* slaves and *lawful* masters. Hayden added these two qualifiers (the original reads "the right of slaves to kill their masters") to strengthen the point he is making: that the rhetoric of slavery seeks carefully to conceal its internal contradictions. If slavery poses as a "natural" institution (that phrase already a contradiction), then the discourse of slavery poses as a "natural" language, thus detracting from the ideological assumptions on which it rests. This is precisely what Hayden's subtle changes in language emphasize in this instance.

By making these seemingly authentic texts part of the poem, Hayden draws further attention to the problematic truth-value of historical documents. In the same way that "justice" is a matter of conforming to certain laws, historical truth is a function of rhetorical conventions. "Middle Passage" both exposes and unsettles such conventions in order to redefine and reinscribe the idea of history and historical truth. Consider the following lines in this regard:

> "8 bells. I cannot sleep, for I am sick
> with fear, but writing eases fear a little
> since still my eyes can see these words take shape
> upon the page & so I write, as one
> would turn to exorcism."
>
> (*AA*, 119)

What writing supposedly exorcizes here is the fear of being contaminated: "'A plague among our blacks—Ophthalmia: blindness—& we / have jettisoned the blind to no avail.'" The spreading of this "terrifying sickness" represents a gradual loss of control, both over the ship's destination and over one's destiny:

What port awaits us, Davy Jones'
or home? I've heard of slavers drifting, drifting,
playthings of wind and storm and chance, their crews
gone blind, the jungle hatred
crawling up on deck.[16]

If writing (here in the form of a slaver's logbook) creates an illusion of control and of an authority already in the process of being eroded, it does so by "exorcizing" a threatening reality, or better, by containing the disturbing inconsistencies of reality within the ordered patterns of linearity. The religious overtones of this kind of exorcism are readily apparent, especially in connection with the mocking plea to grant "safe passage to our vessels bringing / heathen souls unto thy chastening" (*AA*, 118). But if exorcism, in the religious sense, is a form of "chastening," of restoring the purity of the soul and the kind of innocence associated with Christian mythology, it is also, more generally, a way of negating otherness, that is, cultural differences of any sort. Exorcism, then, becomes a *self-imposed* blindness resulting from the failure (or refusal) to acknowledge the legitimate existence of other cultures and creeds in order to avoid being "contaminated" by them. This ironic play on the religious justification of slavery is indeed effective, but Hayden's language penetrates the myth of purity even more deeply. Hayden's language reaches down to the ideological core of American society: its Puritan heritage. The implications of Hayden's attack on the narrow-mindedness and intolerance of Puritanism are clarified by a statement from Octavio Paz's meditations on the same subject. He contends that for the Puritans and their North American descendents, "every contact is contamination. Foreign races, ideas, customs, and bodies carry within themselves the germs of perdition and impurity. Social hygiene complements that of the body and soul."[17]

For Hayden, the kind of writing to which we generally attribute the status of historical documentary and thus a certain truth-value is characterized precisely by such practices of "social hygiene," which is of course but a euphemism for slavery in its many forms. In this way, the written chronicles of the slave ships' voyages render visible in their own rhetoric the underlying ideological structures and strictures of North American imperialism: historiography becomes a mechanism of defense against cultural otherness and difference, against everything, in short, that would challenge ("contaminate") existing social institutions. Hayden's is a struggle not only against historical slavery; his struggle is also against the linguistic vestiges of slavery manifest in the continued confinement of Afro-Americans by a language that denies not only their complex historico-cultural identities, but their humanity: for him, the difference between such phrases as "sweltering cattle," "chattel slaves," and "black poet" is one of the degrees only.

As a poet, Hayden is particularly sensitive to ideological constraints placed upon him by certain forms of language. Sharing "the deep immortal human wish, / the timeless will" to freedom that comes to be embodied in Cinquez, Hayden is careful not to replace old shackles with new ones. Nor is his definition of freedom simple and commonsensical. No easy resolutions conclude "Middle Passage." While Cinquez unquestionably evolves into an emblem of freedom in the same way that Frederick Douglass does in the poem that closes *Angle of Ascent*, the former's freedom is significantly conceived in terms of a return to his native land. We may say that, in some sense, Cinquez is an epic hero who survives the "Voyage through death" and returns from it a wiser man. But Hayden did not, in final analysis, write an epic poem. In fact, his revisions of the poem on the whole show that he carefully excised all vestiges of the epic mode from the *Phylon* version of "Middle Passage," most notably the prelude, whose repetition of "It was long, long after ... " perpepuates the convention of linear temporality.[18] Moreover, as the revisions of the poem's final lines particularly indicate, he was not satisfied with weaving "a hero's garland for Cinquez" in the way that John Quincy Adams did when he renamed Cinquez and his companion Grabeau:

> Cinque and Grabeau [declares Adams] are uncouth and
> barabarous names. Call them Harmodius and Aristogiton,
> and go back for moral principle to the fierce and
> glorious democracy of Athens. They too resorted to *lawless violence*, and
> slew the tyrant to redeem the
> freedom of their country. For this heroic action they
> paid the forfeit of their lives: but within three
> years the Athenians expelled their tyrants themselves,
> and in gratitude to their self-devoted deliverers
> decreed that henceforth no slave should ever bear
> either of their names. Cinque and Grabeau are not
> slaves. Let them bear in future history the names
> of Harmodius and Aristogiton.[19]

Hayden's phrase "Roman rhetoric," a revision of "lavish rhetoric" which also replaces the line "*Jus suum* is the view of the *viejo* [meaning Adams]" in the poem's initial version, effectively invokes this passage from

Adams's elaborate discourse on personal liberty and its allusions to the *sic semper tyrannis* motif.[20] However, as a careful reading of the above citation reveals, Adams's argument does not advocate the abolition of slavery. By renaming Cinquez, he indeed creates a "superb Homeric image," but this rhetorical gesture and the historical analogy on which it so eloquently draws hardly constitute an attack on the system of slavery. The fact that many slaves in the Americas were actually named after Roman or Greek heroes not only renders Adams's analogy suspicious, but also reverses the positive symbolism of his act of renaming: in both historical and rhetorical terms, this baptism signifies not liberation, but another kind of enslavement. Hayden seems well aware of the inappropriateness of re-dressing Cinquez as a classical hero and promptly eliminates the "superb Homeric image" from the final text of the poem. This specific revision already suggests that Hayden's concept of freedom in "Middle Passage" is infinitely more complex and problematic than Adams's defense of *personal* liberty. This complexity is reinforced by the deletion of the reference to Homer, which removes the poem even further from any possible epic resonances. Let us, then, compare the poem's two endings:

I. The deep immortal human wish
the timeless will:
    Cinquez its superb Homeric image,
    life that transfigures many lives
    life that defines our history upon these shores.
Borne from that land
    our gods false to us, our kings betraying us
like seeds the storm winds carry
to flower stubbornly upon these shores.

(*Phylon*, 1945; p. 53)

II. The deep immortal human wish
the timeless will:

    Cinquez its deathless primaveral image,
    life that transfigures many lives.

Voyage through death
to life upon these shores.

(*AA*, 123)

As freedom's "deathless primaveral image," Cinquez is now invested with a much broader and more flexible mythological significance than in the previous version. Hayden wrests Cinquez away from Adams's stale neo-classical clichés that detach him from his cultural context to charge him with a different definition of freedom. Hayden thus transforms, as he frequently does, an historical character into a poetic paradigm, into a trope. In the process of transforming he effaces and invalidates the image of Cinquez that represents Adams's "Roman rhetoric" and, connected with that, the legal rhetoric of the trial that reduces the Africans' identity to the terms *ladinos* and *bozales*.[21] Either inscription of identity, the heroic and the legal, is constraining in that it is conceived from within the rhetorical (and ideological) bounds of slavery. The choice here appears to be between a barbedwire pen and a gilded cage, to recall two of Hayden's previously mentioned images.

Extracted from its restrictive historical and rhetorical frames the figure of Cinquez emerges as "deathless" and "primaveral." In its resistance to narrow definitions and semantic stability, it comes to embody the very power of transfiguration that characterizes Hayden's language. Cinquez's new identity transforms the conventional meaning of Middle Passage. Although still identified as "Voyage through death," the Middle Passage can now be comprehended as an internal journey, indeed as a *rite of passage*, which is a figure for Hayden's historical imagination. "Middle Passage" is the visible, textual shape of that imagination and thus of Hayden's ability to transfigure the movement from freedom to slavery into its exact opposite. If Cinquez returns to Africa, Hayden returns to "life upon these shores," which are his native land, but the "chartings" of his own journey through history are love, not "unlove." Hayden's journey, the writing of "Middle Passage," leads toward an understanding of "the claims the living / owe the dead," to borrow a phrase from Jay Wright,[22] toward an understanding of "our history upon these shores." And it is this understanding that transforms chronicles of death into "something rich and strange." From the scattered fragments of "official" histories that Hayden reassembles emerges a text that changes as we behold it, and that changes us in the very act of beholding. *Beholding*, a verb Hayden uses as a figure for reading, creates a strangeness and richness due to the absence of a conventional poetic format, such as the epic, that would arrest the continuous "sea-changes" in Hayden's language. "Middle Passage" is indeeed a "changing permanence," a poem whose linguistic surfaces are as varied as its voices and ultimately as deceptive as the references to calm seas in the slavers' logbooks. The historical (and poetic) truth that emerges from these shifting surfaces is the *limbo* of Hayden's ever-transfiguring poetic imagination.

Notes

1. *American Journal* (New York: Liverright, 1982) 60. Subsequent references to this edition are included in the text as *AJ*.

2. See John Wright's essay-review of *American Journal*, "Homage to a Mystery Boy," *The Georgia Review* 36 (1981): 904–11. Wright does not explore this topic, but the title of his essay in suggestive.

3. *Angle of Ascent* (New York: Liveright, 1966) 8–10. All further references to this edition are included in the text as *AA*.

4. See Wilburn Williams, Jr., "Covenant of Timelessness and Time: Symbolism and History in Robert Hayden's *Angle of Ascent*," in *Chant of Saints. A Gathering of Afro-American Art, Literature, and Scholarship*, ed. Michael S. Harper and Robert B. Stepto (Urbana: University of Illinois Press, 1979) 79–80.

5. *Pictures from Brueghel and Other Poems* (New York: New Directions, 1949) 109.

6. For a more detailed discussion of the relationship between "For a Young Artist" and Gabriel García Márquez's short story "Un señor muy viejo con unas alas enormes" see my "The Logic of Wings: Gabriel García Márquez and Afro-American Literature," *Latin American Literary Review* 13 (1985): 133–45.

7. Quoted in John Hatcher, *From the Auroral Darkness, The Life and Poetry of Robert Hayden* (Oxford: George Ronald, 1984) 37.

8. *The Labyrinth of Solitude. Life and Thought in Mexico* (New York: Grove, 1961) 51.

9. For details about Hayden's historical (and literary) sources see Charles T. Davis, "Robert Hayden's Use of History," *Modern Black Poets: A Collection of Critical Essays*, ed. Donald Gibson (Englewood Cliffs: Prentice Hall, 1973) 96–111; and Fred M. Fetrow, "'Middle Passage': Robert Hayden's Anti-Epic," *CLA Journal* 22:4 (1979): 304–18.

10. The Court's reference point was the treaty between England and Spain of September 23, 1817, which set the terms for the abolition of the transatlantic slave trade and designated June 30, 1820 as legal time limit for the import of Africans (*bozales*) to the Spanish colonies.

11. *Phylon*, V6I (1945): 247–53.

12. The *Phylon* version clarifies the speaker's identity: "Cinquez spared Done José and me" (252). The testimonies of both Pedro Montez and José Ruiz can be found in John Warner Barber, *A History of the Amistad Captives* (1840; New York: Arno Press and the New York Times, 1969) 6–8. Hayden's version of the mutiny and its accompanying circumstances seems very much indebted to Muriel Rukeyser's narrative of the *Amistad* mutiny in *Willard Gibbs* (Garden City, New York: Doubleday Dorxan, 1942) 16–46 (especially 19–20).

13. "Robert Hayden's Use of the History," 102.

14. Manuel Moreno Fraginals has commented at length on the significance of such linguistic changes, both with respect to the naming of slave ships as well as the naming of sugar mills in the Hispanic Caribbean. He suggests that both are indicative of the same clash between religious and economic institutions. See *El ingenio. Complejo económico social cubano del azúcar* (Havana: Editorial de Ciencias Sociales, 1978), 112–26, 264.

15. See Warner, *A History of the Amistad Captives* 31.

16. In the *Phylon* version these lines are neither italicized nor set off from the preceding quotation.

17. *Labyrinth of Solitude*, 24.

18. See *Phylon*, 247–48.

19. John Quincy Adams, *Argument in the Case of United States Vs. Cinque* (1841; New York: Arno and the New York Times, 1969) 86–87.

20. Adams, 82.

21. The license of the transportation of the *Amistad* slaves, signed by the Captain-General of Cuba, misidentifies them as *ladinos*, a term used for blacks long settled in Cuba, instead of designating them *bozales*, referring to recent arrivals from Africa. This fraudulent document and the accompanying testimony by R.R. Madden, a British abolitionist, concerning the illegal practices of the Cuban authorities, played a significant role in the Court's final decision. See Warner, *A History of the Amistad Captives*, 17–18, 22–24, Rukeyser notes that in the translation of this document, *ladino* had wilfully been mistranslated as "sound" (*Willard Gibbs*, 47).

22. *Dimensions of History* (Santa Cruz: Kayak, 1976) 7.

PONTHEOLLA T. WILLIAMS

A Ballad of Remembrance *(1962)*

Between 1941 and 1962, a volume of Hayden's collected poems did not exist, and it was not until 1966 that an American house accepted such a work. However, *A Ballad of Remembrance*, a collection of Hayden's most representative pieces since *Heart-Shape in the Dust*, was published in Europe in 1962 by Paul Breman, who became acquainted with Hayden's works through Rosey E. Pool, who, like Breman, was an expatriate of Holland living in London.

The result of Breman's editing was a substantial compilation of thirty-five poems. Three of them are revised reprints from *The Lion and the Archer*, and ten are revised reprints from *Figure of Time*. At least eight of the remaining pieces are revised versions of poems that first appeared in various periodicals. Thus, about fourteen of the poems in *A Ballad of Remembrance* are new.

The book received favorable, if limited, reviews. Arna Bontemps noted that the "special quality of [his] meticulous art is his synthesis of old and new elements." Hayden, he said, had proved his craftsmanship and in "Homage to the Empress of the Blues" found a middle passage through the dilemma of utilizing folk sources on the one hand and meeting the requirements of New Criticism on the other.[1] Ralph Mills examined the book's strengths and weaknesses, citing "Tour 5" as particularly demonstrative of its "quiet understatement" and "dispassionate observation." He noted Hayden's ability to achieve special effects, including musical ones, especially in "O Daedalus, Fly Away Home." However, Mills felt that these effects were more advantageously used in "Middle Passage," which he felt demonstrated Hayden's capacity for capturing the subtleties of human motives in dramatic fashion.[2]

Four years after *A Ballad of Remembrance* was published, Hayden was awarded the *Grand Prix de la Poésie* for it. Rosey E. Pool, in her press release announcing the award, characterized Hayden as "a remarkable craftsman ... a striking singer ... who gives glory and dignity to America through his attachment to the past, present and future of his race."[3] Certainly the international award was the most impressive evidence of the work's reception. His competitors were the Caribbean poet-playwright Derek Walcott and Christopher Okigbo, a Nigerian. The international, interracial panel of judges included Langston Hughes, Katherine Dunham, Gerald Moore, and Abiolo Wole. Alioune Diop, president of the First International Festival of Negro Arts, presided; and Léopold Sédar Senghor, president of Senegal and a famous poet in his own right, announced the award and later presented it to Hayden in New York City.[4]

Because almost half the volume consists of revisions of poems in the two brochures that preceded it, the work necessarily repeats certain themes; however, the Afro-American cultural hero theme, introduced by "Gabriel" in *Heart-Shape in the Dust*, comes to full flower. Afro-American history was an element in the 1948 and 1955 brochures, but it is the basis for major thematic development in *A Ballad of Remembrance*. The second main emphasis in *A Ballad of Remembrance* is memory poems about his childhood and ghetto life. There are twelve of these in all, four of which are revised reprints. Another major subject is Mexico. During his sojourn there, when he wrote the poems for *Figure of Time*, Hayden kept a notebook in which he entered his observations and experiences.[5] Later, upon his return to Fisk and between 1956 and 1961, he used his notebook to develop the book's seven poems about Mexico. It is the Afro-American history poems, however, that are responsible for the acclaim the volume won.

He was inspired to write his historical poems by a challenge Stephen Vincent Benét issued in *John Brown's Body* (1928). Dissatisfied with his treatment of the Afro-American in his poem, Benét wrote:

> O black-skinned epic, epic with the black spear,
> I cannot sing you, haying too white a heart,
> And yet, some day, a poet will rise to sing you
> And sing you with such truth and mellowness.[6]

In response to Benét's challenge, Hayden undertook to write *The Black Spear*, which was to be a volume of Afro-American history poems.[7] "The Negro people's struggle for liberation and their participation in the anti-slavery movement and the Civil War" was its intended theme. He did not complete the project, but he included one of the best poems from it, "O Daedalus, Fly Away Home," in *A Ballad of Remembrance.*

Taken together, these poems provide a fictionalized chronicle of the Afro-American and his acculturation to America. In "Middle Passage" he treats the origin of the slave trade in Africa as it relates to the development of the new ethnic group—the Afro-American. In "O Daedalus, Fly Away Home" he treats the Afro-American's wishfulfillment mechanism that reflects his discontent with America and his desire to return to Africa. In "The Ballad of Nat Turner" he shows a Messianic figure being thrust up from the agonies of a people that had been uprooted in the early 1600s from their native land, held in bondage in their new home, become an American sub-society, and, if Anthony Wallace's revitalization movements theory is applicable, by the mid-1800s were experiencing the early stages of a revitalization period.[8] In "Frederick Douglass," he treats the Afro-American intellectual activist who fights for his people's freedom. Thus Hayden develops the history of the Afro-American's transition from tribal man to slave, to rebel and soldier, to statesman.

"Middle Passage" tries to achieve a two-fold purpose.[9] Hayden says that he wanted to fulfill Benet's prophecy and to write a poem that would give the lie to bigots who had distorted the Afro-American's history.[10] Though it was inspired by epic intentions and contains elements of the epic, it is not quite that. The traditional epic depicts the values and patterns of the life of an entire people or culture through the experience of a hero who represents in himself certain ideals of that culture. "Middle Passage" attempts through a hero to present the values, both positive and negative, of the slavery era and the Afro-American's historic condition, depicting his dislodgment and displacement from his mother country to an alien land.

The hero of the poem is Cinquez, the captive prince who inspired and carried out the *Amistad* mutiny. This figure, however, blends with the poet-observer, who enunciates "the deep dark immortal human wish / the timeless will to be free" (lines 172–73).

Another epic element in "Middle Passage" is the device of cataloging—the listing of the ships and the listing of the African tribes, all historically authenticated by Hayden's research.[11] It begins *in medias res* with the depiction of ships under full sail carrying slaves in mid-Atlantic. Its tone is dignified. The ending is not without a note of triumph, though this term does not adequately describe the mystical exaltation of the concluding stanzas.

Yet, the poem is not an epic. It is too short. Moreover, it is more lyrical than narrative; whenever a narrative section appears, it is telescoped or fragmented. The issue of religion is handled with great irony and for the purpose of condemnation. Intervention of the gods is lacking. The intervention of John Quincy Adams is the nearest approximation to this convention. And the hero does not engage in monologues; his words as well as his deeds are presented from the reportorial consciousness of the poet-observer.

The poem is set in the classic framework of a journey—one that begins when the African principals leave their villages. The exodus is engineered as much by the African kings who sell their captives to satisfy their greed for "luxuries" as it is by the Spanish greed for gold. The first lap of the journey is to the "factories"—places where the captives are sorted out, processed, and subdued for their coming enslavement. The second lap, the horrific "Middle Passage," is the journey across the Atlantic Ocean to America and slavery. The third lap, only alluded to in the poem, is the journey from the barracoons in America to the plantations.

Part 1 begins with a chilling description of the inhumane treatment slavers gave the Africans aboard various slave ships. Moving from the general to the particular, part 2 presents the reminiscences of a corrupt old slave-trader who is stopped from plying his trade only by the physical toll the tropics take on him—"fevers melting down [his] bones." Ironically his greed for gold is shown as being of a piece with that of the African kings' greed for luxuries. Part 3, the climactic section of the poem, is the poetic recreation of the *Amistad* mutiny, which occurred in 1839 and became a cause célèbre.[12]

The personae are the omniscient poet-observer, the African tribal chiefs and their subjects, the heroic Cinquez, the Spanish captain of the *Amistad*, common seamen, Celestino the mulatto, and the silent voice of John Quincy Adams, who argues the case for Cinquez and his people and who, in fact, argued the case for the *Amistad* rebels.

It is a tribute to Hayden's poetic genius that in the poem, otherwise so brilliantly and uniquely his own, he stands in debt to two poets who demonstrated conflicting views of America. Evident in "Middle Passage" are the techniques T.S. Eliot used in "The Wasteland" and the influence of Hart Crane's vision of crucifixion and resurrection, horror and squalor out of which radiates hope and light. As Crane, in "The Bridge," attempted to forge the American identity, Hayden likewise forges in "Middle Passage" the American identity of the Afro-American.

In part 1, Hayden introduces the technique of fragmentation which Eliot used with striking effect in "The Wasteland." It is a device that lends itself to a vivid portrayal of the disintegration of a society—in "Middle Passage," the historic disintegration of African society. Accordingly, the development of part 1 includes sequential presentation, without transition, of names of ships, a section of a ship's log, a sailor's prayer, a portion of a sailor's letter, and a legal deposition. The Eliot-like motifs that achieve unity are the refrain "Jesus Savior Pilot Me" (a hymn line which creates an ironic commentary), the biblically derived names of ships, and the poet-observer's chorus-like voice.

From a vantage point that spans time and place, the poet condemns the horrors of the Middle Passage, describing it as a "voyage through death" (lines 3–7). He condemns American greed—that of the New England shipping interests as well as that of the southern plantation owners:

> Standing to America, bringing home
> black gold, black ivory, black seed.
>
> > *Deep in the festering hold thy father lies*
> > *of his bones New England pews are made,*
> > *those are altar lights that were his eyes.*
> > (Lines 15–19)

The "altar lights" motif establishes an ironic relationship with Shakespeare's theme of death and resurrection in *The Tempest.* The allusion is to Ariel's speech to Ferdinand that falsely reports the death of Ferdinand's father. Hayden explains that his intention was based on his feeling that there was some connection between the sea change Shakespeare describes and "the change from human beings into things—objects, suffered by the enslaved Africans—the idea that slavery was a kind of death."[13]

Hayden's immediate purpose in using the allusion, according to Charles Davis, is to mock "a less than spiritual transformation."[14] While reminding the reader of a supposed death by drowning, which in reality led to a regeneration through sea change, Ariel's song also portrays a metamorphosis from blindness to new vision. (The sailor writes that "Opthalmia has struck the Captain as well as the Africans aboard the ship.") The line "those are altar lights that were his eyes" may be seen as a scathing indictment of a Christian people with eyes blind to the enslavement of their fellowman. It is a blindness that prevails in the poem until John Quincy Adams, as the champion of human rights, speaks "with so much passion of the right of chattel slaves" (lines 164–65) and their will to be free. When the justice he represents proves not to be blind, it opens the way for the African "to life upon these shores."

According to Elizabeth Drew, Eliot uses the Shakespeare line "Those are pearls that were his eyes" as the central symbol for the whole of Western tradition, which, as he saw it, was lifeless as a pearl. Eliot also used the symbol to suggest metamorphosis from blindness to vision. Drew further notes that Eliot's purpose in making the allusion was to symbolize the transmutation of life into art—a creative act the poet must find, not only through suffering but *in* suffering.[15] Whether in response to the Eliot model or not, Hayden develops this dimension of the metaphor in the sailor's letter:

> "8 bells. I cannot sleep, for I am sick
> with fear, but writing eases fear a little
> since still my eyes can see these words take shape
> upon the page & so I write, as one
> would turn to exorcism.
> (Lines 26–30)

The passage speaks of the transformation from blindness to vision that can be effected through the arts.

The blindness theme is continued in another variation of *The Tempest* motif which appears in part 3:

> *Deep in the festering hold thy father lies,*
> *the corpse of mercy rots with him,*
> *rats eat love's rotten gelid eyes.*
> (Lines 108–110)

In this passage the poet also decries the rotting bodies of his ancestors interred in the holds of slave ships. The contrast of "rotten" with what ought to be living thoughts—"mercy" and "love"—is reminiscent of yet another precedent set by Eliot in "The Wasteland," especially in "Burial of the Dead."

Further reminiscent of "The Wasteland" is the use of several voices, some of them ghostly, including those of the poet-observer, of the praying sailor, of the old slaver, and of the attorneys who speak for the Spanish deponents. As in "The Wasteland," though to a lesser extent, Hayden shuffles history, past and present, in his depiction of the African's "coming to life upon these shores."

Hart Crane's epic "The Bridge" also influenced the shaping of "Middle Passage." After announcing his vision of hope, which he contrasted to Eliot's negations,[16] Crane attempted to create, through the use of history and folklore and of his key bridge symbol, the American identity, achievement, and future hopes. It is, certainly, a subject matter for a myth that could support an American epic. This is a vision similar to that of Hayden's poem—a vision that creates an Afro-American identity around the central metaphor of the "Middle Passage" and a vision that carries, indeed, a constructive note of hope.

At the time he composed "Middle Passage," Hayden was a young man with certain identifiable ideas about Afro-American history, justice, and social change. He was, however, a poet who was making a search in himself for a new iconography that would inform his poetry along with the beliefs he had accepted. He was tossed up to rhetorical heights by his reckless faith in his poetic genius and scholarship; yet he was brought to a more even keel somewhat later by his stern sense of self-discipline and self-criticism. The true extent of these flights of optimism and the degree of his self-discipline and self-criticism cannot be known. Hayden said that the working sheets of "Middle Passage" are long since lost.[17] Nonetheless, there are four published versions of the poem: version A, in *Phylon* (1941); version B, in *Cross Section* (1945); version C, in *A Ballad of Remembrance* (1962); and version D, in *Selected Poems* (1966).

The painstaking revisions of "Middle Passage" from 1945 to 1966 produced a poem that won the acclaim of eminent critics and fellow-poets. A passage from the letter that Allen Tate wrote to him about the poem will indicate the measure of that approval: "I am especially moved by 'Middle Passage,' a beautifully written poem. The power is in the restraint and the purity of diction."[18] More important is the fact that the poem was produced by a black poet speaking of black history and heritage in the most sophisticated traditions of twentieth-century western poetry.

In "The Ballad of Nat Turner" Hayden turns to the second stage of Afro-American acculturation in America.[19] Turner is a black cultural hero who, having been a part of the mass movement of Africans to America, suffers the stress of enslavement and consequent acculturation and is in revolt. He was the slave of a Virginia planter, Benjamin Turner. The ballad recreates the ecstatic vision which led to a Messianic mission and resulted in a revolt of some Virginia slaves.[20] The poem falls into two distinct but related parts, with each part developing a particular set of circumstances. Dialogue in the poem is indirect; the tragic situation that the content treats is not presented with the simplicity of his earlier "Gabriel." Rather, the style is richly allusive and symbolic, and the tone is religious, ecstatic, and visionary.

The first section of the poem, stanzas 1 through 5, delineates the conditions of stress in the slave sub-society to which Turner reacts:

> Then fled the mellows, the wicked juba
>   and wandered wandered far
> from curfew joys in the Dismal's night.
>   Fool of St. Elmo's fire.
>
> In scarey night I wandered, praying,
>   Lord God my harshener,
> speak to me now or let me die;
>   speak, Lord, to this mourner.
>
> And came at length to livid trees
>   where Ibo warriors
> hung shadowless, turning in wind
>   that moaned like Africa,
>
> their belltongue bodies dead, their eyes
>   alive with the anger deep
> In my own heart.

The imagery in stanza 1 evokes the ideal pastoral setting—"mellows" and "curfew joys." The hero, however, has come to see it as deceptive. He perceives that the toned-down quality of this environment hides the harshness of a "wicked juba," an evil dance which casts a spell, or St. Elmo's fire, which can mislead ships at sea. From this reality he flees to the night of Dismal (Swamp).[21] But he flees in vain, for once in Dismal he is confronted with the apparitions of Ibo warriors "turning in wind / that moaned like Africa." What he sees is his suffering Mother Africa contemplating her emasculated sons brought to a cultural death in America that is as final as that of the dead, hanged and swollen-tongued. He calls on his newly adopted Christian God.

God answers in the second half of the ballad, stanzas 6 through 17. The answer is a revelation given through an apocalyptic vision. Unlike Bahá'u'llah in the Garden of Ridwan, who prayed surrounded by benevolent presences in the midnight air, Turner prays in Dismal, where he is surrounded by hostile, evil presences.

And wild things gasped and scuffled in
  the seething night; shapes
of evil writhed upon the air,
  I reeled with fear, I prayed.

In this vision the spiritual presences are like those in Hawthorne's "Young Goodman Brown." He is transported by his fervor and is shown an awesome revelation. Though the description of what he sees is couched in mystical language, it demonstrates that Hayden was continuing to forge the specialized language of religious transport which he began in his Bahá'i poems:

Sudden brightness clove the preying
  darkness, brightness that was
itself a golden darkness, brightness
  so bright that it was darkness.

When the personae in the vision appear, Turner sees that they are "angels at war / with one another" and that they are engaged in "holy battle." His description of this battle faintly recalls the war imagery used in the battle scene in Book VI and the expulsion scene in Book I of *Paradise Lost.* The Miltonic echoes seem evident in stanza 10, in which occurs such imagery as "The shock of wing on wing and sword / on sword," and in stanzas 12 and 13:

    I saw oh many of
  those mighty beings waver,

waver and fall, go streaking down
  into swamp water, and the water
hissed and steamed and bubbled and locked
  shuddering shuddering over

Nonetheless Turner's description of the holy war and his response to it bears the unmistakable imprint of Hayden's signature in its reflection of his early religious beliefs. This may be seen in the allusions to fundamentalist religion. An example occurs in Turner's emotional response to the vision he beholds

the fearful splendor of that warring.
  Hide me, I cried to rock and bramble.

Hide me, the rock, the bramble cried.
    How tell you of that holy battle?

Lines 2 and 3 of this stanza echo the Afro-American spiritual, "There's No Hiding Place Down Here," which was probably based on Amos 2:10–22, a passage that gives the prophet's description of judgment day. A second example occurs in stanza 11:

for the wheel in a turning wheel which is time
    in eternity had ceased
its whirling, and owl and moccasin,
    panther and nameless beast

The allusion in lines 1 and 3 is to an Afro-American spiritual that owes its primary source to Ezekiel 1:15–21, "Vision of the Wheels." Once again, as he does in "Sunflowers: Beaubien Street," Hayden makes symbolic use of one of the most striking of all of Israel's prophets. A man of God, a visionary, and iconoclast, and a prophet of hope, he ministered to the Israelites for at least twenty-two years, during the Babylonian captivity when they were becoming forcibly acculturated to an urban and alien way of life. Ezekiel's message was one of warning, to bring Judah to repentance and true faith in God, and also one of comfort and hope for the future, especially in his promises for the restoration of Israel. Moreover, his teachings promoted the idea of individual responsibility and divine retribution. The wheel allusion, then, refers to Ezekiel's inaugural vision in which he is called to be a prophet of God. Ezekiel is shown the omniscience of God—the chariot wheel-within-a-wheel that transports God from Jerusalem to Babylonia. And Ezekiel is commissioned to speak to the rebellious nation, summoning them to hear the word of God.[22] Turner, himself a zealot, a mystic, an avid reader of the Bible, and a leader of the slaves about him,[23] could have seen the similarities between his situation and that of Ezekiel. Certainly it seems to be the rationale which informs Hayden's design in the poem.

Another dimension of the poem which bears Hayden's distinctive signature is his portrayal of local color. It is the particular cachet of the southern swamp that he evokes in the poem. In stanza 11, lines 3 and 4, the creatures he names are precisely the inhabitants of such places: "owl and moccasin, / panther and nameless beast." In stanza 13, his references to swamp water and his description of its activity further and accurately develop the verisimilitude of the region.

Stanzas 14 and 15 recreate the birth of Turner's messianic mission at the moment it is revealed that, like his own, the conqueror's faces are black:

> and I
>
> beheld the conqueror faces and, lo,
> they were like mine, I saw
> they were like mine and in joy and terror
> wept, praising praising Jehovah.

The last two stanzas develop Turner's resolution of his problem and further describe his religious experience as a crucible in which he knows a death and a rebirth:

> Oh praised my honer, harshener
> till a sleep came over me,
> a sleep heavy as death. And when
> I awoke at last newborn
>
> and purified, I rose and prayed
> and returned after a time
> to the blazing fields, to the humbleness.
> And bided my time.

The closing work in *A Ballad of Remembrance* is "Frederick Douglass."[24] It is also the final Afro-American history poem in the book. It may be considered thematically in terms of the Afro-American's search for freedom and dignity; structurally, as a Hopkinsean sonnet.

The sonnet is a tribute to the Afro-American writer-orator, abolitionist, reformer, who rose against formidable odds to become a leader in the service of mankind. He spent the first twenty-one years of his life as a slave, separated from his parents. He was taught how to read by his owner's wife and then forbidden by her to do so. He was threatened with emasculation by a slave-breaker. When he was twenty-one years of age, he escaped from slavery; and, within the subsequent four years, he had become an internationally known abolitionist, writer, and reformer. By the time he was forty-six years of age, he had become a confidant of President Abraham Lincoln.[25]

The subject matter of the sonnet is confined to a definition of the significance of freedom, a definition of the inherent qualities of man's need to be free, and a tribute to Douglass that recognizes these qualities in him:

> When it is finally ours, this freedom, this liberty, this beautiful
> and terrible thing, needful to man as air,
> usable as earth; when it belongs at last to our children,
> when it is truly instinct, brainmatter, diastole, systole,
> reflex action; when it is finally won; when it is more
> than the gaudy mumbo jumbo of politicians:
> this man, this Douglass, this former slave, this Negro
> beaten to his knees, exiled, visioning a world
> where none is lonely, none hunted, alien,
> this man, superb in love and logic, this man
> shall be remembered. Oh, not with statues' rhetoric,
> not with legends and poems and wreaths of bronze alone,
> but with the lives grown out of his life, the lives
> fleshing his dream of the beautiful needful thing.

Lines 1 to 3 show elements of the natural environment indispensable to human existence on this planet, each of which is equated with freedom, to show how utterly essential freedom is to man. Lines 4 and 5 show man's absolute dependence on freedom in the same sense as man's existence is dependent on certain biological components of his body's characteristics and functions. Freedom is more, he goes on to say, than the "gaudy mumbo jumbo" of "politicians"—a satirical image which evokes not only the ambiguity of the politicians but the deviousness (as the poet sees it) of the lawmaker. Lines 7 through 11 recall Whitman's use of incremental repetition to support his presentation of an idea. Hayden begins by speaking of his subject first as a man, then as a person identified by name, then as a "former slave," then as a representative of a "race," yet endowed with the persisting vision of a world in which such disabilities may have become only memories of a painful past. To this capacity for envisioning a better future, he adds Douglass's further positive attributes"logic" and "love." In line 8 the dominant features of his subject's life are telescoped, with "lonely," "hunted," "alien" as the key words. From line 10 to the end of the poem, while paying tribute to the part played by imaginative artists in perpetuating the memory of Douglass, Hayden shows that the actual persistence of Douglass's example and influence transcends the rhetoric expressed in statues, or even presumably in the Emancipation Proclamation itself. The grandest testimony of all to the greatness of Douglass is eloquent, Hayden says, in the "lives"—Afro-American lives certainly, but also the lives of all[26] the beaten yet hopeful persons before and after Douglass—of those who had embodied, or were to embody, the great reformer's "dream of the beautiful needful thing."

The poem provides an impressive example of how sound can support sense. This feature of the lyric is of crucial importance in promoting the achievement of "inscape" and "instress," which he was committed to do in taking Hopkins's sonnets as his model. Vocabulary creates images which combine with rhythm and sound to capture the unique totality of the subject, thus achieving Hopkins's "inscape" or vividness. Likewise, as his choice of specific words promotes "thisness," or the essence of the person and the idea of the preciousness of freedom in the poem, Hayden achieves Hopkins's "instress."

Hayden's choice of words in respect to their brevity and relative simplicity is not without significance here. Of the 103 words, 85 are one-syllable words, 26 are two-syllable words, and only one is a four-syllable word. Such choices make for directness and force. In several instances, the sound is an almost exact parallel to the sense, even in syllable count and manner of articulation: "diastole," "systole," "reflex," and "mumbo jumbo" may serve as examples. "Mumbo jumbo" serves also, because of its African origin, to help Hayden develop a special Afro-American flavor in this poem. Hayden's word usage is conducive to the richly subtle alliterative slant characteristic of this poem. He also has selected words which contribute to the sprung rhythm effect for which he was indebted to Hopkins (see line 5 for example).

Although Hayden has said that he wrote the poem when he was reading Hopkins, it is an interesting probability that he may have got his syncopated effect in this and other poems from Afro-American jazz. Line 3 of the sonnet provides a good example of Hayden's metrics; the line opens with a dactyl and is followed by an iambic, a trochaic, two more iambics, and a foot with two unstressed syllables followed by a stressed syllable and another unstressed syallable. This irregular line with its interposed downbeats is one of syncopation much like that of jazz.

The entire sonnet is made up of only two sentences. In the first, the thought is asserted; in the second, it is developed. Lines 1 through 11 (center) contain a periodic sentence made up of a series of conditional dependent clauses followed by an independent clause that drives home the point—"this man shall be remembered." Lines 11 through 14 contain an antithesis made up of two negative statements in which the clause "this man shall be remembered" is understood. The major divisions of thoughts are so interwoven that the sonnet structure becomes subordinate to meaning rather than vice-versa. Hayden uses run-on lines to emphasize his views. Similarly, in the first part the order of the sentence structure with three semicolons is used to contain his major points, only to release them at once with greater force. A similar structure is used in the second part, this time with a series set off by commas. Hopkins's "Duns Scotus's Oxford" provides an interesting structural parallel to this lyric.

Closely related to his Afro-American history poems but actually an Afro-American folk theme poem is "O Daedalus, Fly Away Home." It is the sole reprint from Hayden's prize-winning Hopwood Collection, and it is the poem that finally rewarded Hayden's efforts to have his work appear in *Poetry*.[27] The poem is a skillful blend of Afro-American folk and classical subject matter. An epigraph included in the first two versions of the poem indicates that it is based on the "Legend of the Flying African," which Hughes and Bontemps state is a part of the folklore of the Georgia Sea Island blacks.[28] This dramatic poem of six stanzas develops the speaker's invitation to a girl to dance with him:

Drifting night in the Georgia pines,
coonskin drum and jubilee banjo.
    Pretty Malinda, dance with me.

Night is juba, night is conjo.
    Pretty Malinda, dance with me.

Night is an African juju man
weaving a wish and a weariness together
    to make two wings

O fly away home fly away.

Do you remember Africa?

Enchanted by the night, the music, and the girl, the speaker reflects on his slave heritage and his African roots. He recalls that his "gran" was one of those slaves who escaped slavery by flying back to Africa:

My gran, he flew back to Africa,
just spread his arms and
flew away home.

The classical Daedalus image compliments the "flying gran" image. The images together symbolize the blend of Western civilization with that of Africa, which the Afro-American actually represents.

African words and the names of African religious figures create a diction that promotes the voodoo theme so important in the lyric. The voodoo theme in "A Ballad of Remembrance" was a negative force that drew the observer into the charade of the Mardi Gras dance; in "Incense of a Lucky Virgin" it was treated as an unsuccessful potion that failed to bring her man home to a deserted mother. It is also used in "Witch Doctor"—a long character sketch included in *A Ballad of Remembrance* in which Hayden examines a modern avatar of a witch doctor who practices a mixture of voodooism and quasi-religious fundamentalism.[29] In "O Daedalus, Fly Away Home," however, voodooism is pictured as a positive force that effects escape from a dehumanizing plight. In the original legend, according to Bontemps, on a certain plantation there was an old man to whom the slaves turned for help when their suffering became unbearable. He would whisper a magic formula to them that was inaudible to others, whereupon he transformed them into winged creatures who flew back to Africa.[30] Thus the poem demonstrates the truth of Ralph Ellison's perceptive critique that Afro-Americans in their folklore "[back] away from the chaos of experience and from ourselves," in order to "depict the humor as well as the horror of our living."[31]

Hayden's use of literary voodooism draws from the well of folklore that is an integral part of the Afro-American literary tradition. In this respect he joins a series of Afro-American writers from Paul Laurence Dunbar to Jean Toomer to Ralph Ellison. Hayden, furthermore, could not have been unmindful of the example set by W.B. Yeats in his artistic use of Irish folklore.[32]

Notable among the memory poems of Hayden's childhood are those about his adoptive father who died in 1938.[33] As early as his first volume Hayden had answered his need to make a statement of filial love for him. In "Obituary," the most outstanding of a group of three in *Heart-Shape in the Dust*, he eulogized his adoptive father as a devoutly religious patriarch. In "This Grief," he expressed faith that his sorrow would pass and leave him "Unbowed, unbroken / scarred and wise," (lines 7–8).[34] In "Rosemary"—a title reminiscent of its symbolic use with Shakespeare—for the first time Hayden expresses the thought that he did not appreciate his father while he was alive.[35]

He never lived for us
Until he died;

We never knew him
Till he moved
Beyond the need
Of our too laggard knowing.

It remained, however, for "Those Winter Sundays" to capture the essence of Hayden's particular regret: "time lost is spent."[36] In its surface meaning the lyric is about a working father who rises earlier than the other members of his family each day, including Sundays, to make the house warm.

Sundays too my father got up early
and put his clothes on in the blueblack cold,
then with cracked hands that ached
from labor in the weekday weather made
banked fires blaze. No one ever thanked him.

I'd wake and hear the cold splintering, breaking,
and smell the iron and velvet bloom of heat.
When the rooms were warm, he'd call,
and slowly I would rise and dress, fearing

the chronic angers of that house, speaking
indifferently to him, who'd driven out
the cold and polished my
good shoes as well. What did I know,
what did I know of love's austere and lonely offices?

In one of his favorite ironic uses of romantic conventions—that of drawing an analogy between external nature and human actions—Hayden poses the "blueblack cold" of predawn Sunday mornings in a reflection of wintry family relationships that are lacking in the warmth engendered by love and mutual consideration. The phrase "chronic angers of that house" suggests the corrosiveness of the actual relationship. The image evokes a milieu of long-standing, deeply rooted resentments that resist all efforts to be eradicated. Confronted with this prospect, the boy is reduced to indifference or, in another view, the need to resort to an adolescent ploy of seeming unconcern. One is reminded of the "quarrels and shattered glass" and of "elders" who "after each unrelenting day" were "shouting angry," a situation from which the same boy escaped in his fantasy world as a daredevil rider on "circus-poster horses."

Another poem, "The Whipping," gives the reader a further clue as to the nature of the relationship between the boy and certain adults.[37] It is a lyric about a woman who exhausts herself by whipping a boy to achieve her personal catharsis. Developed from the point of view of the poet-observer, the spectacle recalls Hayden's own childhood experience. What he remembers is not the humiliation of having his head caught between the woman's knees while she applied blows to his posterior, but:

> the fear
> worse than blows that cruel
>
> words could bring, the face that I
> no longer knew or loved....

Noting that among the elements of ghetto life is the inhabitants' "cruelty to one another," Hayden states that this "is a sad poem, one that I had to write, almost as an act of expiation."[38]

The third subject group in *A Ballad of Remembrance* is "An Inference of Mexico," a suite of seven poems.[39] It was a great distance that Hayden had to go in order to create his Mexican poems, but only in terms of miles. He already had the interest and the language preparation. Also, his longstanding friendship with Langston Hughes, who had spent some time in Mexico with his father, may very well have had some influence on developing his interest in the Spanish-speaking country. Hughes, together with Arna Bontemps, sponsored Hayden for a Ford Foundation Fellowship in Creative Writing that provided his sojourn in Mexico from 1954 to 1955.

The dominant theme in Hayden's Mexican poems seems to be the reality which lies behind Mexico's appearance. The worst dimension of what he perceives to be Mexico's reality is the stultifying condition of poverty there that either shrouds the victims with apathy or reduces them to a demeaning scramble for subsistence. He reveals these perceptions in what he sees as Mexico's toleration of public begging and prostitution, its preoccupation with death, and its acceptance of poverty as a way of life for many of its citizens.

In contrast to this reality, Hayden ironically poses Mexico's awesome natural beauty—the beauty that the rich *turista* comes to see and enjoy. With the eyes of a painter, in "Veracruz" (poem 2), he sees the ricocheting brilliance of sun on water—the "arabesque ornately green" waves. In "Sub specie aeternitatis" (poem 5), he is struck by the sight of Mexico's "firegreen mountain" and "gothic rocks."

Beyond both the concrete reality of social wrongs and the local color that excites the tourist, Hayden perceives the ancient heritage of the land—a heritage that begins with the brilliant civilization of the ancient Aztecs and their too-exacting gods, of which he writes in "Idol" (poem 3, p. 50) and that includes the Aztec's conquest by the Spanish, who came with the sword in one hand and the Bible in the other to erect the fort and the convent, both of which, in their turn, were to fall.[40] The present point in this continuum is, of course, the plight of the Mexican poor.

These themes find their most successful symbiosis, perhaps, in "Veracruz," which demonstrates a cinematic development. Divided into two parts, it has Hayden's artistry with words, which he uses as a painter uses his brush, to achieve a Gauguin-like impression of the scene he surveys. The personae include several peons and the omniscient poet-observer:

> A shawled brown woman
> squinting against
> the ricocheting brilliance
> of sun and water
> shades her eyes and gazes
> toward the fort,
> fossil of Spanish power
> looming in the harbor.

In stanza 2, standing now at the site of the "fossil of Spanish power," the observer defines the shoreward view:

> the shore
> seen across marbling waves
> is arabesque ornately green
> that hides the inward-falling slum,
> the stains and dirty tools of struggle;

The beauty of the shoreline, of course, represents an appearance which hides a harsh reality.

Hayden is more specific in his characterization of the "dirty tools of struggle" in both "Market" (poem 6, pp. 53–54) and "Day of the Dead" (poem 1, p. 46). For example, the Indian boys who fish and idle in "Veracruz" are, possibly, the same "ragged boys" who "lift sweets" during the week that he writes of in "Market"; they steal in the same market where the "barefoot cripple," crying "Por caridad, por caridad,"

foraging crawls
among rinds, orts,
chewed butts, trampled
peony droppings
his hunger litany
and suppliant before
altars of mamey,
pineapple, mango.

In stanza 3 of "Veracruz," from the vantage point of the "pharos," the observer shifts his attention to the sea which he pronounces the sole reality:

Here only the sea is real
the barbarous multifoliate sea
with its rustlings of leaves,
fire, garments, wind;
its clashing of phantasmal jewels,
its lunar thunder,
animal and human sighing.

The imagery in the stanza, echoing the harshness of the "bickering spray" and "ricocheting" imagery of stanza 1, evokes a reality that is brutal—memories of the Spanish galleons that came with gunpower, some of which sank, but a sufficient number of which remained to take away the riches.

Stanza 4 centers on the poet-observer. Is he overwhelmed by the reality of this ancient heritage of suffering as he was overwhelmed by the Afro-American's plight in "Sonnet To E."? Or is it that this reality serves only to intensify his own sense of inadequacies? In either event, as he does in "Sonnet to E.," and "Monody," again he clearly expresses a death wish:

Leap now
and cease from error.
Escape. Or shoreward turn,
accepting all
the losses and farewells,
the long warfare with self,
with God.

If the poet does, after all, propose a voluntary death for the Mexican peon in "Veracruz," he is not so puzzlingly oblique in showing the prospect of their involuntary death in "Day of the Dead." Here, the advent of death looms so significantly in the peon's life that a special day is set aside in observation of it. Death can be, he says, as commonplace for them as is the candy, the "marzipan skulls," that the children play with, and it can be as certain as is the kwashikoor, so endemic with the Mexican poor, which is as fatal as "almond sweetness"—a lethal potion of cyanide.

On the other hand, it could be the "error" of the peon's spiritual death and degradation through male and female prostitution that overwhelms the poet-observer in "Day of the Dead":

> In flowered shirt, androgynous,
> the young man under palmleaf knives of sunlight
> invites, awaits, obliquely smiles.
>
> Such pretty girls, señor,
> but if instead—

Here, Hayden demonstrates discerning realism and perceptiveness in his treatment of the morally stultifying tentacles that, in his view, have sprung from the peon's economic plight. This dimension of his literary concern, first focused on ghetto blacks, then, successfully, on poor whites, Jews, and European war victims, firmly emphasizes, in *A Ballad of Remembrance*, his thematic stance on the oppressed of all nations. It is a stance that indicts the oppressors and it is one from which Hayden does not waver in his subsequent volumes.

NOTES

1. Arna Bontemps, "A Ballad of Remembrance," review in the *Fisk News* 37, no. 1 (Fall, 1962): 12.
2. Ralph Mills, Jr., review in the *Christian Scholar* 45, no. 3 (Fall, 1962): 337–40.
3. Rosey E. Pool to Robert Hayden, undated note on copy of press release, Hayden's private papers.
4. Ibid.
5. Hayden, "The Poet and His Art," p. 196.
6. Benét, *John Brown's Body*, p. 308.
7. Although Hayden did not complete his projected *Black Spear* volume, in 1942 he entered the poems he had finished in the University of Michigan's Jules-Avery Hopwood competition. He gave that collection of poems the title he had intended to give his projected volume, and it won him first prize.
8. Anthony F.C. Wallace, "Revitalization Movements," *American Anthropologist* 58 (April, 1956): 264–81; Herbert Aptheker, *American Negro Slave Revolts*, pp. 162–292.

According to Wallace, a revitalization movement is a deliberate, conscious effort by members of a society to construct a more satisfying culture. The process of revitalization involves four stages that are analogous to the parenthetical statements of Afro-American history: (1) Steady State (life in Africa); (2) Period of Individual Stress (forceful displacement from Africa); (3) Period of Cultural Discoloration (bondage in America); (4) Period of Revitalization (the numerous slave revolts in English America that began as early as 1663 and included subsequently Turner's, Gabriel Prosser's, and Denmark Vesey's).

9. Hayden, "Middle Passage," A Ballad of Remembrance, pp. 60–66, *Angle of Ascent*, pp. 118–23, *Collected Poems*, pp. 48–54.

10. Hayden, "The Poet and His Art," pp. 179–80.

11. Ibid.

12. Muriel Rukeyser, "The Amistad Mutiny," *Primer for White Folk*, pp. 23–50.

13. Hayden, "The Poet and His Art," p. 178.

14. Charles Davis, "Robert Hayden's Use of History," in *Black Is the Color of the Cosmos: Essays on Afro-American Literature and Culture 1942–1981*, pp. 255–64.

15. Elizabeth Drew, *T.S. Eliot: The Design of His Poetry*, pp. 21, 31, 72–77.

16. Hart Crane, *The Letters of Hart Crane*, p. 90.

17. Hayden, interview, July 3, 1973.

18. Allen Tate to Hayden, December 19, 1967, Hayden's private papers.

19. Hayden, "The Ballad of Nat Turner," *A Ballad of Remembrance*, pp. 68–70, *Angle of Ascent*, pp. 125–27, *Collected Poems*, pp. 56–58.

20. Herbert Aptheker, *Nat Turner's Slave Rebellion*, pp. 132–51.

21. The swamp is located in southeastern Virginia and northeastern North Carolina, extending from near Suffolk, Va., to Elizabeth City, N.C. It is partially located in Southampton County, Va., the site of the Turner revolt. In Turner's time, it was six times as large as it is now. *Encyclopedia Americana*, International ed., s.v. "Dismal Swamp."

22. This part of the discussion is based on Ezechiel 1:15–21; *Encyclopedia Americana*, International ed., s.v. "Ezekiel" and "Book of Ezekiel."

23. Aptheker, *Nat Turner's Slave Rebellion*, pp. 132–51.

24. Hayden, "Frederick Douglass," *A Ballad of Remembrance*, p. 71, *Angle of Ascent*, p. 131, *Collected Poems*, p. 62.

25. Frederick Douglass, *Life and Times of Frederick Douglass*, passim.

26. This last, Hayden makes clear, is his intention in his *Selected Poems* emendation of the "our children" phrase to simply "all."

27. Hayden, "O Daedalus, Fly Away Home," *A Ballad of Remembrance*, p. 67, *Angle of Ascent*, p. 124, *Collected Poems*, p. 55. See also the chronological Bibliography.

28. Hughes and Bontemps, *Book of Negro Folklore*, pp. 62–65.

29. Hayden, "Witch Doctor," *A Ballad of Remembrance*, pp. 18–22, *Angle of Ascent*, pp. 107–9, *Collected Poems*, pp. 35–37

30. Hughes and Bontemps, *Book of Negro Folklore*, pp. 62–63.

31. Ralph Ellison, "A Very Stern Discipline," *Harpers* (March, 1967): 80.

32. Hayden, interview, July 3, 1973.

33. Ibid.

34. Hayden, "Obituary," *Heart-Shape in the Dust*, p. 28, "This Grief," ibid., p. 34.

35. Hayden, "Rosemary," ibid., p. 37.

36. Hayden, "Those Winter Sundays," *A Ballad of Remembrance*, p. 29, *Angle of Ascent*, p. 113, *Collected Poems*, p. 41.

37. Hayden, "The Whipping," *A Ballad of Remembrance*, p. 28, *Angle of Ascent*, p. 112, *Collected Poems*, p. 40.

38. Hayden, "The Poet and His Art," pp. 147, 149.

39. Hayden, "An Inference of Mexico," *A Ballad of Remembrance*, pp. 45–57, *Angle of Ascent*, pp. 89–98, *Collected Poems*, pp. 17–26.

40. For an explanation of the system of *repartimentas*, under which the Indians were to supply labor for gold mines and plantations in return for instruction in the Spanish language and acceptance into the Christian religion, see "Tears of the Indies," *The American Heritage Book of Indians*, p. 99.

BRIAN CONNIFF

Answering The Waste Land: *Robert Hayden and the Rise of the African-American Poetic Sequence*

April 1966 was one of the most eventful and paradoxical months in the history of twentieth-century American poetry. At the Third World Festival of Negro Arts in Dakar, Senegal, Robert Hayden's *A Ballad of Remembrance* was awarded the Grand Prix as the best recent volume of Anglophone poetry. In at least some international literary circles the prestige of this award roughly matched its Olympic title. The first such event to be held on "independent African soil," the festival was sponsored by Léopold Sédar Senghor in conjunction with UNESCO and the Société Africaine de Culture and was attended by over ten thousand people from thirty-seven nations. The other finalists in the poetry competition were Derek Walcott's *In a Green Night* and Christopher Okigbo's *Limits.* Langston Hughes was one of the judges. Also in attendance were Aimé Césaire, Léon Damas, Alioune Diop, Yevgeny Yevtushenko, and Duke Ellington. André Malraux, then French minister of culture, seems to have captured the prevailing spirit when he praised the festival as an indication that Senghor's cultural program was about to shape the "destiny of a continent."[1]

For Hayden, though, the Grand Prix was wildly unexpected. He had not yet published a book with a commercial or university press in the United States, and he was still teaching fifteen hours each semester as an associate professor in the English department at Fisk University. Even the Grand Prix itself, when it first arrived, seemed to do him as much harm as good.

From *African American Review* 33, no. 3 (Fall 1999): 487–504.

In fact, within a few days, while his poetry was being praised in Senegal as the centerpiece of international negritude, back home in Nashville Hayden was being attacked as the scapegoat of choice for a new generation of African-American poets.[2] At Fisk's First Black Writers' Conference a group of writers and students, led by Melvin Tolson, assailed Hayden as the stooge of exploitative capitalists and, all in all, a traitor to his race. For the most part Tolson and his supporters endorsed the "Black Cultural Nationalism" of Ron Karenga, with its declarations that "all art must reflect and support the Black Revolution" and that "any art that does not discuss and contribute to the revolution is invalid." Hayden's crime was that he refused to be labeled a "Negro poet." From the beginning of the conference, and much to the dismay of most of his audience, he insisted that he should be considered, instead, "a poet who happens to be Negro." When he reiterated his position at a panel discussion—which also included Tolson, Arna Bontemps, and Margaret Walker—the advocates of Black Cultural Nationalism reacted as though they had come face to face with the enemy. Tolson's response was perhaps most characteristic. Among other things he declared that "when a man writes, he tells me which way he went in society." "I'm a black poet," he continued, "an African-American poet, a Negro poet. I'm no accident—and I don't give a tinker's damn what you think."[3] One member of the audience even accused Hayden of contributing to the "delusion" of the "young black people" studying at Fisk. In the following months students on the Fisk campus—almost all of whom, as Hayden was well aware, were from backgrounds more privileged than his own—continued to refer to him as an "Uncle Tom" or an "Oreo," believing that he should use the prestige granted by the Grand Prix to authorize and advance their political positions.

I begin with these events for three reasons. First of all, it is in these few days that studies of Hayden almost inevitably find their critical center—and, unfortunately, Hayden's defining moment.[4] From a conventionally biographical perspective this focus might seem reasonable. In the years immediately following the Third World Festival of Negro Arts, Hayden was granted a brief flurry of academic and otherwise official interest. From 1967 to 1969 he was offered a couple of visiting professorships, a permanent position at the University of Louisville, a recording at the Library of Congress, and, finally, the position at the University of Michigan that he would accept and then occupy for the rest of his life. Nonetheless, it is safe to say that even by the end of the 1960s, soon after the Grand Prix and his auspicious association with the negritude movement, and at least until very recently, Hayden would regain and retain his status as, in Julius Lester's words, "one of the most underrated and unrecognized poets in America." This neglect is largely the result of a collective choice—usually implicit but nonetheless clear—that academic critics have made in their descriptions of Hayden's career. Hayden's poetry has rarely been considered in terms of its rich affiliations with the work of major international poets—including Walcott, Okigbo, and Césaire, among many others—as suggested at the Third World Festival. And his poetry has never been seriously considered, at least by mainstream critics, in relation to the major works by younger African-American poets, who have found it a rich resource and an inspiration.[5] Rather, his poetry has been viewed—by his detractors and most of his supporters—as somehow determined by his one-line answer to the "Negro question," as it was framed by his opponents at the Fisk conference. For Tolson and the younger writers of the emerging Black Arts Movement, Hayden eventually came to be viewed as a poet of some ability—and some minor historical significance—whose work is irreparably limited and dated because it is not sufficiently concerned with issues of race. Even Arna Bontemps, who was often sympathetic with Hayden's work, would conclude after the Fisk conference that Hayden "doesn't really like that Negro thing." Meanwhile, for a handful of more conservative critics and editors Hayden's poetry has also maintained a kind of marginal interest—and, ironically, for much the same reason. For instance, in the influential *Norton Anthology of Modern Poetry* Richard Ellmann and Robert O'Clair begin their introduction to Hayden's poetry by stating that Hayden "did not subscribe to any esthetic of Black poetry." They describe his poetry in terms of his interest in the work of Countee Cullen, Carl Sandburg, Edna St. Vincent Millay, and "the English classics," and then include a selection of Hayden's poetry that would seem to suggest, to a reader unfamiliar with his career, that he must have been trying to write a kind of race-free poetry. In either case Hayden's critical reception has served, more than anything, to obscure and diminish his most formidable accomplishments.

Second, when viewed in the context of the history of American poetry over the past thirty years, the events of April 1966 point to an even more striking neglect. Recent criticism has remained oblivious to one of the most remarkable developments in contemporary literature: the rise, in part out of Hayden's poetry, of the African-American poetic sequence. Because of their particular moment in history, I think, the conferences in Dakar and Nashville were bound to have mixed legacies. Despite the notable absence of the more politically "radical" American writers, the Third World Festival of Negro Arts did help make the rich history of negritude known beyond the cultural centers of Paris and Dakar. At the same time, as a formative moment in the

American debate over a "black aesthetic," bringing together a number of still neglected writers on the verge of academic awareness—if not legitimacy—Fisk's First Black Writers' Conference helped expand the audience of such poets as Margaret Walker and Amiri Baraka, among others, and the second conference of 1967 would generally be recognized as the impetus for Gwendolyn Brooks's movement toward African poetic forms and what has been called a "new Black consciousness."[6] Nonetheless, the universalizing grandeur with which Hayden was praised, on the one hand, and the vehemence with which he was attacked, on the other, suggest that the two conferences, like most events that end up being reconstructed as defining moments, obscured just about as much as they revealed. After all, the often contentious politics surrounding the emerging postcolonial African and Caribbean literature—still loosely grouped at the Dakar conference under the title "négritude"—was just about as foreign to Hayden's sensibilities as the cultural politics of the Fisk conference.[7] A Bahá'í by faith, Hayden was committed to abstinence from partisan politics of any kind. Beginning just about a decade later, however, American poets would be better prepared to draw directly from the legacy of Hayden's poetry—at once individualistic and engaged, local and international, highly crafted and improvisational. Clearly conscious of Hayden's example, in recent years such poets as Michael S. Harper, Jay Wright, and Brenda Marie Osbey have been writing highly ambitious poetic sequences, firmly grounded in history, that invoke distinctly heterogeneous heritages with a wide range of formal experimentation.

Third, if the events of April 1966 are located in the context of a more extensive literary history, Hayden becomes an even more significant figure. His career spans a crucial period, from the early 1940s through the early 1970s, and his poetry eventually plays a major role in the emergence and development of what I have come to call "posttraditional" poetry. This poetry is largely informed by its author's paradoxical stance toward literary tradition. The posttraditional poet is certainly conscious—in fact, often intensely conscious—of tradition. At the same time, though, he or she manages, in one way or another, to view any distinctly literary tradition as historically contingent. Most often, the posttraditional poet uses thise sense of contingency to construct from disparate sources a personal heritage—provisionally, heterogeneously, willfully—in order to address some perceived historical crisis or, especially in recent years, some immediate social need.

Posttraditional poetry has its most conspicuous origins in the mid-1920s, when, just about simultaneously, the leading canonizers of high modernism began to take radical measures to address what seemed to them a profound schism between their most revered traditions and their peculiar historical interpretations of postwar Europe. At this time, writing in Venice, Ezra Pound began to juxtapose paradisal visions with Dante's *Inferno* and Major Douglas's economics. At the same time, in London, T.S. Eliot, recently established as a cultural icon, began his second "career" as poetry editor at Faber and Gwyer, redefining himself as a "reactionary" man of letters in what was in effect an elaborate attempt to counterbalance his own philosophical uncertainty with a millennial vision of Christian culture. Meanwhile, in Ireland William Butler Yeats set out on his first deliberate effort to distance himself from his early romantic nationalism—a truly strange journey, by way of a highly personal reclamation of an Anglo-Irish heritage, that would eventually lead him, in the last days of his life, to the striking embrace of common humanity in "The Circus Animals' Desertion" and "Cuchulain Comforted."

By the middle of their careers these poets were writing as though tradition—as they knew it—was about to come to an end, under the assault of a debased and debasing culture. They cultivated their notions of historical crisis in ways that resulted not only in reactionary cultural politics but also, eventually, in an understanding that, if the sense of literary culture they so cherished could be threatened and even destroyed by the forces of history, then any canon, indeed any culture, might be considered radically contingent.

Of course, at least since the Bollingen Prize controversy of 1949, the efforts of later poets and critics to come to terms with this legacy—especially its disturbing mixture of poetic innovation and reactionary politics, its vast international influence and intense Eurocentrism—has amounted to a kind of collective anxiety attack. By now, though, it has become clear that these often embarrassing ancestors have contributed largely—and, politically speaking, despite themselves—to the rise of a posttraditional poetry that has been growing, at least since the mid-1980s, more explicitly heterogenous and more international, both in its sources and its influence, in such works as Adrienne Rich's *Your Native Land, Your Life* (1986), Seamus Heaney's *Station Island* (1983), and Derek Walcott's *Omeros* (1990). Considered more broadly, a distinctly posttraditional stance has become increasingly apparent in the linguistic heterogeneity of contemporary Irish poets like Nuala ni Dhomhnaill and Medbh McGuckian, in the communal heritage evident in the prison poetry and autobiographical writing of Jimmy Santiago Baca, and in the remarkable emergence of contemporary poetry by American Indians. For these later poets any approximation of a tradition—any communal or even personal heritage—is conceived pragmatically, as one instrument among many others with which they can engage a world that is at once overwhelmingly various and desperately in need.

In this essay I will focus primarily on Hayden's "Middle Passage," the long early poem that would remain his most significant contribution to the development of posttraditional poetry. In "Middle Passage" he developed an experimental poetics that could examine racism, directly and specifically, by telling an episode of its history in a number of contending voices. Even at this early point in his career Hayden was able to challenge the modernists' sense of social crisis and give voice to his personal doubts about modernism's moral limitations—in terms that would not even be suggested at the conferences at Dakar and Fisk. In this sense "Middle Passage" is crucial to any reconsideration of Hayden's career. It anticipates his later "Negro history" poems, including "Runagate Runagate," "The Ballad of Nat Turner," and "Frederick Douglass." It also anticipates a number of Hayden's poems in widely varied historical contexts—most notably "A Ballad of Remembrance," "Night, Death, Mississippi," "Belsen, Day of Liberation," "El-Hajj Malik El-Shabazz," and the important later sequence, "Words in the Mourning Time"—in which he explores, often in brutal detail, the psychology and consequences of racism and xenophobia. Throughout this poetry, as William Meredith has put it, "there is scarcely a line of his which is not identifiable as an experience of Black America."[8]

Eliotic Intonations

For American poets of Hayden's generation the development of a posttraditional poetry almost inevitably involved some kind of direct confrontation with received modernism. Hayden was certainly no exception. Beginning his career in the early 1940s, he was conspicuously aware of the previous generation's legacy, particularly as it was perceived in the academy. In this view a few designated "masterpieces," the most conspicuous of which was *The Waste Land*, tended to appear as the culmination—both in the sense of the highest attainment and in the sense of the end—of a predominantly English tradition. The posttraditional impulses in the work of the established modernists—Yeats's provisional reconstructions of his own heritage in his final poems, for instance, or the philosophical and linguistic uncertainty of Eliot's "Little Gidding"—were not yet recognized or had not yet appeared.

Hayden's confrontation with this legacy can be seen in two contrary tendencies of his critical writing. On the one hand, he was prone to monumentalize Eliot's work—as would most academics of his time—by locating it at the end of the Great Tradition. In an overview of "Twentieth Century American Poetry," written for a 1973 textbook entitled *The United States in Literature*, he begins with a surprisingly conventional narrative account of modern poetry in which he acknowledges "the supremacy of Auden and Eliot" in the 1940s and then finds his conclusion in a description of "The Love Song of J.Alfred Prufrock" and *The Waste Land* as expressions of "the spiritual emptiness of industrialized civilization."[9] On the other hand, having been raised in Detroit's Paradise Valley, Hayden was also unusually aware, for an academic of his time, of the persistence of folk culture, jazz, and popular song throughout modern poetry. So even in his textbook account he mentions, along the way, the influence of these populist forces on the work of Edwin Arlington Robinson, Robert Frost, Carl Sandburg, Edgar Lee Masters, and the writers of the Harlem Renaissance—among many others.

Only on rare occasions in his critical writing could Hayden put aside this characteristic ambivalence—and, in doing so, move beyond the positions of both the "academicians and purists" and the Black Cultural Nationalists. Near the end of his career, in an address to the Library of Congress, he was finally able to articulate a more nuanced and culturally grounded understanding of "poetry as a medium, an instrument for social and political change":

> Poetry *does* make something happen, for it changes sensibility. In the early stages of a culture it helps to crystallize the language and is a repository for value, belief, ideals. The *Griot* in African tribes keeps names and legends and pride alive. Among the Eskimos the shaman or medicine man is a poet. In ancient Ireland and Wales the bard was a preserver of the culture.

From a perspective with this range of cultural and historical reference, the conventional academic canon of the midcentury—which usually seemed, with Eliot in his place, so complete—suddenly appears temporary, limited, and relatively inconsequential. So, in the same passage, Hayden is able to reconsider poetic tradition in terms that are personal, pragmatic, provisional, and moral:

> A point to consider: What would I as a poet do if my people were rounded up like the Jewish people in Germany under the Nazis? Claude McKay's sonnet "If We Must Die"; the poems of the Greek poet Yannis Ritsos that were recited and sung by men and women fighting in the streets for the freedom of their country; Pablo Neruda, William Butler Yeats, Emily Sachs, Muriel Rukeyser, Gwendolyn Brooks, Walt Whitman; they stand out as poets even if you dislike their politics. To be a poet, it seems to me, is to care passionately about justice and one's fellow human beings.[10]

In this construction of a living poetic heritage Hayden no longer sees tradition as a "line of development" leading toward an inevitable poetic conclusion. He is arranging writers, in heterogeneous combinations, to address a particular historical problem with a poetic vision of justice and compassion.

One irony in Hayden's situation is that, obvious political differences aside, this general method of overcoming the canon of the day is something he shared not only with a number of his contemporaries but also, in a way he himself never recognized, with the canonized modernists themselves. Like Yeats, Pound, and Eliot—especially in the later stages of their careers—Hayden's most basic tendency was to reconstruct a standard canon and, at the same time, to locate himself outside this canon in a way that highlighted its limitations and, ultimately, its historical contingency. In this sense his method was similar to that of philosophers like Nietzsche and Heidegger, as Richard Rorty has described it, when they redescribed their predecessors in terms of a tradition that seemed, in some sense, to have reached its end. Canon construction then became a strategy for dealing with "the problem of ironist theory ... the problem of how to overcome authority without claiming authority."[11] In this sense, at least from the mid-1920s on, each of the major modernists eventually came to see himself as Hayden saw Eliot: at the end of the English poetic tradition, as, in some manner of speaking, the last poet.

Still, for those of us who have entered the academy well after the rise of postmodern theory, I think it is difficult to appreciate just how common, and at times overwhelming, the monumentalizing view of Eliot was in the 1940s. Overcoming *The Waste Land* was a problem Hayden shared with such different poets as H.D. when she wrote her *Trilogy*, William Carlos Williams when he wrote the first four books of *Paterson*, and even Charles Olson, early in the next decade, when he began *The Maximus Poems*. As these poets progressed through the 1940s and 1950s, they were not worried, as their predecessors had been, that tradition, as they knew it, was about to end and that therefore there might no longer be anything of significance to write; rather, they were driven, and at times practically inebriated, by a sense of freedom they associated with the end of tradition, in the conventional academic sense of the term. That is why, just when literary criticism was being established in an unprecedented state of institutional security and influence within the academy and mainstream critics were settling on a totalizing view of poetic tradition, a number of American poets were undertaking some of the most ambitiously experimental work of the century.

That is also why, no matter how monumental high modernist poetics might have seemed to be when Hayden began his career, his confrontation with *The Waste Land* should not be construed as the kind of agonistic struggle against "belatedness" imagined by Harold Bloom in books like *The Anxiety of Influence*, *A Map of Misreading*, and *Agon*. Hayden's revision of Eliot's poetics was far more conscious and strategic than Bloom's Freudian mythology would allow and more engaged with history than Bloom's metaphysics and his preoccupation with private irony have ever permitted him to recognize. In the writing of his poetry, Hayden understood from the start that all acts of literary influence, and most of all those involving any kind of "alternative" tradition, take place in a world in which power is distributed unequally. As Edward Said has written of narrative literature in relation to European imperialism, even the most essentialist accounts of influence always retain, in some form, traces of the relationship between master and disciple, even master and slave.

In "Middle Passage" Hayden's revisionist strategy is calculated most of all to challenge Eliot's poetics by drawing upon historical sources alien to Eliot's social world. He originally meant to use this poem as the opening piece in a volume to be entitled "The Black Spear," in which he would attempt to "correct the misconceptions and to destroy some of the stereotypes and clichés which surrounded Negro history."[12] Though Hayden never finished "The Black Spear," an early manuscript version, without "Middle Passage," won the Hopwood Award for creative writing in 1942 when he was a graduate student at the University of Michigan, and many of the poems later appeared, extensively revised, in the fifth section of his *Selected Poems* of 1966.

Several critics have discussed the significance of "Middle Passage" to Hayden's career-long effort to incorporate revisionist history into his poetry. At the same time, however, most of the critics who have noticed the connections between Hayden's poetry and Eliot's have assumed that Hayden was, at least in matters of poetics, little more than a dutiful disciple, learning matters of technique from the master and in some cases imitating him directly.

In fact, the only readers who seem to have understood the kind and degree of confrontation involved in Hayden's reading of Eliot are those younger poets who have turned to Hayden's poetry as a resource for continuing innovation. For instance, Michael S. Harper has referred to "Middle Passage" as, in part, an "answer" to *The Waste Land*—that is, a poetic and historical challenge rather than a reverent echo. Harper recognizes that Hayden tried, through his knowledge of diverse poetic traditions, to move "beyond many of the experiments steeped in conscious modernism."[13] According to Harper, "Middle Passage" recalls "the schizoid past's brutalities" in order to confront Eliot's poetry with "a broad and pungent social reality." Along similar lines Jay Wright has written that "Middle Passage" alters Eliot's famous claim that a poet's fundamental responsibility is to language—and at the same time answers the criticism of many of Hayden's "younger contemporaries"—by demonstrating that "a language has a history and a relationship to other languages" that is more complex, and far more political, than Eliot ever imagined.[14] To these poets Hayden's view of Anglo-American modernism is much like that of Houston Baker in *Modernism and the Harlem Renaissance:* even though such iconic figures as Eliot and Joyce and Pound confronted the "changed condition of humankind" in the early twentieth century with "seriousness and sincerity," to use Baker's words, they also "mightily restricted the province of what constituted the tumbling of the towers, and they remained eternally self-conscious of their own pessimistic 'becomings.'"[15]

As he worked on the manuscript of "The Black Spear" in New York City during the summer vacation of 1941, Hayden immersed himself in the various histories, journals, notebooks, and ships' logs related to the slave trade in the Schomburg collection. Most significantly, at least for "Middle Passage," he also read the account of an 1839 slave mutiny on a schooner named the *Amistad* in Muriel Rukeyser's remarkable biography of the theoretical chemist Willard Gibbs. Gibbs's father, Josiah, was for most of his life a retiring professor of theology and sacred literature at Yale; in his more daring moments he was an amateur practitioner of the new German philology. But when a group of slaves who had seized control of the *Amistad* mysteriously appeared on Long Island, only to be thrown in jail, the elder Gibbs came to their aid, teaching them some English and finding translators for their legal defense among the African laborers in the ports of New York. He also seized the opportunity to begin a study of Mendi grammar.

Still, Hayden could not effectively use his research to answer *The Waste Land* until he had established a critical understanding of Eliot's poetics. At the end of the summer of 1941 he returned to Michigan, where he continued his research and enrolled in a course taught by W.H. Auden. Under the influence of Auden's teaching Hayden's understanding of modern poetry, and Eliot in particular, was caught in an intellectual landslide. Auden still spoke of Eliot as a close friend, and regarded him as the leading arbiter of current literary taste, but he was also in the midst of a prolonged, difficult moral questioning of his own earlier poetry. Most of all, in 1941 Auden was struggling to reconcile his early leftist politics with his recent reading of modern theology, especially the Christian realism of Reinhold Niebuhr—often deliberately obscuring his earlier positions but still subjecting his poetry to the questions of conscience raised by the rise of Nazism, the fall of the Spanish Republic, and the ongoing war in Europe. Auden's understanding of Christianity was significantly different from Eliot's increasingly millennial vision of a homogeneous Christian culture, and before long, most notably in *For the Time Being*, he would reject Eliot's peculiar fusion of social crisis and reactionary ideology.

Auden's efforts to remake himself as a Christian intellectual led him to challenge the very idea of a stable literary canon. A couple of years before Hayden met him, in his "New Year Letter," Auden had satirized the prevailing concept of literary influence, the idea that anyone who dares to write poetry must face "interrogation" by "the grand constructions of the dead." Dismissing this kind of purely literary anxiety, Auden had claimed for the poet a radical freedom to reshape the canon in order to serve immediate social needs, moral imperatives, and even personal whims:

> Each one, so liberal is the law,
> May choose whom he appears before,
> Pick any influential ghost
> From those whom he admires most.

By the time Hayden came along, Auden's method of teaching involved an apparently endless rearrangement of texts in constellations that were provisional, deliberately unconventional, and often downright playful. Another of Auden's students at Michigan, Donald Pearce, has described Auden's teaching at this time as driven by a "sense of verbal text as interdisciplinary conflux, or event ... of convergent-and-explosive text."[16] Tossed into one of Auden's textual "confluxes," Eliot's works could never appear as sacred, or as secure, as they were so often made out to be: for instance, in the reading list for Auden's course in the fall of 1941, Eliot's essays and *Family Reunion* appear alongside more than two dozen other books, including Kierkegaard's *Fear and Trembling*, Nietszche's *The Case of Wagner*, and Rimbaud's *Season in Hell*.

As eccentric as they must have seemed to many of his poor students, Auden's exercises in textual convergence were motivated by a developing sense of moral purpose. Mostly through his reading of Niebuhr, Kierkegaard, and Charles Williams, Auden had recently come to believe that the individual is far more capable of moral action than any larger social group can ever be. Primarily for this reason, the undermining and reconstruction of an authorized tradition was more than just the individual poet's prerogative. At the very least it was a moral responsibility. At best it could be a religious vocation.

Before long, all of these revisionary forces—the Negro history, the understanding of tradition as an array of cultural fragments provisionally constructed by an individual writer, the commitment to canon reconstruction as a moral imperative—would provide Hayden with his own means of answering *The Waste Land.*

Though "Middle Passage" was not finished in time for the Hopwood contest, "The Black Spear" manuscript did include a preliminary response to Eliot. This poem is far less impressive than "Middle Passage," but it does suggest just how quickly and systematically Hayden was developing his own revisionary poetics. "Schizophrenia" is a superficially Eliotic poem in two voices, each of which speaks a refrain with variations. The first voice recalls *The Waste Land*'s "heap of broken images" and its nearly exhausted anguish in the face of cultural and spiritual disintegration:

> We were trying to harvest the fragments
> of our scattered spirits,
> but it was the blitzkrieg's year,
> and the bombs were falling.

"The blitzkrieg's year" is only the most obvious among many symptoms of a culture so fragmented, so far beyond any hope of repair, that it seems to have come to the end of its history. The war continues, somehow, beyond human agency; yet, at the same time, it is all too ordinary, something like the weather. "Schizophrenia"'s second voice supplies the predictable metaphoric connection between this cultural catastrophe and personal insanity. For this second voice the falling bombs are little more than background noise for a series of private nightmares: "I saw a man in a cracked gold mirror / and a man in surrealist streets"; "I saw a pale girl, savage of eye, / fondling a headless doll"; and so on. Like a conspicuously modernist Parsifal, he has set out on a quest of some significance, apparently, but he is unable to figure out where he should go or what he should do: "One of these tasks is mine, / and the other is mine, / but which is mine they won't tell me." Needless to say, it is never clear just who "they" might be, these unhelpful shades. But that hardly seems to matter either, since, as it turns out, within a few lines both of the poem's speakers discover that they are locked up "in padded cells."

Poetically, the most basic problem with "Schizophrenia" is that its two voices sound far too much alike to answer each other—let alone anyone else—in any very meaningful way. Even if they are meant to be spoken by the same person, they could hardly support any respectable diagnosis of schizophrenia—perhaps clinical depression or echolalia or some such thing, but not schizophrenia. And, more important, these voices seem to be far too distant from recognizable events for "the blitzkrieg's year" to have any historical resonance, even in a time of war. Both voices echo Eliot's diction, syntax, rhythms, and repetitive phrasing, almost to the point of parody but never to any discernible purpose.

Still, at this early point in Hayden's career I think this little experiment proved to be very valuable: he learned that he could not answer Eliotic despair, in any very useful way, with his own rendition of Eliotic despair. By doing Eliot in two very similar voices—voices that just about any reader of poetry in the 1940s would find familiar—he discovered that all this preoccupation with the "tumbling towers" of some universalized Western culture, the "split shards / of the major illusion," could be patently self-indulgent. In "Schizophrenia" the speakers' vaguely nostalgic longing to recover the "shattered spirit" of the past only hides their mutual impulse to turn the harshest realities of the ongoing war, the falling bombs, into an analogue for some vaguely personal anxiety, just as *The Waste Land*'s compulsive allusions and nervous voices tend to obscure the social conditions of post–World War I London.

"Middle Passage"

For all "Schizophrenia"'s shortcomings—Hayden would never include it in any of his published collections—the poem's halfhearted experiment in Eliotic voices soon developed into a more pointed and far more powerful response. In "Middle Passage" Hayden once again explored the theme of cultural "schizophrenia" but this time within the historical context provided by his research on the slave trade. This historical material gave him the means by which he could abandon the kind of psychological posturing—the inevitable blending of dreams and consciousness, self and other, world war and private neurosis—Eliot's poetry had helped make fashionable.

"Middle Passage"'s most significant element of "social reality," as Harper would put it, was provided primarily by Rukeyser's account of the strange series of events set in motion by the *Amistad* mutiny. When the mutiny occurred, the *Amistad* held fifty-three Africans who had until recently been part of a much larger group, probably captured in one of the local wars fought, in those days, primarily for the acquisition of slaves. They had already been dealt by traders in Sierra Leone, sent under a Portuguese flag to the thriving market in Havana, bought by two Spaniards named Ruiz and Montez, placed in irons, and shipped off once again, this time to Guanaja, the main port of Principe. Their capture and transportation violated the decree of Spain of 1817—and, for that matter, "all the treaties then in existence" among European countries and the United States.[17]

Until the fourth night after the *Amistad*'s departure from Havana, their crossing was much like countless others on the Middle Passage. Hayden makes this point by constructing the poem's main narrative so that it emerges in the midst of fragments drawn from assorted accounts of earlier journeys. In this way he is able to tell the story of the *Amistad* against a background of sickness, madness, fire, rape, and other cruelties:

> "Deponeth further sayeth *The Bella J*
> left the Guinea Coast
> with cargo of five hundred blacks and odd
> for the barracoons of Florida:
>
> "That there was hardly room 'tween-decks for half
> the sweltering cattle stowed spoon-fashion there;
> that some went mad of thirst and tore their flesh
> and sucked the blood:
>
> "That Crew and Captain lusted with the comeliest
> of the savage girls kept naked in the cabins.

On that fourth night, however, the *Amistad*'s journey took an unusual turn. After just about all of the ship's crew had gone to sleep, having spent much of the day battling a storm, the slaves managed to get hold of machetes being sent along to cut sugar cane in the New World. Led by a man named Cinquez, they quickly seized control of the ship, killing the captain and the cook, who had threatened them throughout their journey. Then, because they believed they would need experienced sailors to navigate back home, they decided to spare the lives of Montez, Ruiz, and a cabin boy who had helped them as a translator.

This decision backfired. For sixty-three days Montez and Ruiz managed to delay their return, guiding the ship east by day and then turning northwest by night when they knew their captors would be unable to judge their direction. Zigzagging across the Atlantic in this way, the *Amistad* soon became the subject of local legend, with reports in the American press of a "phantom ship" following a route so incomprehensible that it must be driven by ghosts. When the *Amistad* finally landed at Montauk, Long Island, the Africans were thrown in the county jail. Accordingly, in "Middle Passage" it is Montez and Ruiz, suddenly set free, who tell this part of the story:

It sickens me
to think of what I saw, of how these apes
threw overboard the butchered bodies of
our men, true Christians all, like so much jetsam.
Enough, enough. The rest is quickly told:
Cinquez was forced to spare the two of us
you see to steer the ship to Africa,
and we like phantoms doomed to rove the sea
voyaged east by day and west by night,
deceiving them, hoping for rescue,
prisoners on our own vessel, till
at length we drifted to the shores of this
your land, America, where we were freed
from our unspeakable misery.

The story of the *Amistad* provided Hayden with a narrative framework within which he could include accounts of cruelty, from various sources, that make *The Waste Land*'s sense of "horror" seem timid and self-indulgent. But what would turn out to be just as important—at least for Hayden's development as a poet—was Rukeyser's less dramatic account of the series of trials and political maneuvers that began once the *Amistad* had landed on Montauk. This portion of the Gibbs biography, along with courtroom testimony by Montez and Ruiz published a hundred years earlier in John Barber's *A History of the Amistad Captives*, provided Hayden with a vision of a less personal, more historically grounded kind of schizophrenia: the assorted moral duplicities in mainstream American culture that sustained the slave trade. In these accounts he discovered a labyrinth of hypocrisy and rationalization so intricate that, to account for it with any degree of accuracy, he needed to master a more complex and ironic interplay of contending voices.

When the *Amistad* slaves landed on Long Island, they were surprised to discover that their arrival in a "free state" did not mean they would be set free. Of course, they "claimed freedom, charging Ruiz and Montez with assault, battery, and false imprisonment" (Rukeyser 36–37). Of course, for their part Montez and Ruiz claimed possession of the *Amistad* and its passengers.

Strangely, though, they were not the only ones to make such a claim—not by a long shot. Led by a Captain Green, who lived down the road, a group of Long Islanders also "claimed salvage on the vessel, the cargo, and the slaves," on the grounds that they had been the first to speak to Cinquez and his men when they had come ashore looking for water. Still another claim was made by a certain Lieutenant Gedney who, having seen the *Amistad* approaching Montauk, thinking it must have been a pirate ship and hoping for an opportunity to revive his languishing career, had ordered his own crew to follow. Meanwhile, the Spanish minister, with the support of the pro-slavery press in the United States, claimed the ship and its "cargo" for Spain, arguing that the trials should be held in Cuba since "a 'trial and execution' in Connecticut was not as good." Not to be outdone in a matter of patriotic duty, the local district attorney "claimed that the Africans should be held, according to the 1819 Act, subject to the pleasure of the President." Secretary of State John Forsyth and Attorney General Felix Grundy intervened, trying to keep the proceedings within federal jurisdiction so they might be able to turn the slaves and cargo over to "persons designated" by the Spanish minister. Even President Van Buren considered getting involved—he too was inclined to return the ship and the slaves to Spain—until he realized that he lacked an extradition treaty.

All things considered, it is hardly surprising that, in Hayden's account, Montez and Ruiz are perplexed. Most of all, they have trouble understanding how some Americans—especially the members of the antislavery movement who are sponsoring the Africans' defense—fail to recognize their right to what they consider their own property. When Hayden gives them a chance to speak for themselves, they focus their astonishment primarily on John Quincy Adams, who has taken up the cause of the *Amistad* slaves and will eventually argue for their freedom in their final appeal before the Supreme Court. When the events of the poem take place, Adams is seventy-three years old and returning to court after a thirty-two-year hiatus. Even by his own account, he is not in very good shape, with "a shaking hand, a darkening eye, a drowsy brain, and with all of my faculties dropping from me one by one, as the teeth are dropping from my head." To the Spanish slavers he seems to have been transported from the Roman Empire, rhetorically extravagant and oblivious to the practical demands of their very modern business:

> We find it paradoxical indeed
> that you whose wealth, whose tree of liberty
> are rooted in the labor of your slaves
> should suffer the august John Quincy Adams
> to speak with so much passion of the right
> of chattel slaves to kill their lawful masters
> and with his Roman rhetoric weave a hero's
> garland for Cinquez. I tell you that

we are determined to return to Cuba
with our slaves and there see justice done. Cinquez
or let us say "the Prince"—Cinquez shall die.

Ironically, it is with this slaver's speech that "Middle Passage" enters a maze of moral contradictions: between the law of New York and the broader political interests of the federal government; between the "Christian" slave traders, whose legacy of violence and lust has been documented throughout the poem, and the so-called apes who have spared their lives; between the slaves' perception of the United States, during the journey, as "mirage and myth" and these strangely "civilized" events that occur once the ship reaches the "actual shore"; between the talk of liberty in the free states and the "roots" of this liberty in slave labor; between the familiar language of Montez and Ruiz, confident in its sense of a culture shared with educated Americans, and the increasing isolation of the poem's main narrative voice, as it traces the history of "dark ships" that move like "Shuttles in the rocking loom of history."

Within this narrative framework Hayden uses his historical sources to turn Eliot's own poetics against his restricted vision of cultural decline. In "Middle Passage" Hayden makes use of *The Waste Land's* abrupt shifts between multiple voices, its cryptic quotations, its central symbols of fire and water, its references to the sea as the site of transformation, and its mythical hero who must journey through the land of the dead in order to restore a vital society. He even includes a bitter variation on Eliot's variations on Shakespeare. The two passages from *The Tempest* used by Eliot—Ariel's song, "Full fathom five thy father lies," and Ferdinand's lament for his missing father—are displaced from Prospero's magic island, compressed, and relocated in the hold of a slave ship:

Deep in the festering hold thy father lies,
the corpse of mercy rots with him,
rats eat love's rotten gelid eyes.

By establishing this doubly ironic relationship between his poem, *The Waste Land*, and the Shakespearean original, Hayden undermines the cultural nostalgia that Eliot characteristically imposes upon such passages: the search among the ruins for a once-coherent civilization, the pained intimations of moral decline, the longing almost beyond hope for some reconstruction of the fragmented past that might bring spiritual redemption. To put it another way, in Hayden's allusions the passages from earlier texts do not appear as a bulwark against the ruinous forces of modernity; they, too, have been transformed so that they carry the indelible marks of history in their imagery and even in their music. After "Middle Passage"'s accounts of, among other things, ophthalamia, starvation, death by fire, and live people fed to sharks, *The Waste Land's* method of allusion seems painfully literary.

That is the most important difference between "Middle Passage" and "Schizophrenia." In "Middle Passage" Hayden appropriates Eliot's poetics with this distinct purpose—and, in doing so, he develops a morally engaged, pragmatic poetics that would eventually align his work with the posttraditional poetry of a younger generation. Most fundamentally, his answer to *The Waste Land* demonstrates just how Eliot's poem struggles toward moral condemnation, without being able to establish any convincing or consistent moral ground. In this way Hayden is able to exploit a radical philosophical uncertainty that is one of the pervasive features of Eliot's poetry but is typically obscured by Eliot's later pronouncements on culture and religion. At the center of *The Waste Land's* moral universe, as Eliot and others have noted, is the vision of Tiresias, old and blind, "throbbing between two lives." According to Eliot's famous notes, Tiresias is "the most important personage in the poem, uniting all the rest":

> I Tiresias, old man with wrinkled dugs
> Perceived the scene, and foretold the rest
> I too awaited the expected guest.
> He, the young man carbuncular, arrives,
> A small house agent's clerk, with one bold stare,
> One of the low on whom assurance sits
> As a silk hat on a Bradford millionaire.

Of course, Tiresias' vision turns out to be the most famous—and discouraging—seduction in twentieth-century poetry:

> Flushed and decided, he assaults at once;
> Exploring hands encounter no defence;
> His vanity requires no response,
> And makes a welcome of indifference.
> (And I Tiresias have foresuffered all
> Enacted on this same divan or bed;
> I who have sat by Thebes below the wall
> And walked among the lowest of the dead.)

With its shifts between vatic proclamation and mock-heroic deflation, this passage brings *The Waste Land's* method of allusion close to that of English neoclassical satire, with its characteristic manner of exposing contemporary pretensions by holding them up to the standards of an idealized past that is deceptively made to seem available by the imitation of conventional poetic form. But, as Ezra Pound understood, I think, in some of his revisions of Eliot's typescript, such a method is fundamentally irreconcilable with either the poem's sense of irreparable fragmentation or its striving to give voice to distinctly modern anxieties. On the other hand, without the ironies generated by its classical and neoclassical allusions, this passage would suggest that Eliot's vision of Western civilization's impending doom must somehow wrench its moral authority from a voyeuristic commentary on an uninspired sexual fling—as if sexual boredom were the end of the world.

In "Middle Passage" Hayden places a reply to Tiresias' vision at his poem's center, both spatially and thematically. For Hayden the heart of darkness resides in the speech of an anonymous slave trader who, in the course of twenty prosperous years, has come to view his work, from its basic sources to its net profits, as an ordinary business. Loosely based on Theodore Canot's account of his own career in his *Adventures of an African Slaver*, it is a passage that, I imagine, must have been noticed by the judges at the Senegal conference, given their tendency to view both literature and racism in the context of colonialism:

> Aye, lad, and I have seen those factories,
> Gambia, Rio Pongo, Calabar;
> have watched the artful mongos baiting traps
> of war wherein the victor and the vanquished
> Were caught as prizes for our barracoons.
> Have seen the nigger kings whose vanity
> and greed turned wild black hides of Fellatah,
> Mandingo, Ibo, Kru to gold for us.
>
> And there was one—King Anthracite we named him
> fetish face beneath French parasols
> of brass and orange velvet, impudent mouth
> whose cups were carven skulls of enemies:
>
> He'd honor us with drum and feast and conjo
> and palm-oil-glistening wenches deft in love,

and for tin crowns that shone with paste,
red calico and German-silver trinkets

Would have the drums talk war and send
his warriors to burn the sleeping villages
and kill the sick and old and lead the young
in coffles to our factories.

By placing this speech at the center of "Middle Passage," Hayden also develops the strategy of moral implication he uses when Montez and Ruiz contrast Adams's rhetoric to the economic realities of slavery in America.[18] By including this particular slaver's voice, he is able to widen his net of implication: the speech is effective precisely because it seems so familiar, the words of a man who has simply been carried along in a job that leads him to everyone from local rulers like "King Anthracite" to "factory" workers at the barracoons to lawyers in New York.

Passages like this one suggest that Hayden's rejection of Black Cultural Nationalism, almost twenty-five years later, was primarily determined by the already formidable achievement of his own poetry. He would never be a "Negro poet" if that meant—as it certainly seemed to mean to his audience at the Fisk conference—that he could not mimic for his own purposes the voices of lynchers and common slavers. He would never be a Negro poet if that meant he could not use such impersonations to implicate, among many others, the African kings whose vanity and greed were so necessary to the slave trade, especially in its early years when white men rarely entered Africa's interior. And he would never be a Negro poet if that meant he could not give full voice to historical characters like Montez and Ruiz in order to account, accurately and with sufficient moral complexity, for the contending political and social forces at work when the *Amistad* captives finally landed in New York.

But, even more fundamentally, in his work of the early 1940s Hayden sets out to restore to poetry the sense of contingency by which a particular historical moment—say, for instance, a mutiny aboard a Spanish slave ship—appears vividly uncertain and, for that reason, at that moment, human action is potentially prophetic. The fragmentary narrative in the final lines of *The Waste Land* depends, more than any other passage of the poem, upon the myth of Parsifal, in various incarnations, searching for the Chapel Perilous in his quest to restore, and reconnect, the natural and social orders. *The Waste Land's* other more or less religious allusions—most notably, the vision of the disciples on the road to Emmaus and the ritualistic ending of the

Upanishads—are more than anything else variations on this theme. This overarching mythic structure and the poem's dominant narrative voice imply that these apparent fragments are ultimately unified in the refuge of a collective unconscious—or some such half-concealed repository of cultural memory and meaning—where they dwell, in their more complete forms, beyond the changes and challenges of history. In this way Eliot strains poetic metaphysics just about, but not quite, to the point of breaking. Or, to put it another way, in *The Waste Land* Eliot stops just on the verge of the posttraditional.

On the other hand, by rescuing Cinquez from obscurity—that is, by returning him, through poetry, to living history—Hayden asserts the possibility that an unlikely individual, even after one of the most convoluted journeys through the Middle Passage and the American courts, can act in a manner that "transfigures many lives." In the end, despite the eloquence of Montez and Ruiz—and the many others who claimed to own him—Cinquez did not die for his part in the mutiny. Somehow, Adams managed to revive his long-neglected skills as a litigator, and the Supreme Court ultimately ruled that Cinquez should be released to the missionary society for transportation back to Sierra Leone—along with those other slaves who had managed to survive their journey, imprisonment, and legal odyssey. By ending "Middle Passage" with a poetic account of Cinquez's survival, Hayden transforms *The Waste Land's* theme of transformation. He replaces "mirage and myth" with historical revision and continuance. Even more important, in contrast to Eliot's nostalgia for a stable tradition, supported by an equally stable social order, Hayden ends with a prophetic voice capable of resurrecting the suppressed past in, and beyond, the present:

> The deep immortal human wish,
> the timeless will:
>
> Cinquez its deathless primaveral image,
> life that transfigures many lives.
>
> Voyage through death
> to life upon these shores.

And, so, a "deep immortal human wish" finds expression in the poetic image—but what is most important is that the poem does not end there. The couplet at the center of this concluding passage balances two visions of Cinquez: for an instant he is equally a figure within the poem and an individual living in a historical moment. But the sequencing of the couplet's two lines, like the larger movement of this passage, suggests that the poetic image aspires to the status of an individual life, which can transfigure many other lives through prophetic action. The poem and the historical life invest each other with meaning, in a common world, for "life upon these shores."

Hayden and the Contemporary African-American Poetic Sequence

Of all the consequences of the literary politics of April 1966, probably the strangest is that Hayden's poetry—with its radical contingency, historical detail, moral complexity, and formal experimentation—would be so persistently ignored or undervalued by scholars and critics. This neglect can be interpreted within a number of contexts: for instance, the conflict between the cultural politics of New Criticism, in the years of its greatest domination in elite universities, and the Black Arts Movement, as it shaped one generation's discussion of African-American poetry; or the recent ascendancy of African-American novelists like Alice Walker and Toni Morrison; or the declining status of contemporary poetry within the academy over the past forty years or so, with the tendency to relegate poetry to creative writing programs; or the increasing influence of theories that seem to be more readily proved by narrative fiction and, in some cases, popular culture.

But none of these contexts really does much to lessen the irony, or the larger significance, of Hayden's situation. Just as critical approaches more sympathetic to history and issues of race have gained academic acceptance and influence, African-American poets have produced a body of work that is, I think, unprecedented in the degree to which it adapts innovative poetics to address historical and racial issues. Yet the criticism has remained virtually oblivious to the poetry. Hayden himself anticipated this problem when he said, in one way or another, any number of times, that discussions of "race and poetry" always seem to turn into discussions of "race."

So, for the most part it has been left to a younger generation of African-American poets to claim and continue Hayden's legacy. These poets have generally begun their careers with a clear recognition of the limitations of both Black Cultural Nationalism, with its tendency toward the kind of rigid political proscription that led to Tolson's denunciation of Hayden, and New Critical aestheticism, with its tendency to ignore race altogether and treat Hayden as a kind of minor formalist. At the same time, these poets have recovered some of the more useful affinities between African-American poetry and international negritude that were merely suggested by the conference in Dakar.

Most of all, these more recent poets have drawn from the approach to historical poetry that Hayden began to develop in "Middle Passage." By demonstrating that literary tradition—like history itself, as it is actually being lived—is radically contingent, Hayden made it easier for younger poets to view any given tradition as provisional, even improvisational. To put it in the more familiar terms of literary history, these poets have extended many of the poetic experiments of modernism while historicizing the modernists' sense of historical crisis—that is, the peculiar dread of impending chaos and social disruption, the barbarians-at-the-gates mentality, that so often characterizes the later canon formations of Yeats, Eliot, and Pound.

For instance, in his sequence "Debridement" Michael S. Harper extends Hayden's experiments in multiple voices and historical disjunctions. Using a prosody derived in part from jazz, "Debridement" comments upon a more recent but equally "schizoid" episode of the recent past: the Vietnam War, in which the poem's main character inadvertently wins a Medal of Honor, and the years immediately following, in which he returns to the projects, only to be berated by "militants" then shot and killed by a white store manager who is frightened to see "a car filled with blacks" parked in his neighborhood.[19] Shifting, often with the syncopation of a Charlie Parker solo, between Cambodia, the Projects, and the hospital where its main character dies, "Debridement" depends upon a sense of history in which the past remains oddly alive in the present and in which it seems that poetry—in particular, a distinctly posttraditional poetry—can provide the resources necessary to bring this past to judgment in a manner that serves the needs of the present.

Hayden's legacy also endures in the poetic sequences of Brenda Marie Osbey, with their multiple voices, disjunctive narratives, and heterogeneous cultural traditions. In works like "Ceremony for Minneconjoux," *In These Houses*, and most of all the book-length narrative poem *Desperate Circumstances, Dangerous Women*, Osbey's féfé women recreate a local history of New Orleans' Tremé district, in heterogeneous voices rich with the rhythms of island songs, okono drums, hoodoo chants, and "root ends / against tamborines."[20] Fittingly, Osbey begins the final sequence of *In These Houses* with a tribute to Hayden, a variation on his poem "O Daedalus, Fly Away Home." In this poem Hayden adopts a popular legend from Georgia Sea Island: "It was believed there were certain Africans who, after being brought here as slaves, flew back to Africa. They had magic power and, as I say in the poem, they could just spread their arms and fly away."[21] Drawing from the personal reminiscences of former slaves, Hayden recounts these legends in a kind of juba, accompanied by "coonskin drum and jubilee banjo." Osbey's tribute recalls not only Hayden's "Daedelus" but also the end of "Middle Passage":

> amid all the laughter
> i manage to fly away home
> have yet to perish
> in the sea.[22]

In her poetry, as in Hayden's, legend functions as both local history and living literature. A "tradition" of this kind is not something preserved by the purifiers of language against the corrupting influences of common culture—whether within the boundaries established by the range of allusion and other restrictive gestures of modernist poetics or within the institutional practices of the academy. A tradition of this kind is woven by the individual poet from the strands of assorted heritages still alive within her community. It still serves immediate purposes. It is a means of survival.

It seems to me that Hayden's legacy is apparent in similar ways in Melvin Dixon's "Tour Guide: *La Maison des Esclaves*," Yusef Komunyakaa's "Blues Chant Hoodoo Revival," Elizabeth Alexander's "The Venus Hottentot," and, perhaps most significantly, Jay Wright's *Dimensions of History* and *The Double Invention of Komo*. One way of looking at these works would be to say that they are part of one of the richest—and least appreciated—traditions in modern American literature, a tradition that undoubtedly includes Hayden as a shaping and presiding presence. It is also certainly true that all of these works draw, in one way or another, from what Robert Stepto has called, in a discussion of Wright's poetry, "the tangle of black traditions binding the Americas to West Africa."

But in remarkable ways all of these works point to a more fundamental lesson that should be drawn from the strange events of April 1966, from Hayden's calculated response to Eliot's poetics—and from the kind of reconsideration of Hayden's career that I am advocating. Terms like *tradition* and *influence* can only be applied to this poetry in a manner that is self-conscious and ironic, if at all. This poetry is so highly attuned to historical, social, cultural, and moral disjunctions that it never pretends to resolve, through direct appropriation of an established poetic convention, any injustice or hypocrisy that remains unresolved in the society at large. Instead, this poetry uses improvisation and linguistic heterogeneity as a means of constantly redescribing, and cultivating, human complexity and dignity.

So, I think it would be more accurate and more useful to say that this poetry—which might be called, rather loosely, the contemporary African-

American poetic sequence—builds on Hayden's legacy by constantly renegotiating relationships between contending traditions and contending social orders. Each of these poets reconstructs, at will, a heritage that is at once personal and historically grounded, continuous and progressively hybrid, in order to serve immediate social need.

To put it another way, for more than fifty years now Hayden's work has been one of the most persistent forces moving poetry in the direction of the posttraditional.

NOTES

From African American Review 33, no. 3 (Fall 1999): 487–504.

1. Janet G.Vaillant, *Black, French and African: A Life of Léopold Sédar Senghor* (Cambridge: Harvard University Press, 1990), 323. Clearly, the significance of the festival's location was not lost on its organizers or its participants. The first festival had been held in 1956 at the Sorbonne—as Vaillant notes, "the center of French scholarship"—and the second in 1959 in Rome, "The Capital of Christian Europe."

2. Rosey Pool, a member of the "Grand Jury" for Hayden's Grand Prix and for many years the leading advocate of his poetry, proclaimed that "at Dakar the words 'Negro' and 'Negritude,' Negro-ness, took on new meaning and dignity." She also used the example of Hayden to invest "negritude," in particular, with unusually extended, personal, and religious overtones: "In light half-nightmare and half-vision he speaks of the face of Baha'u'llah. prophet of the Bahá'í faith, in whose eyes Hayden sees the suffering of the men and women who died at Dachau and Buchenwald for their specific *Negritude.*" Rosey Pool, "Robert Hayden: Poet Laureate," *Negro Digest* 15 (June 1966): 39–43. In his keynote address at the Fisk conference Saunders Redding was more upbeat: he drew loud applause by referring to negritude as a "relatively inexplicable mystique." See David Llorens, "Writers Converge at Fisk University," *Negro Digest* 15 (June 1966): 55.

3. See Llorens, "Writers Converge," 62–63. More than a decade later, in his 1978 address at the Library of Congress, Hayden would respond to this particular comment. At one point in a dialogue between "the Poet" and "the Inquisitor" (a figure "more like Chekhov's Black Monk than anything else"), the Poet rebukes his adversary with the phrase, "As if you give a tinker's damn about poetry." Robert Hayden, *Collected Prose*, ed. Frederick Glaysher (Ann Arbor: University of Michigan Press, 1984), 4, 15.

4. The three book-length studies of Hayden, each of which begins with a biographical overview and then proceeds to critical analysis of his poetry, are typical in this regard, though they vary in their estimation of the degree to which the events of 1966 would ultimately shape Hayden's career. Fred M. Fetrow accurately describes the changes in Hayden's critical reception following the International Prize and the Fisk Conference. Pontheolla Williams uses Hayden's response to the conference—his rejection of Black Nationalism and his continued determination not to be bound by any kind of "Black Aesthetic"—as the central message of her "Biographical Sketch" and as the recurrent theme of her critical analysis. John Hatcher entitles his chapter on Hayden's life in the 1960s "The Crucial Years" and begins the critical portion of his book with an attempt to focus Hayden's career by accounting for his response to "The Problem of a 'Black Aesthetic.'"

5. The notable exception is Robert Stepto, who considers Hayden, Michael S. Harper, and Jay Wright as three poets who develop "post-modernist expressions" anticipated by the ending of Ralph Ellison's *Invisible Man.* Robert B. Stepto, "After Modernism, After Hibernation: Michael S. Harper, Robert Hayden, and Jay Wright," in *Chant of Saints*, ed. Michael S. Harper and Robert B. Stepto (Urbana: University of Illinois Press, 1979), 471. Also, in his introduction to the *Selected Poems of Jay Wright* Stepto suggests that "from the view of literary history" Hayden's "Middle Passage" might be "the poem behind Wright's art," since it anticipates Wright's attention to "the tangle of black traditions binding the Americas to West Africa."

6. D.H. Melhem, *Gwendolyn Brooks: Poetry and the Heroic Voice* (Lexington: University Press of Kentucky, 1987), 154.

7. A general idea of the academic consensus on the dimensions of négritude, at about the time of the Dakar conference, is provided by Lilyan Kesteloot's rather conservative survey, described in chapters 21 and 22 of her book *Black Writers in French: A Literary History of Négritude*, trans. Ellen Conroy Kennedy (Philadelphia: Temple University Press, 1974).

8. William Meredith, foreword to Hayden, *Collected Prose*, vi.

9. Hayden, *Collected Prose*, 45–49.

10. Ibid, 11.

11. Richard Rorty, *Contingency, Irony, Solidarity* (New York: Cambridge University Press, 1989), 105.

12. Hayden, *Collected Prose*, 162.

13. Michael S. Harper, "Remembering Robert Hayden," *Michigan Quarterly Review* 21, no. 1 (1982): 184.

14. Jay Wright, "Desire's Design, Vision's Resonance: Black Poetry's Ritual and Historical Voice," *Callaloo* 10, no. 1 (1987): 18.

15. Houston Baker, *Modernism in the Harlem Renaissance* (Chicago: University of Chicago Press, 1987), 4.

16. Donald Pearce, "Fortunate Fall: W.H. Auden at Michigan," in *W.H. Auden: The Far Interior*, ed. Alan Bold (Totowa, N.J.: Barnes and Noble, 1985), 157.

17. Muriel Rukeyser, *Willard Gibbs: American Genius* (New York: Doubleday, 1942), 18.

18. Hayden uses a similar strategy in "Night, Death, Mississippi," in which a later episode in American racism is described through the voice of one of its villains—an old man who, as his son is out taking part in a lynching, looks back with a nearly sexual excitement to the times when he too could join in the torture and killing.

19. Michael S. Harper, *Images of Kin: New and Selected Poems* (Urbana: University of Illinois, 1977), 110.

20. Brenda Marie Osbey, *Ceremony for Minneconjoux* (Lexington: Callaloo, 1983), 6.

21. Hayden, *Collected Prose*, 174.

22. Brenda Marie Osbey, *In These Houses* (Middletown, Conn.: Wesleyan University Press, 1988), 33.

FRANK RASHID

Robert Hayden's Detroit Blues Elegies

In the 1930s, the young Robert Hayden began to write poems set in his neighborhood, Detroit's Paradise Valley. Decades later, the mature artist, long removed from the "vanished rooms" and "dead streets" of his youth, returned to them in his poetry. Paradise Valley, which, in the 1950s, was sacrificed to urban renewal, increasingly became the subject and not merely the setting for his poems. "By then," he said, he had "gained enough psychic or emotional distance" to compose these poems based on his youth (*Prose* 139), and, though they appeared sporadically, he saw them as part of a group.[1] In them, he filtered his recollections through the Afro-American and European artistic traditions in which he schooled himself. Hayden applied the principles of two such traditions—the blues and the elegy—to the concrete circumstances of Afro-Americans in Paradise Valley.

Although the blues and the elegy both offer strategies for coping with adversity, elegies usually consider general, universal topics: death, ruin, the nature of change itself, whereas blues normally react to immediate and specific changes in life: loss of a lover, a job, money; movement from one locale to another. The elegist usually writes to make sense of an irrevocable loss, whereas the blues artist often includes in the work a way to reverse the condition or at least mollify the sadness. As a young poet, Hayden wrote

From *Callaloo* 24, no. 1 (2001): 200–226.

blues poems about Depression-era Detroit. As he matured, he concentrated more on the elegiac, although the blues experience remains. The Detroit poems of his later career are elegies in their expression of loss over a vanished place and absent people and blues in their resurrection of the Paradise Valley experience. They examine the miseries and coping strategies of long-gone Paradise Valley people.

Late in life Hayden commented that "the good old days in the Detroit slums had never been good" (*Prose* 20), but these poems do not merely bemoan the wretchedness of urban existence. Inherent in the blues and elegy—and in Hayden's use of them—is a protest against injustice, violence, and death itself. City life provides resources to confront these forces. Hayden's integrative and communitarian impulses led him to appreciate the "beauty," "gentleness," "vividness of life," and "intensity of being" of Paradise Valley, as well as its "violence and ugliness and cruelty." He recalled the "people who retained ... a sheltering spiritual beauty and dignity ... despite sordid and disheartening circumstances" (*Prose* 141).[2] While disdaining much that is called "protest poetry," Hayden disagreed with W.H. Auden, his mentor, about what poems can accomplish, writing that "poetry does make something happen" and that "to be a poet ... is to care passionately about justice and one's fellow beings" (*Prose* 9, 11).

Hayden's Detroit poems fit into the contexts of urban literature and Afro-American urban literature. Although the city they present is a fallen habitat of poverty, crime, and sin, it is also the locus for a potentially harmonious and just community. Charles Scruggs writes that, even when seeming least likely, "the idea of a visionary city is a durable and ongoing tradition within black urban literature." He argues further:

> The city as a symbol of community, of civilization, of home—this image lies beneath the city of brute fact in which blacks in the twentieth century have had to live. This kernel has never been lost. It is one of the aspirations expressed in an ongoing dialogue that the Afro-American community has with itself, a dialogue that sets a city of the imagination, the city that one wants, against the empirical reality of the city that one has. (4–5)

Hayden's urban poetry is visionary in this sense. His Bahá'í belief, in his words, "in the fundamental oneness of all races, the essential oneness of mankind, ... [and] the vision of world unity" strongly influences his mature poetry (*Prose* 200). To Hayden, the poet's role "is to affirm the humane, the universal, the potentially divine in the human creature" (*Prose* 119-20).

Despite its harshness, his early life in Detroit introduced him to these possibilities. He recalled that although he experienced prejudice, he played with white youngsters in Paradise Valley, and he notes frequent acts of kindness between members of different races. Pontheolla T. Williams suggests that "the insight and compassion gained from his own interracial experiences and mixed ancestry" contribute to his "humanistic worldview" (8). In reviving the city of his past, Hayden revives "a symbol of community, of civilization, of home."

Paradise Valley provided Hayden with models of integrative experience other than those involving race. His elegiac recollections become occasions for meditation on religion and morality as experienced in Paradise Valley. His poems record his youthful fascination with the street scene: gambling, prostitution, raucous music, and violence. Unknown to his foster-parents, he ran errands for prostitutes (Williams 11-12) Moreover, at some point in his youth, he began to experience profound confusion about his own sexuality. He was acutely aware of the supposed differences between the sinners and the saved, and he knew, too, that some who on Sundays worshipped with his family at Second Baptist Church behaved differently the rest of the week. In the city he learned tolerance and found acceptance. As Hayden composed elegies about the blues in his past, he found sources of sadness and hope. While integrating poetic traditions, he uncovered the foundations of integrated human community.

I.

The three broad meanings of the *blues* all bear on Hayden's Detroit poems. The first describes a mood of depression or sadness often but not exclusively linked with the Afro-American experience; the second refers to any artistic expression of this mood; and the third consists of specific musical and poetic forms of this expression.[3] Although Hayden experimented only briefly with specific blues forms, the blues tradition clearly informs his subsequent thinking and writing.

"Literature about Detroit," Dorothy H. Lee asserts, applying the second meaning above, "is often like all African American literature, a blues." Hayden's Detroit poems certainly fit Lee's rather general definition of the genre: "narratives of suffering that convert pain to beauty by shaping it into art" (313). They also embody Ralph Ellison's classic definition:

> The blues is an impulse to keep the painful details and episodes of a brutal experience alive in one's aching consciousness, to

> finger it jagged grain, and to transcend it, not by the consolation of philosophy but by squeezing from it a near-tragic, near-comic lyricism. As a form, the blues is an autobiographical chronicle of personal catastrophe expressed lyrically. (90)

Hayden's Detroit poems are a lyrical "autobiographical chronicle" of down times, joblessness, poverty, family strife, loneliness, austerity, sordidness, crime, and violence. The poverty and discord of his childhood, he later wrote, gave him "a deep ambivalence toward life and a sense of alienation nothing could alter" (Prose 21-22). In mood, even when not in form, Hayden's poems convey the blues of urban living.

True to the blues tradition, however, they do more than mourn about the city's miseries. They also present the richness and humor of Paradise Valley. They delight in the characters who walked its streets, sat on its porches, sang in its churches and theatres, and danced in its music halls. Above all, they admire the perseverance of the Valley's residents, despite its violence, poverty, and injustice. Houston Baker notes this quality in blues artists and their performances: "Even as they speak of paralyzing absence and ineradicable desire, their instrumental rhythms suggest change, movement, action, continuance, unlimited and unending possibility" (*Ideology* 8). A blues aesthetic offers strategies for transforming the uncertainty of Detroit life, ways to contain it, name it, and recognize its potential, even as one bemoans its immediate effects. The sadness of a specific blues lyric thus is for Hayden only part of a larger vision of human spirit and community. In a 1972 interview, he observes that "a typical effect of authentic old-time blues" is to "make people feel happy-sad" (*Prose* 144), and in the lecture notes for his college literature courses, he refers to Langston Hughes's view that although blues songs are "generally sad," they make the audience laugh. Hayden told his students that blues songs (and other songs and stories that belong to the black tradition) "reflect not only the harshness of the life they celebrate but also the fortitude, hopefulness and determination with which the rigors of life were faced.... Out of despair comes a song, and out of misery laughter" (HP 54/8).

As a young poet, Hayden experimented with the eight-bar blues stanza and its ABCB ballad rhyme-scheme which Langston Hughes had employed in "Sylvester's Dying Bed" among other poems (Tracy 79). Two poems in Hayden's *Heart-Shape in the Dust* (1940) explicitly transfer blues themes and techniques to Depression era Detroit. Direct references to the auto industry in "Shine, Mister?" and to Hastings Street in "Bacchanale" indicate that Hayden is consciously joining a Detroit blues tradition. Otherwise, the poems, in a manner typical of the blues, focus on the generic misery of unidentified representative speakers. In "Shine, Mister?" economic conditions force the speaker into menial labor and the "no-job blues":

> Ford ain't hirin
> Shine em up,
> Shine, mister?
> Briggs is firin.
>
> Man at Cadillac
> Said: Gwan back home.
> Went and played me a number
> But it wouldn't come.
>
> Asked for a shovel On the W.P.A.,
> Man said: Uncle Sam
> Ain't handin out today.
>
> Shine em up,
> Shine, mister, shine?
> Got in a crap game,
> Luck was ridin high
> oh, rent-money, eatin-money!
> When the cops come by.
>
> They throw me in jail,
> Put me on the show-up line,
> Slap me in the mouth
> And make me pay a fine.
>
> Standing on the corner
> With these no-job blues;
> Leave this hard-luck town
> if I had some walkin-shoes.
>
> Standing on the corner
> Tryin to make a dime
> Lawd, a po workin man
> Has a helluva time.

Shine em up, mister,
Shine? (*Heart-Shape* 42)

Even though economic conditions, hard luck, the "man," and the police thwart every opportunity, the resourceful speaker persists in his attempt to get "rent-money, eatin-money." Even shining shoes is a temporary expedient. He gains control of his sadness by singing and naming his blues, which never shut down the possibility of escape from the conditions that inspire them.

The speaker of the ironically titled "Bacchanale" employs another traditional response—drinking—after losing his factory job and after his lover has taken up with a Hastings Street man; still his plan to "git high" results from his belief in the possibility of earthly "joy" and his resourceful search for it:

Gonna git high,
High's a Georgia pine,
Can't laugh,
Don't wanna cry:
Gonna git high.

Factory closed this mawnin,
Done drawed that last full pay;
One of these Hastings studs
Done coaxed ma brown away.
A little likker,
O a little gin

Makes you fergit
The fix you in.

What the hell's the use'n
Miseryin on? ...
Wonder what I'll do when
Ma lush money's gone.

There must be some joy,
There's gotta be joy somewhere
For a po colored boy
This side the sky.

> Gonna git high. (*Heart-Shape* 44)

This speaker knows his "lush money" will run out, but he willingly exhausts it in his search for "joy somewhere" this side of heaven. Although he does not share the work ethic of the shoe shiner, he does reject "miseryin' on." He'd rather "fergit / the fix" he is in. Again the blues presents strategies for relief from misery and belief in possibility.

Although Hayden does not employ the blues stanza in his later poems, he does use the blues aesthetic in other ways. "Homage to the Empress of the Blues" describes the cause-effect relationship between communal human suffering and its artistic expression. In the poem, Hayden recalls the night he heard Bessie Smith sing at Detroit's Koppin Theater:

> Because there was a man somewhere in a candystripe silk shirt,
> gracile and dangerous as a jaguar and because a woman moaned
> for him in sixty-watt gloom and mourned him Faithless Love
> Twotiming Love Oh Love Oh Careless Aggravating Love,
>
> She came out on the stage in yards of pearls, emerging like
> a favorite scenic view, flashed her golden smile and sang.
>
> Because grey laths began somewhere to show from underneath
> torn hurdygurdy lithographs of dollfaced heaven;
> and because there were those who feared alarming fists of snow
> on the door and those who feared the riot-squad of statistics,
>
> She came out on the stage in ostrich feathers, beaded satin,
> and shone that smile on us and sang. (*Poems* 32)

Emphasizing private and public sources of misery—the injustices of love and of society—the poem blurs the lines between art and life, artist and audience. Smith's voice emerges from the audience's experience, just as the "sad juba songs" and sunflowers in "Sunflowers: Beaubien Street" (*Heart-Shape* 12) spring from their "dooryard loam." In commenting on "Homage," Hayden links the southern roots of the blues and of the people, with their particularly northern miseries. He recalls that at the Koppin Theater concert, Smith sang the classic, "Backwater Blues," which emerged from the Mississippi flood experience. However, she was also, as Hayden remarks, "singing about the uncertainties and sorrows of life as poor Negro people knew them—especially those who had not been out of the South very long" (*Prose*

144–45). In Hayden's poems, human acts of love, creation, desperation, and revolution often come from intense pain; the particular modes of Afro-American artistic expression, including the blues, result from shared experiences of private and public grief.

In this poem, Bessie Smith's art serves those who suffer from "careless love," from domestic insecurity and anxiety, and from hostile environmental and societal forces. Even the pictures, which, Pontheolla Williams suggests, are "torn" from magazines (60)—to cover up the exposed laths of the homes' inner walls—cannot hide the slow decay of these frame dwellings. Hayden says that he refers to "the fears," "anxieties," and "insecurity" of the urban environment, the "violence" of the people themselves, and the "menace of white authority—policemen, welfare workers, landlords." By "fists of snow," he adds, he means both the cold of winter and the "spiritual coldness, the threat of hostile forces" (*Prose* 146). By linking the pathos of the experience in the South and North, and by referring explicitly to the blues tradition, Hayden joins Detroit folk artists and factory workers in creating a blues expression specific to Detroit.

II

"Homage to the Empress of the Blues," like Langston Hughes's "The Weary Blues," belongs to the general tradition of blues writing, despite the absence of conventional blues stanzas. Its focus on a specific human being, rather than on a nameless representative figure, links it with Hayden's elegies. Hayden's mature work is rooted in the specific. He writes of specific historical figures and events and of specific personal acquaintances and incidents. Hayden often venerates his subjects, be they people, places, or events. We see this in his titles and subjects: the "homages" to Bessie Smith and Paul Robeson, and the poetic tributes to William Hayden, Frederick Douglass, Paul Laurence Dunbar, Malcolm X, Nat Turner, Cinquez, Tiger Flowers, and the "Queen of Sunday," and in his consistent concern with the elegiac.

Hayden, as poet, had an elegiac disposition. Especially in advanced age—"the elegy time," as he calls it in one poem—he concentrates on transience and loss, on specific human deaths as well as on absent friends and family and vanished surroundings. He makes use of the techniques of classical elegy: the "*ubi sunt*" motif and the meditation on ruin.[4] He also demonstrates his awareness of the elegiac strategies used by others—notably believers in conventional Christian formulas—to grapple with tragedy and loss. He often uses the word *elegy*, either as a title, within a work, or in description of a work. In his poems, he focuses on two main elegiac subjects: human death and loss of place.

The poems that combine the blues tradition with elegiac subjects are more concrete than "Shine, Mister?" and "Bacchanale," which present the hardships of nameless individuals who have journeyed to Detroit. Four poems focus on William Hayden, the poet's foster-father and a source of his earliest inner conflicts. Robert Hayden recognized his great debt to his foster-parents, who, out of kindness, took on the burden and expense of raising this cast off child. But their personal shortcomings and the unusual domestic arrangement made for a turbulent upbringing. The young foster-son—with his poor eyesight, scholarly bent, and skeptical disposition—challenged the understanding of William Hayden, a simple, religious man who had little formal education. One of the Southerners attracted to Detroit's industry, William found only hard work and low pay delivering coal (Hatcher 5–7).

In his foster-son's poems, William emerges as a man who held to his principles despite the hardship of his life and the criticism of those closest to him. These blues-elegies, taken together, combine William's own understanding of his predicament, his strategies for retaining dignity, and the poet's deep regret for his own "laggard" appreciation of this man.

Hayden calls Section 5 of "Beginnings" (1975) "The Crystal Cave Elegy." It describes William's reaction to the well-publicized 1925 entrapment of spelunker, Floyd Collins, in a Kentucky cave. As Williams (148) observes, the poem links Collins' fate and the predicament of the senior Hayden, a former coal miner now trapped in Paradise Valley. As he reads the news accounts of the rescue attempts, Pa Hayden recognizes their shared fate:

> Poor game loner
> trapped in the rock
> of Crystal Cave,
> as once in Kentucky coalmine
> dark (I taste
> the darkness yet)
> my greenhorn dream of
> life. Alive down there
> in his grave. Open
> for him, blue door. (*Poems* 129)

Like Collins, Pa Hayden is a "poor game loner" who is "alive down there/ in his grave." He has escaped the mine, perhaps, but not the harshness of working with coal, and he still tastes, quite literally, the mine's "darkness." In probing the reasons for his foster-father's concern for Collins, Hayden gives William his own elegiac voice. Later, in "Elegies for Paradise Valley," Hayden attributes to the character Crip a similar capacity for perceiving shared tragedy despite racial and ethnic differences.

Two early elegies, "Obituary" and "Rosemary" appear in Hayden's 1940 *Heart-Shape in the Dust.* "Obituary" (28), like "Those Winter Sundays," pays particular attention to William's hands, described as "gnarled and hard," and concentrates on his firm religious faith rooted in scripture, "the rock of the word." An early attempt, its conventional rhythm and rhyme undercut the intense feelings that inspire it. The more compressed "Rosemary" conveys more in only six lines because it presents the conflicts surrounding the senior Hayden and the deep regret with which the adult poet recalls him:

> He never lived for us
> Until he died;
> We never knew him
> Till he moved
> Beyond the need
> Of our too laggard knowing. (*Heart-Shape* 37)

In life, William needed the understanding of his family, but in passing to death, he has "moved / Beyond the need." In death, he has transferred the need, the knowledge, and his life itself to those who now are left only with the longing of remembrance.

"Those Winter Sundays" makes the same point. Pa Hayden rises on Sunday as he does on every day of the week; his "cracked" and aching hands receive no relief on this day of rest. Still "tasting the darkness," he rises to more coal-work:

> Sundays too my father got up early
> And put his clothes on in the blueblack cold,
> then with cracked hands that ached
> from labor in the weekday weather
> made banked fires blaze. No one ever thanked him.
>
> I'd wake and hear the cold splintering, breaking.
> When the rooms were warm, he'd call,
> and slowly I would rise and dress,
> fearing the chronic angers of that house,

Speaking indifferently to him,
who had driven out the cold
and polished my good shoes as well.
What did I know, what did I know
of love's austere and lonely offices? (*Poems* 41)

Pa Hayden has not left the harsh work of the mine. Unable to articulate his love in any other way, he performs two menial tasks, shoveling coal and shining shoes, in the cold and dark to serve the members of his family. Although he can alter the home's physical conditions, he cannot, in life, alter the emotional coldness and darkness that prevail there. Like "Rosemary," the poem focuses on the family's—specifically the speaker's—response to the man's self-sacrifice, the "too laggard" knowledge of his service and love, the regret intensified by Hayden's poignant repetition of "What did I know."

This is an urban poem: the coldness, the "weekday weather" comes inside, and the city's injustice, racism, and poverty chill the house. The poem, however, focuses on the responsibility of the individuals themselves for their thanklessness, anger, and indifference. In "Shine, Mister?" Hayden treats shoe-shining as the last resort, a debasement of self in order, paradoxically, to retain some dignity. When brought inside and performed for a family, shoe-shining indicates devotion but also suggests a level of desperation, a last resort to secure not physical but emotional sustenance. The pressures of an antagonistic society certainly victimize this man, but the intense regret at the poem's end is personal; the speaker knows that nothing in his behavior relieved the cracks and aches inflicted by the outer weather and that his own coldness made them worse. He also recognizes the true heroism in one who performs "love's austere and lonely offices"—even to the point of self-abasement—in the face of the hostility, indifference, and injustice of society and even of the family he serves.

These elegies sing both William and Robert Hayden's blues. They reveal the hardship and sadness William faced as he confronted a cold urban environment and a chilled domestic one, and they convey Robert's regret about his own part in William's misery. More important, they present the blues strategies each man uses to contain his sadness. William's consists of deep faith, hard work, and service. What he does, he does well. Lacking the opportunity to serve in return for William's kindness, Robert finds only in the poem a way to expiate guilt and contain sadness.

III

Several poems concentrate on icons of local and national Afro-American culture. As Hayden pays tribute to these heroes and heroines, he examines the effect of their lives and deaths on Paradise Valley residents, who have invested in them their own aspirations. These "urban" elegies recall the well-known person's death to reveal the complexity of the community's response. Hayden expresses consistent interest in the conflict between the reactions of conservative church-going members of the community and the reactions of the freewheeling devotees of street culture. He frequently mentions his own youthful deceptions in negotiating between both environments.

Hayden's friend, the poet Michael Harper, properly invokes Keats's "negative capability" to describe Hayden's method of handling the uncertain and mysterious ("Remembering" 185). Hayden often recalls the complexities and uncertainties of his childhood and youth, but in these blues-elegies, he does draw conclusions and take positions. When he writes in the first person singular of actual persons and experiences, he may present them as sources of controversy, but, in paying tribute to them, he almost defiantly renders a personal judgment, usually in opposition to conventional wisdom and morality. Even when he uses the voice of a member of the community, a position emerges. He recognizes the strategies his subjects employ to contain their sadness and retain their dignity, and, in forming his own appraisal, he arrives at artistic strategies that allow him to master his own emotional confusion.

Hayden's first-person voice directs the early version of "Homage to Paul Robeson" which appears in Harper's "Remembering Robert Hayden" and in several worksheet drafts (HP 41/21). Although this version lacks the concise intensity of the one Hayden eventually published (*Poems* 157), it does provide a dramatic occasion in Hayden's recollection of Robeson's pro-labor appearance in downtown Detroit's Cadillac Square in the 1930s:

> Crossing Cadillac Square today,
> I suddenly thought
> It's more than forty years since that afternoon
> when crowds of us with flags
> and cardboard signs gathered in the Square
> to hear magnificent Paul Robeson
> sing the Union cause, sing us,
> the poor, the marginal.

> Call him deluded, say that he
> was duped and by half-truths
> finally betrayed.
> I speak him fair,
> recalling in his hour
> the power and compassion of his art
> that day (all is blurred),
> the noble presence that exalted us. (Harper 186)

"I speak him fair." Hayden renders a clear judgment about Robeson whose own multiple artistic strategies convey sufficient "power and compassion" to diminish what Yeats calls the "mere complexities" of human existence. Hayden introduces the hero to the city and its residents and examines their diverse responses before revealing his own conclusion.

In "Free Fantasia: Tiger Flowers," Hayden ponders the significance of the 1926 middleweight champion and the life he represented. Then his speaker recalls his own youthful response before presenting his adult elegiac tribute:

> The sporting people
> along St. Antoine
> that scufflers'
> paradise of ironies
>   bet salty money
> on his righteous
>   hook and jab.
>
>   I was a boy then, running
>   (unbeknownst to Pa)
>   errands for Miss Jackie and
>   Stack-o'-Diamonds' Eula Mae.
>   ... Their perfumes,
>   rouged Egyptian faces.
>   Their pianolas jazzing.
>
> O Creole babies,
> Dixie odalisques,
> Speeding through cutglass
> dark to see the macho angel
>   trick you'd never

turn, his bluesteel prowess
  in the ring.

Hardshell believers
amen'd the wreck
as God A'mighty's will. I'd thought
  such gaiety could not
die. Nor could our
  elegant avenger.

The Virgin Forest
by Rousseau
its psychedelic flowers
towering, its deathless
  dark dream figure
death the leopard
  claws—I choose it
now as elegy
  for Tiger Flowers. (*Poems* 130–31)

The street is a major force in this poem, for that is where Tiger Flowers was hero. St. Antoine Street, one of Paradise Valley's major north-south corridors, was, in Hayden's memory, the scene of its most colorful characters and activities: "St. Antoine: St. Anthony: pronounced by Detroiters St. Antowine. Detroit's Beale Street. Respectable people shunned it as the devil's" (*Prose* 18). Hayden, who appreciated the irony in the name "Paradise Valley," saw St. Antoine as the haven of ironic conflicts: having a saint's name, it becomes "the devil's" habitat. Adding to the irony, the street's gamblers bet their "salty" money (Hayden's variants: "evil," "easy," "scuffler's") on Tiger Flowers' strong "hook and jab," which are not necessarily delivered with his right hand (Flowers was a left-handed puncher) but are definitely "righteous": Since he is the black Americans' "elegant avenger," his boxing represents their own moral battle against cultural racism.[5]

The speaker confesses to his youthful involvement in the street life, his undercover errand running for prostitutes, and his exposure to their risqué music. The poem's early worksheet drafts emphasize the eroticism of their world and the speaker's fantasies which link Tiger Flowers, the public symbol of heroic black masculinity, with the provocatively hidden world of Miss Jackie and Eula Mae.[6] Despite these fantasies, he recognizes that Flowers is out of their reach, and that they can only hope to observe his "bluesteel prowess/ in the ring." However, even this would elude them, since they are the victims of a "wreck," on the way to a Tiger Flowers fight. In 1927, aggressively seeking to regain the title, Flowers fought 19 times, winning two Detroit bouts, on June 17th and November 9th. One week after the latter fight, however, Flowers himself died, mysteriously and unexpectedly, during a routine operation to repair scar tissue above his eye.

It may seem that Flowers' death is the "wreck" which the "hardshell believers/ amen'd." However, the poem separates the deaths of the two women from that of Flowers:

> ... I'd thought
> such gaiety could not
> die. *Nor* could our
>
> elegant avenger. (my emphasis)

Hayden's worksheet drafts explicitly distinguish the accident which took the lives of the prostitutes from the boxer's demise.[7] Moreover, Theodore ("Tiger") Flowers was much closer to the "believers" at Second Baptist Church than to the "gaiety" of Jackie, Stack-o'-Diamonds, and Eula Mae. A devout Christian, his other nickname, "The Georgia Deacon," was accurate: He served as a deacon in his Georgia church and was known to pray audibly in his corner before his fights. In fact, while the believers may have found vindication in the "wreck" involving the prostitutes, Flowers' death must have puzzled them.

Both events apparently had a dramatic effect on the young Hayden, and the poem expresses this blow to his youthful hope for permanence. The joy and power, the vitality and righteousness, the mysterious eroticism in adult sexuality—all that intensifies the experience of life in Paradise Valley—is subject to even more potent forces. Absorbed in this rich complexity, the speaker finds the "hardshell believers"' cruel but "proper" reaction unsatisfactory. At first, he only wistfully remembers his own disillusionment upon discovering that joy and power pass away, but as an adult, he gains experience, understanding, and artistic sensibility that allow him to "locate" Tiger Flowers and the environment in which he fought. Some have questioned the appropriateness of the Rousseau painting in this context, but Hayden's speaker is definite not only about the painting, but about his own power in selecting it. By changing to the present tense, he insists that this is his considered response: "I choose it/ now as elegy...." He *now* can take on the power and gaiety in a way he could not before. The "elegy" not only mourns death but masters it. The very outlandishness of the choice brings the speaker/poet his power, asserting his own identity and knowledge. Few others, it is safe to say, would have made this connection. The painting, he insists, is the elegy, but his choice makes the painting a part of the poem. He brings to the poem the features in the painting which inspired its choice:

> its psychedelic flowers
> towering, its deathless
>   dark dream figure
> death the leopard
>   claws....

Hayden's intentional scrambling of the grammar gives us the painting's elements, and the painting itself provides the logic behind his selection: A deep orange-red sun hangs over a verdant jungle glade, thick with vegetation. All plant life appears huge. In the scene's center, the painting's smallest figures, a leopard and a black man, lock in struggle. The man's darkness is featureless, like that of a shadow. As on Keats's urn, all is deathless, despite the presence of death. The painting's sun will never set, the flowers will blossom forever, the man and the leopard will struggle eternally. The painting's "gaiety" will "not die," nor will its "dark dream figure." Infused by brilliance and power, the painting, as elegy, lives on. Just as Keats refers to the urn as an "unravished bride," this "virgin forest" remains untarnished by time and life.

The suggestiveness and eroticism of the painting's images also must have inspired its choice for this "free-fantasy." On one level, of course, the "deathless / dark dream figure" represents Tiger Flowers in combat with "death the leopard." But the boxer's feline nickname also links him with the leopard, and the "dark dream" figure of the poem's final version has its source in the worksheet drafts' startling description of the foliage: "sexdream flowers." Moreover, while an obvious parallel exists between the forest and the street and the "psychedelic flowers" and the "Dixie odalisques," the boxer's last name identifies him with the flowers as well. Through the painting-elegy, the "elegant avenger" who in life appealed to both saints and sinners comes to stand for inclusiveness of experience. He represents all elements of this battle: the forces of life ("deathlessness") and "death," humanity and nature, fauna and flora, masculinity and femininity. The elegy renders Hayden's personal judgment. He separates himself from the "hardshell believers" and uses his particular knowledge and sensibility to pay tribute to a hero and a way of life.

The "hardshell believers" do not question their certainties after the deaths of Miss Jackie and Eula Mae. However, the sordid secrecy uncovered in the unexpected death of one of their own leaves them less sure. The faithful in "Mourning Poem for the Queen of Sunday" cannot "amen" this "wreck"; too many questions remain.

Lula Butler Hurst is the "Queen of Sunday." A well-known singer of gospel music at Second Baptist, Detroit's oldest Afro-American church and the congregation to which the Haydens belonged, "Madame Butler" died violently at the hands of her lover. The poem, which, as Fred Fetrow notes, bears some resemblance to a gospel hymn (*Robert Hayden* 80-81), consists of three short-lined stanzas, divided by two stanzas with longer lines, which comment on the singer and her death. Hayden's speaker presents the different levels of mourning about the ironies of her death:

> Lord's lost Him His mockingbird,
> His fancy warbler;
> Satan sweet-talked her,
> four bullets hushed her.
> Who would have thought
> she'd end that way?
>
> Four bullets hushed her. And the world a-clang with evil.
> Who's going to make old hardened sinner men tremble now
> and the righteous rock?
> Oh who and who will sing Jesus down
> to help with struggling and doing without and being colored
> all through blue Monday?
> Till way next Sunday? (*Poems* 38)

She is one of Hayden's ironically captivating Paradise Valley characters, "sweet-talked" by the Devil, and thus ominously "lost" to the Lord in life as well as in death. The speaker calls her God's "mockingbird," both complimenting her singing and suggesting that her different voices have "mocked" God. The world still rings "with evil"; the "old hardened sinner men" as well as "the righteous" still need her to shake them; the victims of poverty and racism still need her to "sing Jesus down" to help them endure the other six days. Ironically, the one who helped so many get through the week was herself "struggling" until "next Sunday." The refrain—"Who would have thought / she'd end that way?"—indicates apparent bewilderment at the discovery of her dual life. This is undercut, however, by the obvious overstatements of traditional elegiac strategies, including a purposely-melodramatic appeal to cosmic grief:

> All those angels
> in their cretonne clouds and finery
> the true believer saw
> when she rared back her head and sang,
> all those angels are surely weeping.
> Who would have thought
> she'd end that way?

The speaker posits that the "true believer" needs reassurance that the angels join in grief over this death and its circumstances.[8] The sordid events of the urban underworld may be difficult to reconcile with a standard Christian vision, but this speaker lives close to such events, and the poem's form suggests that the purpose of ritual is not to separate the congregation from Sunday's fallen queen, but to find a way to include her and all sinners, to return her to the fold. The final two stanzas continue the debate between religious belief and urban experience:

> Four holes in her heart. The gold works wrecked.
> But she looks so natural in her big bronze coffin
> among the Broken Hearts and Gates-Ajar,
> it's as if any moment she'd lift her head
> from its pillow of chill gardenias
> and turn this quiet into shouting Sunday
> and make folks forget what she did on Monday.
>
> Oh, Satan sweet-talked her,
> and four bullets hushed her.
> Lord's lost Him His diva,
> His fancy warbler's gone.
> Who would have thought,
> who would have thought she'd end that way?

As the poem ritualistically reconciles the true believers with the singer-sinner, it also mourns her and pays tribute to her as artist. Through the community's response, we recognize her as one who wears the mask for the sake of her art.

Despite her now-acknowledged "sinful" life, she has made "the righteous rock" and she has sung "Jesus down." The poem, therefore, pays tribute to the complexity of the singer-sinner-artist. Had she been only a one-dimensional character, there would have been no poem. The speaker's need to reconcile the artist and the community intensifies the poem's mourning.

IV

Hayden carries on the discussion about conventional morality in several poems culminating in "Elegies for Paradise Valley." As he focuses on the tensions in the Valley itself, Hayden recalls the ways the older generation attempted to maintain fragile homes and families despite the powerful forces that would eventually destroy the neighborhood; he observes the erasure of his early experiences of integration; he links human deaths with the vanishing of the people and landmarks of Paradise Valley. As in other poems, he considers the Valley residents' strategies for weathering their hardships, managing their weaknesses, and comprehending their mortality. Most important, he develops his own strategies based upon his attraction to the "otherness" pervasive in urban life. Through these strategies, Hayden conveys his version of the visionary city that Charles Scruggs feels is a "durable and ongoing tradition within black urban literature."

"'Summertime and the Living....'" (*Poems* 39), like "Free Fantasia: Tiger Flowers," focuses on an adult speaker's recollection of the Valley's environment and culture. Hayden mentions that the poem is "partly an elegy" for his foster-parents and their peers, who sheltered the children in the midst of hardship and deprivation.[9] The first stanza introduces a third-person adult, who "recalls" his boyhood's imaginative blues-strategies, his capacity to use fantasy to escape his environment. The planting of sunflowers is much less willful than in "Sunflowers: Beaubien Street." These sunflowers, "unplanned"—like the children, like Hayden himself—do not "hold in thrall/ The cruel, sweet remembrance of Down Home." Instead, they serve as a "tough-stalked and bold" poor people's alternative to the thin-stemmed delicacy of roses, which, as the rest of the poem shows, only appear when the people die.[10] The boy transports himself above the violence and urban foliage to the circus world. Like the "danger zones" of Tom Swift and Kubla Khan in "Names" (*Poems* 171), the circus posters, stapled to the trunks of ailanthus trees (also "unplanned" and seemingly omnipresent in Detroit's inner city), inspire imaginary escape to other worlds and identities; the boy need not attend the circus in order to remove himself from the angry, broken life of the street.

The second and third stanzas develop the contrast between sunflowers and roses as they concentrate on the "elders" and explain the domestic anger Hayden mentions in "Those Winter Sundays" and explores in "The Whipping" (*Poems* 40). The ironic ease of summer in this poem, as in the Gershwin lullaby-aria which provides its title, is the adults' way of protecting the child from the dystopia they inhabit. They tell the boy the pleasant lie that there is such a thing as a "poor folks' time/ of year." Only as an adult can he articulate what, in Hopkins' words, his child's "heart heard of, ghost guessed": these were summers without roses, without vacations, without release; the "living" was "easy" only in contrast to the harshness of the northern winters. But there were still communal blues strategies. With no other affordable way to relax, they would attempt to forestall their "shouting" anger and recover "on broken steps" from broken days and restless nights by fanning "hearsay" or "quietness." Underlying all, he now realizes, was the presence of the "blight" (again, Hopkins' word) even more ominous than that of the ghetto: the hand-held fans advertising funeral homes, the absent roses, the solemnity; these reminders of mortality add intensity to the pressures of living poor. After all, these were people who came here in hope of an easier, more secure existence. With their "Mosaic eyes," they directed and empowered their children, even though they could not themselves reach the Promised Land.

The poem tells us about the speaker as well as about his elders. Although he has grown in his ability to name the springs of his sorrow, his adult blues-strategy resembles that of his boyhood. Just as he could imaginatively escape the circumstances of his life back then, he can now imaginatively return so powerfully to his elders that he actually "feels their Mosaic eyes / upon him," even though they have "long since" passed through those funeral parlors, whose fans gently guided their living voices through the evening air.

In the final stanza, Hayden leaves the elders and returns to the setting of the Paradise Valley streets. His powers of imagination call back their vitality and the contrast between religious fundamentalism and the "wickedness" of the streets in a manner similar to that of "Free Fantasia: Tiger Flowers" and the appearance of its boxer-hero:

Then grim street preachers shook
their tambourines and Bibles in the face
of tolerant wickedness;
then Elks parades and big splendiferous
Jack Johnson in his diamond limousine

set the ghetto burgeoning with fantasies
of Ethiopia spreading her gorgeous wings. (*Poems* 39)

In the midst of the contrasting visions of the "grim street preachers" and those who practiced "tolerant wickedness" (the "wicked" are as usual to Hayden more inclusive) arrive instances of awe-inspiring possibility and unity for all.[11] The poem's significant inclusion of Jack Johnson and his ostentatious display of wealth adds considerably to this scene. Of course, the "diamond limousine" represents in the particular terms of American (and Detroit) materialism his triumph over the oppressive white society. However, it does more than empower the Valley residents with the possibility of making it in America. Suddenly, they, too, imagine another time and place; they transcend America and transport their own identities. They envision the "gorgeous wings" of ancient Africa extended in an image of transcendent power and unity. From the community itself, therefore, emerge collective strategies for erasing misery and calling up a noble legacy. The city, however briefly, becomes the locus of not misery but possibility.

Hayden often finds opportunities for visionary transport and transcendence in the city's streets and institutions. The rider of circus horses in "'Summertime....,'" the reader of stories and poems in "Names," the viewer of movies in "Double Feature" (*Poems* 172), the listeners to Bessie Smith in "Homage to the Empress of the Blues" all become "other for an hour or two" because of the venues for art and entertainment—libraries, concert halls, arenas, theatres—which serve the urban population. The church, too, can serve this purpose. However, in Hayden's works, organized religion's restrictive vision diminishes opportunities for imaginative freedom provided by art and popular culture; and blind faith can leave its possessors vulnerable to the manipulations of clerical con artists, such as the subject of "Witch Doctor" (*Poems* 35), not an elegy but a brilliant expose, or Madam Artelia in Section IV of "Elegies for Paradise Valley."

One elegiac poem demonstrates the way in which organized religion can thwart the urban environment's opportunities for otherness. In "The Rabbi," Hayden calls up his early experience of ethnic and cultural diversity before the mysterious forces of adult religion erase it:

Where I grew up, I used to see
the rabbi, dour and pale
in religion's mourner clothes,
walking to the synagogue.

Once there, did he put on
sackcloth and ashes? Wail?
He would not let me in to see
the gold menorah burning.

Mazuzah, Pesach, Chanukah
these were timbred words I learned,
were things I knew by glimpses.
And I learned schwartze too

And schnapps, which schwartzes
bought on credit from "Jew Baby."
Tippling ironists laughed and said
he'd soon be rich as Rothschild

From their swinish Saturdays.
Hirschel and Molly and I meanwhile
divvied halveh, polly seeds,
were spies and owls and Fu Manchu.

But the synagogue became
New Calvary.
The rabbi bore my friends off
in his prayer shawl. (*Poems* 9)

No poem more succinctly captures the experience of growing up in Detroit, where one can taste the sweetness of diversity only to have it rapidly dissolve. During the brief periods when a neighborhood is integrated, children of different cultures play together, partake of one another's food, language, and customs; they can even comprehend the often disparaging ways that other members of their races regard one another. Hayden never lost his affection for these playmates; he recalls them again in a meditation on the Holocaust: "From the Corpse Woodpiles, from the Ashes" (*Poems* 46).[12] Yet the adult world, epitomized here in the grim rabbi, refuses to let him in; he cannot be "other," even "for an hour or two," by visiting the synagogue and experiencing its tantalizing mysteries, comparable in their way to the sexuality hidden in the rooms of Miss Jackie and Eula Mae.

The Jewish and Afro-American adults have a primarily economic relationship, based on a shared understanding of their respective roles. Although they privately demean one another, the storeowners and their customers understand the game. The customers, the "tippling ironists," know that the Jewish storeowners profit from their "swinish" violations of the Jewish sabbath. The "tippling ironists" not only increase the wealth of the businessmen, but also finance their eventual exodus from the area. In what historian Sidney Fine calls "a familiar pattern of neighborhood succession" in Detroit, Jews move out, and blacks move in (409). The child, left behind, feels abandoned. To him, the change is momentous, historic, a move from the Old Testament to the New, one that he does not welcome, since it means the loss of his close friends and imposes a new "Calvary" on him. In the last lines, the adult figuratively assigns his playmates' mysterious disappearance to the rabbi and his "prayer shawl." Religion here divides and separates. Yet briefly, the city works, long enough to inspire a vision of its integrative possibilities.

V

These possibilities influence Hayden's broadest and deepest exploration of his past, "Elegies for Paradise Valley" (*Poems* 163–70). Integrative in form and content, this set of eight poems uses blues strategies to resurrect the Valley's diverse characters and their struggle with life's uncertainties and death's certainty. "Elegies" explores the themes of other poems; however, this set introduces a much wider array of characters, concentrates more intensely on human death, and takes more obvious delight in the richness of Paradise Valley.

"Elegies" resurrects as it recollects. Two of its main characters, Uncle Henry ("Crip") and Madam Artelia resurfaced in Hayden's memory as he worked on the series.[13] It calls back 25 people who have died or vanished: the anonymous (the junkie in the opening lines), the famous (Bert Williams, Jellyroll Morton, and Kid Chocolate), the familiar (Uncle Crip, Ma, Auntie, and Melissabelle), and the "characters" of the neighborhood: Madam Artelia, "Belle the classy dresser," "stagestruck Nora," "fast lola," "snuffdipping Lucy," "Tump the defeated artist," "Les the huntsman," "gentle Brother Davis," "dopefiend Mel" and "Jim" the "Watusi Prince."[14] "Elegies" examines different traditions of mourning the dead: Two wakes—Crip's and the Gypsy king's—are main settings. The series also employs different methods—including a séance and an *ubi sunt*—of calling on the dead. Hayden uses the elegy to locate the self amid the contrasting personalities and conditions of the Valley. He finds the traditional elegiac impulse—the link between love and death—in the Valley's people and places. In the shared confrontation of mortality, he discovers the source of a communitarian urban vision.

The judgmental Christian believers from "Free Fantasia: Tiger Flowers" reappear in "Elegies," but, at first, they work in concert with sinners to protect the children from the dangers of the outer world:

> .... Godfearing
> elders, even Godless grifters, tried
> as best they could to shelter
> us. Rats fighting in their walls.

In this futile struggle the very structures of protection harbor danger, but life is rarely simple in the ghetto, and this is the source of its delight as well as its danger. In the alley just outside these walls—in fact, next to the speaker's boyhood bedroom window—"A junkie died in maggots." An even more hostile force exists in 1920s Detroit:

> I saw the hatred for our kind
> glistening like tears
> in the policemen's eyes.[15]

Natural and societal forces conspire against the children's well being. The second elegy points out that there was "no place for" the nurturing, individual attention recommended by Swiss educational reformer Johann Pestalozzi, and "no time of starched/ and ironed innocence." In this environment, both saints and sinners recognize a common purpose in protecting children.

Uncle Crip was one of the sinners. The companion of Hayden's "Aunt" Roxie, Crip was "murdered" while gambling. The "Godfearing elders" predictably "amen" this wreck:

> Unsaved, old Christians
> gossiped; pitched
> from the gamblingtable
> Lord have mercy on
> his wicked soul
> face foremost into hell.[16]

But Crip befriends the young boy. One of the Valley's interesting "wicked" characters, Crip appears in five of the eight "Elegies": dancing, singing, laughing, pronouncing, and possessing the added virtue, in the boy's eyes, of being "unsaved."

His first appearance, in the third elegy, is in his casket. Hayden's speaker attaches particular attention to its location, noting, as a sensitive child well might, that the dead body occupies the former location of a symbol of new life:

> Waxwork Uncle Henry
> (murdered Uncle Crip)
> lay among floral pieces
> in the front room where
> the Christmas tree had stood.

In death, Crip's Christian name replaces the one bestowed by the injuries of life. The impressionable youngster associates flowers with death, as Hayden thereafter always would, and naturally recalls the Nativity celebration's centerpiece. These contrasts continue as the poem concentrates on one significant mourner:

> Mister Hong of the
> Chinese Lantern (there
> Auntie as waitress queened it
> nights) brought freesias, wept
> beside the coffin.

Others probably wept and brought flowers, but Hayden singles out this instance of cross-cultural mourning. The restaurateur (perhaps Sam Hong, who lived at 2011 St. Antoine) testifies to Crip's character, countering the brusque judgments of the "old Christians."[17]

Mention of the coffin suggests another association of ideas and more combinations of images of life and death:

> Beautiful, our neighbors
> murmured; he would be proud.
> Is it mahogany?
> Mahogany—I'd heard
> the victrola voice of
>
> dead Bert Williams
> talk-sing that word as macabre
> music played, chilling
> me. Uncle Crip
> had laughed and laughed.

The neighbors' murmuring about the casket inspires memories of the living, laughing Crip, who introduced the boy to the humor and music of black America, including that of Bert Williams, whom W.C. Fields called "'the funniest man I ever saw and the saddest man I ever knew'" (Locke 164).[18] The young boy is chilled by the recognition that the voice coming over the phonograph belongs to a dead man. But the adult poet adopts the Victrola's role, playing the voices of the dead: Williams' talk-singing and Crip's laughter.

The phonograph returns in the sixth elegy, once more associating Crip with the music of the "sinful" and, here, with its suggestive sexuality. The boy, confused but attracted, "scrounges for crumbs" of the "sweet sweet jellyroll" even at church. He is attracted to female and male, the choirlady and Crip. Carrying over the ending of the fifth elegy, Hayden creates in the sixth a perversely comic liebestod. The "vanished rooms" and "dead streets" of the Valley "tell ..."

> Of death. Of loving too:
> Oh sweet sweet Jellyroll:
> so the sinful hymned it while
> the churchfolk loured.
>
> I scrounged for crumbs:
> I yearned to touch the choirlady's hair,
> I wanted Uncle Crip
>
> to kiss me, but he danced
> with me instead;
> we Balled-the-Jack
> to Jellyroll
>
> Morton's brimstone
> piano on the phonograph,
> laughing, shaking the gasolier
> a later stillness dimmed.

The setting is again the living room: site of Christmas celebrations, wakes, and moments of overt laughter tinged by the speaker's emerging sexual ambivalence. Birth and death, love and laughter, anxiety and fulfillment, all are at home in this "vanished room." In Crip, the boy experiences an elder whose expressions of affection, though not the kisses he craves, are not "austere and lonely" and whose strategies for coping include song, dance, and laughter. When Hayden returns to these moments, in the eighth and final elegy, he makes it clear that while the "precocious" child understands the "Old Christians'" precepts, he also comprehends the roots of his own hidden distress. He expresses undisguised gratitude to the "godless grifter" who in dance taught him his own blues strategy:

> We'd dance there, Uncle
> Crip and I,
> for though I spoke
> my pieces well in Sunday School,
>
> I knew myself (precocious
> in the ways of guilt
> and secret pain)
> the devil's own rag babydoll.

Dance masquerades sexuality, both revealing and disguising one's own status as the devil's plaything. Through dance, one can be, in the words of Ellison's vet, "hidden right out in the open" (*Invisible Man* 154). It also serves as a strategy for controlling appetites and denying pain, as in Hughes's "Evenin' Air Blues," in which a starving speaker says he dances

> To drive my blues away,
> Cause when I'm dancin'
> De blues forgets to stay. (Hughes, *Collected Poems* 225)

Crip introduces the young boy to black cultural expression as an alternative behavioral code to the Sunday school pieces he masters but finds inadequate.

The poem resurrects Crip much more effectively than does the beautifully drawn Madam Artelia, who is herself resurrected in the fourth elegy. The young boy, his step-mother, and his aunt visit the medium, hoping to contact Crip in the afterlife. Artelia bears some relation to the poet, who also uses the imagery of different cultures and religions to contact the dead. However, the "part Seminole" Artelia—with her "AfroIndian features" and "Gypsy dress," her incense-burning miniature Buddha, "silver crucifix" and "plaster Jesus of the Sacred Heart"—is a cross-cultural and multi-denominational fraud, differing from Hayden's "Witch Doctor" in the obviousness of her fakery and the humor in her portrayal. Only Auntie is taken in by Madam's performance:

She went into a trance,
Auntie said afterward, and spirits talked,
changing her voice to suit
their own. And Crip came.

Happy yes I am happy here,
he told us; dying's not death. Do not grieve.
Remembering, Auntie began to cry
and poured herself a glass of gin.
Didn't sound a bit like Crip, Ma snapped.

Recognizing that this voice and these sentiments could not have emerged from Crip in any condition, Ma cryptically verifies that Artelia is a charlatan. We recognize her phoniness in the tawdriness of her surroundings, not only her eclectic statuary, but also her flowers (omnipresent in Hayden's death-scenes) which are wax. Like Eliot's Madame Sosostris, her powers are undercut from the beginning by her subjection to the very force she claims to control:

Whom now do you guide, Madam Artelia?
Who nowadays can summon you to speak
from the spirit place your ghostly home
of the oh-riental wonders there
of the fate, luck, surprises, gifts

awaiting us out here? Oh, madam,

The question is in part rhetorical, since this elegy is the poet-medium's summoning of her from her actual "spirit place" and "ghostly home" in life (her places of business) through memory and creative expression. This elegy is a séance:

... how clearly you
materialize before the eye

of memory....

Of course, like Artelia, the poet engages in artifice to summon the dead, but the place from which he summons them—the past—is actual, and he does not pretend that they can tell us any more now than they did in life.

In the fifth elegy, Hayden employs two traditional poetic modes—the *ubi sunt* and the ballade—to realize the possibilities and limitations of elegiac recall.[19] He continues to use "the eye of memory" to resurrect the Valley's characters, but the very act of recall is an admission that they are beyond the reach of the living. The *ubi sunt* is an act of honest resurrection of the first the women and then the men of Paradise Valley:

And Belle the classy dresser, where is she,
Who changed her frocks three times a day?
  Where's Nora, with her laugh, her comic flair,
  stagestruck Nora waiting for her chance?
Where's fast Iola, who so loved to dance
She left her sickbed one last time to whirl
in silver at The Palace till she fell?
  Where's mad Miss Alice, who ate from garbage cans?
  Where's snuffdipping Lucy, who played us 'chunes'
on her guitar? Where's Hattie? Where's Melissabelle?
  Let vanished rooms, let dead streets tell.

Where's Jim, Watusi prince and Good Old Boy,
who with a joke went off to fight in France?
  Where's Tump the defeated artist, for meals or booze
  daubing with quarrelsome reds, disconsolate blues?
Where's Les the huntsman? Tough Kid Chocolate, where
is he? Where's dapper Jess? Where's Stomp the shell-
shocked, clowning for us in parodies of war?
  Where's taunted Christopher, sad queen of night?
  And Ray, who cursing crossed the color line?
Where's gentle Brother Davis? Where's dopefiend Mel?
  Let vanished rooms, let dead streets tell.

In these two stanzas, Hayden turns his kaleidoscopic memory on the range and variety of the Valley's characters and their blues. All have strategies for dealing with dissatisfaction and defeat. Laughter, sex, dance, music, alcohol, and drugs figure in the battle against poverty, madness, and alienation. All have ways of being or attempting to be "other": changing clothes, acting, clowning, escaping to the military, cross-dressing, and crossing the color line. Identity challenges, damages, and maddens these Valley residents, as it did Hayden himself. Their lives were poor enough, but death and urban renewal rob them of any legacy, since the streets on which they walked and the rooms in which they dwelt are "dead" and "vanished." Only the elegy creates a place for their memory.

The black residents of Paradise Valley do not suffer their privations by themselves. Desolate in many ways as their existence is, they find in the local group of Gypsies a people whom they can regard with disdain. In the seventh elegy, the parents' warnings about the Gypsies reflect their prejudice. As a group, the Gypsies are seen as dangerous; as individuals, their leaders are mystifyingly "dark," "sinister" and "dirty":

> Our parents warned us: Gypsies
> kidnap you. And we must never play
> with Gypsy children: Gypsies
> all got lice in their hair.
>
> Their queen was dark as Cleopatra
> In the Negro History Book. Their king's
> Sinister arrogance flashed fire.

like the diamonds on his dirty hands.[20]

Despite the queen's darkness, the adults perpetuate stereotypes and react with suspicion to appearances and behavior they do not understand. Their antipathy toward the Gypsies intensifies the breakthrough that occurs when death intervenes. Crip, significantly, in life as in death communicates the hard but simple lessons which death best teaches. "Quite suddenly," the Gypsy King dies, and Crip, quite simply, notes the connection between the gypsies' "clamoring in grief" and that of the black Valley residents:

> They take on bad as Colored Folks,
> Uncle Crip allowed. Die like us too.

This is Crip's admission, a lesson he learns as he observes the mourning Gypsies and recognizes in their ostentatious grieving first a common response to death and then a common experience in dying. Having already read the third and fourth elegies, we note the deep truth of this lesson which, in dying, Crip also teaches. "Colored folks" aren't alone in "taking on" over death; they are in league with Gypsies and Chinese and the range of humanity from the globe in between.

The diversity of urban life fosters this intense awareness of the forces that divide and connect human beings. In this elegy's last stanza, the speaker, drawing from Crip's lesson, recognizes the links between blacks and Gypsies, in life as well as in death:

> Zingaros: Tzigeune: Gitanos: Gypsies:
> pornographers of gaudy otherness:

aliens among the alien: thieves,
carriers of sickness: like us like us.

Based on shared mortality, we understand our shared identity, our common interests and purposes. Paradise Valley is home to those for whom every culture has a name and upon whom all peoples impose judgments and stereotypes. Crip's recognition culminates in acknowledgment of their common sorrows and strategies. Within these Detroiters, Hayden discovers the common source of the elegy and the blues.[21]

Notes

1. Hayden recognizes the link between several of these poems in a May 13, 1976, letter to his friend, poet Michael Harper: "'Elegies' is, I think, complete as it stands, though 'Tiger Flowers,' 'Winter Sundays,' 'Summertime,' etc., should some day all be grouped with the other poems in 'Elegies for Paradise Valley'" (Nicholas 1006). Hayden's lists and early plans in the Hayden Papers (HP) of the National Baha'i Archives indicate that he intended to group these poems. I will henceforth refer to materials in the Hayden Papers by box and file number.

2. In interviews (*Prose* 79–203), Hayden commented often on the contrasts of Paradise Valley life and people. The memoirs he began to write contain several pages (*Prose* 17–27) of his conflicting thoughts about his Detroit upbringing.

3. Among the many scholarly discussions of the blues, I find Houston Baker's *Blues, Ideology, and Afro-American Literature*, Steven C. Tracy's *Langston Hughes and the Blues*, and Ralph Ellison's "Richard Wright's Blues" helpful.

4. The ruin motif appears in the allegorical "Prophecy" in *Heart-Shape in the Dust*. "Fog rolled hoarse elegies over the ruins / Of the gutted city in the valley below" (21). It is also present in "Bone-Flower Elegy," written near the end of Hayden's life:

In the dream I enter the house
  wander vast rooms that are
    catacombs midnight subway
      cavernous ruined movie-palace.... (*Poems* 185)

5. Although Hayden was no athlete, he surely felt the keen interest in boxing that was pervasive in Paradise Valley even before its most famous resident, Joe Louis, became the World Heavyweight Champion. Earlier Afro-American boxers like Tiger Flowers, Jack Johnson, and Kid Chocolate are prominent in Hayden poems. As late as 1961, Hayden listed colorful quotations from a *New Yorker* article on prizefighting in his notebook (HP 31/9).

6. Early drafts of this poem include several fantasies in which the two prostitutes (given several names) succeed in luring Flowers "beyond those fringed portieres." The drafts also indicate that the young Hayden's image of Flowers is based on placards he saw in those centers of Afro-American masculine culture: the Paradise Valley barbershops. In these fantasies, perhaps, the young Hayden sought to reconcile the feminine and masculine worlds and the two dimensions of the self:

... I never
saw the sin burning
like incense beyond those
fringed portieres.
    Maybe
Tiger Flowers
did. Lean and muscular
on the placards
in the barbershops (The
Star, The Wolverine, The Peerless),
spare unsparing stylish
macho punisher in the ring. (HP 47/13)

    Creole babies
    Dixie odalisques
    oh they cooled him
    with their fans
in a paradise of ironies
    Who remembers him?
    But I imagine him
moving naked, lean,
exotic as his name (HP 47/12)

... Tiger Flowers,
the macho
angel trick
    they'd never turn.

Daddy, come into my parlor
    let me cool you with my fan
Step into my parlor, Daddy,
    where I keeps my peacock fan (HP 47/12)

7. Churchfolks called the wreck the will of God.

I thought you were too beautiful to die.
Tiger too is dead who'd never die. (HP 47/14)

I thought they were too beautiful to die
in the wreck the pious called the work of God
as they sped through whiskey dark to see
stylish Tiger Flowers in the ring. (HP 47/14)

Although I have not found a report of this accident in Detroit records, it could have occurred elsewhere. The fights took place in large cities all over the country, including Grand Rapids and Toledo. It is provocative to imagine the two women as earlier versions of today's sports groupies, following their "macho angel" around to different fights. The youngster, enchanted with them as well as with the "elegant avenger," would have been deeply affected by their "wreck," followed by the boxer's death.

8. I must register a minor disagreement with Fred Fetrow's otherwise fine reading of the poem in *Robert Hayden.* Fetrow suggests that the "true believer" is Madam Butler herself (80), but I find little in the poem to support this interpretation. I believe "true believer" refers to the churchgoer. Like the poem's speaker, this believer is moved to such sentimental visions by Madam Butler's performance. Madam Butler is now powerless to project what these "angels are surely" doing. The worksheet drafts support this interpretation. In different versions the "true believer" is replaced with "we" or with "true believers" (HP 43/39, 43/40). Also note the reference to "true believers" in "Electrical Storm" (*Poems* 6).

The precision of Hayden's description of the angels makes me wonder whether he had in mind some actual painting or stained glass representation in Second Baptist Church. Its present decor includes no such representation in the church proper, and photographs of the choir in its loft above the sanctuary from the 1920s are inconclusive. The Church's historian, Dr. Nathaniel Leach, recalls no angel representations in the church. The present outer doors of the church do have stained glass angels, although not exactly in "cretonne clouds."

9. For Hayden's extended comments on the poem, see the interview with Paul McCluskey reprinted in *Collected Prose* (140–43).

10. Hayden links roses and sunflowers (by their absence) in "Approximations," an elegy for his mother. The third section describes the wintry landscape around her grave:

> Not sunflowers, not
> roses, but rocks in patterned
> sand grow here. And bloom. (*Poems* 11)

11. In his prose recollection of St. Antoine, Hayden, using the same imagery, mentions the effect of such parades on this otherwise contentious community: "... nobody quarreled when the Colored Elks or the Colored Masons or Woodmen stepped it off along St. Antoine. The music, the precision of the drill teams, the polish and gleam and sparkle, the ribbons and badges. Ethiopia spreading her gorgeous wings" (*Prose* 19).

12. In early drafts of "The Rabbi," Hayden repeatedly asserts that he "wanted somehow to love" the mysteries of Judaism because he "was in love with Abe and Molly" (HP 45/45). (Hayden, typically, puts these characters through several name changes in these drafts.)

13. Letter of Hayden to Michael Harper (May 13, 1976):

> ... something strange happened as I worked and reworked them [the "Elegies"], for Uncle Crip ('Crip' because he limped) began to take over, and I let him, though I hadn't thought about him in years, I guess. And 'Madam Artelia' the medium (she was actually known in the neighborhood as 'Madam' Williams)—she must have signaled me from the spirit world, though I'm grateful she didn't materialize before me the night I lay in bed suddenly remembering her. (Nicholas 1007)

Even though the adult Hayden had "not thought about him in years,'" Crip's death must have traumatized him as a child. Elsewhere (HP 40/2) he mentions that his reaction was so severe that the adults later told him his hair turned gray.

14. Hayden's 1968 worksheets for these poems reveal a fascinating evolution. He envisioned a series of poems, "For Paradise Valley," made up of several subjects that eventually became parts of "Elegies" as well as other poems and subjects he explored but did not complete. Dramatic changes in emphasis occurred: Crip does not appear in the early drafts and lists of topics, but Jim Champ/ Jim Campbell, mentioned only briefly in Section V ("Jim, Watusi prince and Good Old Boy, / who with a joke went off to fight in France") is thoroughly explored. Hayden describes him as "my idea of a Zulu prince" and "an African Valentino," who "was full of life" and "always laughing." He recounts the reaction to Jim' s death in World War I, when Hayden was about four years old, and observes: "A slum child knows what death is before he knows anything else, I do believe" (HP 30/2). A draft of an apparent dedication lists several Paradise Valley residents and concludes:

> For all of you, you ghosts, you presences, revants [sic], alive or dead,
> that crowd around me, caress or threaten me,
> I write this in your memory, invoke you to be free of you, recall you
> to forget, summon you now to silence you. (HP 40/2)

15. For two excellent discussions of the climate of racism in Detroit in this century, see B.J. Widick's *Detroit: City of Race and Class Violence* and Thomas J. Sugrue's *The Origins of the Urban Crisis: Race and Inequality in Postwar Detroit.*

16. The suggestion has been made that these lines refer to the "unsaved" Gypsy King, but, like the rest of Section VIII, they definitely describe Crip. The early drafts consistently portray Crip as a gambler. This is from one version of Section VIII:

> Uncle died unsaved
> the pitiless pitying whispered
> pitched face foremost
> into hell. (HP 40/3)

17. "At the age of twelve or thirteen I even knew a few words of Chinese, because Kuni, the son of the owner of the Chinese restaurant where my aunt worked for so many years off and on, and I were friends and went to the Detroit Institute of Musical Arts together for violin lessons" (*Prose* 26).

18. In the early 1950s, Hayden composed several drafts of a poem about Bert Williams (HP 38/34).

19. Hayden to Harper, May 13, 1976:

> I suppose I'm risking something with the near-ballade in Part V, but I'm willing to take the chance. Years ago I wrote two ballades on Paradise Valley people—Lord, the place was full of eccentrics, real "characters"!—and I adhered to the rhyming pattern. I've no idea where those poems are today and in the process of trying to re-write them from memory combined them and then decided to write my own kind of ballade. Are the good grey poets of my generation now returning to the old forms? I seem to see evidences of

this. Elizabeth Bishop had a vilanelle [sic] in a recent *New Yorker*, for instance. Maybe there will be a "return," though I for one am not convinced that this is the thing to do. (Nicholas 1007)

The early drafts to which Hayden refers eventually surfaced. They are now in the Hayden Papers, Box 38, Folder 27.

20. Hayden writes of his secret love for Gypsies and his admiration of their "otherness": "Fantasy people / costumed in sex and electric flowers" (HP 41/1). His recollections of Hallowe'en in Paradise Valley (Prose 19–20 and HP 30/2) indicate his childhood love of gaudy costumes and the anonymous otherness they supposedly provided.

21. I am grateful to the Marygrove College Faculty Development Committee and the staffs of the National Baha'i Archives in Wilmette, IL; the Burton Historical Collection of the Detroit Public Library; and the Marygrove College Library. I thank Mary Helen Washington, Barbara Johns, Alvin Aubert, and Kim Stroud for their encouragement, advice, and support.

Works Cited

Baker, Houston A., Jr. *Blues, Ideology, and Afro-American Literature: A Vernacular Theory*. Chicago: University of Chicago Press, 1984.

Ellison, Ralph. *Invisible Man*. New York: Vintage, 1989.

———. "Richard Wright's Blues." *Shadow and Act*. New York: Random, 1964. 89–104.

Fetrow, Fred. *Robert Hayden*. Boston: Twayne, 1984.

Fine, Sidney. "Chance and History: Some Aspects of the Detroit Riot of 1967." *Michigan Quarterly Review* 25 (1986): 403–23.

Harper, Michael S. "Remembering Robert Hayden." *Michigan Quarterly Review* 21 (1982): 182–88.

Hatcher, John. *From the Auroral Darkness: The Life and Poetry of Robert Hayden*. St. Petersburg: George Ronald, 1984.

Hayden, Robert. *Collected Poems*. Ed. Frederick Glaysher. New York: Liveright, 1985.

———. *Collected Prose*. Ed. Frederick Glaysher. Ann Arbor: Univ. of Michigan Press, 1993.

———. *Heart-Shape in the Dust*. Detroit: Falcon, 1940.

Hughes, Langston. *The Collected Poems of Langston Hughes*. Eds. Arnold Rampersad and David Roessel. New York: Knopf, 1994.

Lee, Dorothy. "Black Voices in Detroit." *Michigan Quarterly Review* 25 (1986): 313–28.

Locke, Alain. *The New Negro: An Interpretation*. New York: Arno, 1968.

Nicholas, Xavier, ed. "Robert Hayden and Michael S. Harper: A Literary Friendship." *Callaloo* 17 (1994): 975–1016.

Scruggs, Charles. *Sweet Home: Invisible Cities in the Afro-American Novel*. Baltimore: Johns Hopkins University Press, 1993.

Sugrue, Thomas J. *The Origins of the Urban Crisis: Race and Inequality in Postwar Detroit*. Princeton: Princeton University Press, 1996.

Tracy, Steven C. *Langston Hughes and the Blues*. Urbana: University of Illinois Press, 1988.

Widick, B.J. *Detroit: City of Race and Class Violence*. Rev. Edition. Detroit: Wayne State University Press, 1989.

Williams, Pontheolla T. *Robert Hayden: A Critical Analysis of His Poetry*. Urbana: University of Illinois Press, 1987.

EDWARD M. PAVLIĆ

"something patterned, wild, and free": Robert Hayden's Angles of Descent and the Democratic Unconscious

[Interviewer] *It is nearly a cliché to say that Robert Hayden has the best underground reputation of any poet in America. How do you respond to that?*

[Hayden] (Laughs.) I say Hear! Hear! (Hayden, *Collected Prose* 203)

The diver had to admit that he couldn't surface again alone, without help.... Certainly, for me, an admission of almost complete defeat.... Well, this sounds like melodrama, sure enough, but it's ice cold reality of which I speak. (Hayden, in a letter to Michael Harper [Nicholas 997])

Poetry is really distilled empathy. (Yusef Komunyakaa, *Blue Notes* 126)

In "Answering 'The Waste Land': Robert Hayden and the Rise of the African American Poetic Sequence," Brian Coniff shows how Hayden's historical poems alter assumptions about the intersection of history and modernist poetics. Coniff terms modernist poetics such as Hayden's "post-traditional." He explains that the "post-traditional poet is certainly conscious—in fact, often intensely conscious—of tradition. At the same time, though, he or she manages, in one way or another, to view any distinctly literary tradition as historically contingent.... Most often ... to address some perceived historical crisis" (489). He follows with brilliant readings which show how Hayden's historical vision goes beyond the mainstream modernist

From *African American Review* 36, no. 4 (Winter 2002): 533–555.

grounding in "private neurosis [that] Eliot's poetry had helped make fashionable" (496). Coniff supplies crucial insights into how African-American approaches to modernism emerge from the distinctive features of black encounters with the history of modernity. Like all modernisms, African-American modernisms have one foot in the "historical" past, one in the "cultural" present. While they've attracted almost no critical attention at all, Hayden's poems set in his cultural present contribute to this *cultural axis* of black modernism.

Like all notable African-American modernist artists, Hayden understood that confrontations with modernity are historically contingent. Indeed, nearly all of the scholarship devoted to Hayden concerns his treatment of nineteenth-century subject matter in poems such as "Middle Passage," "Runagate Runagate," "The Ballad of Nat Turner," and "Frederick Douglass." Very little has been written about Hayden's nuanced appreciation of how modernist poetics are *culturally* contingent. For all the histrionics surrounding Hayden's "universalism" and his refusal to join the Black Arts Movement in the late 1960s, Hayden's poems are replete with deeply resonant images of immediate black cultural reality through which he explores the complex interactions between psychological depth and cultural tradition. Hayden's poetry consistently demonstrates the ability to excavate the interlocking historical and cultural contingencies and freedoms of black subjectivity while eluding the oppositional politics which confined the political and cultural era in which he lived. In these poems he explores the classic modernist intersections between objectivity and subjectivity, intimacy and abstraction. He combines the oppositional poles to achieve points of view and review impossible from one or the other. In the present essay, using "The Diver" as the methodological paradigm, I show how Hayden's artistic vision achieves a *depth* of perception from which the divisions that inform oppostional politics become unstable. Far from a naïve universalism, as "The Diver" images and the epigram above confirms, the pressure of that depth perception was as dangerous for Hayden as it was necessary to the (post) tradition of black modernism.

The result is Hayden's complex poetic vision of the strife and possibility embedded in America's fragmented intra-and inter-racial /cultural landscape. In his best work, Hayden derives, sustains, and refines this vision in relation to his excavation of what I'll call the *democratic unconscious.* In this space, Hayden explores the ever-shifting, non-rational nature of the unconscious to create montages of democratic exchange. Hayden's approach can be understood in relation to Freud's assertion that, because "urges with contrary aims exist side by side in the unconscious," its structure "embraces mutually incompatible details" (44). For many modernists, this structure threatened to unleash dangerously anti-social and irrational impulses which might destroy the rational structures of Western civilization. For Hayden and others confined by segregation, the threats can be understood as potentially liberating cultural/political advances. The relationship between images within and between Hayden's poems invokes the fluid structure of psychic depth to resee the world and meditate on the limitations of, and possibilities beyond, racial, cultural, and existential oppositions in American life.

The sources of Hayden's vision are unusually complex. In *From the Auroral Darkness: The Life and Poetry of Robert Hayden*, John Hatcher suggests that Hayden's modernism has three principal ingredients: W.H. Auden's modernist technique, the Bahá'í religion's approach to modernity, and Hayden's own intimately distant creative approach. In his "Introduction" to Hayden's *Collected Poems*, Arnold Rampersad notes that Auden saw "Marxism and ultranationalism as, in different ways, inimical to the flourishing of art.... [thus, he] proposed a modernist poetry of technical and meditative complexity, in which judicious erudition and imagination ... were vital elements" (xviii). In "A 'Romantic Realist,'" Hayden cryptically described his graduate study with Auden as "a strategic experience in my life" (118). Hayden's non-ideological, or anti-dogmatic, approach to composition was not solely the result of Auden's influence. Recalling experiences before he'd met Auden in his third-person autobiographical sketch "From *The Life*," Hayden writes that, before he went to graduate school, "venturing to read his poems for the members of the [Detroit] John Reed Club, he was scathingly criticized for his lack of political awareness. And he was often accused of being too much the individualist and not willing to submit to ideology" (25). As Hatcher notes, in classes, speeches, and interviews, Hayden often repeated "Auden's notion of poetry as a process of solving for the unknown.... 'In poetry you are really solving *x*, looking for the unknown quantity. You are trying to say what cannot be said any other way—and, in some poems, you are trying to say what cannot be said at all' " (70). While saying the impossible implies an improvisational approach to composition, Hayden was a relentless and meticulous reviser. Hatcher quotes a 1976 interview in which Hayden shows his unapologetic attitude toward the rigors of poetic craft: " 'If I have a missionary zeal about anything, it is this. Technique is very important to me. I've not spent my life as a poet just to put words together any old way' " (89).

Although some critics look at Hayden's cultural (black), religious (Bahá'í), and artistic (modernist) moorings, as incompatible, in his best poems the elements converge and confirm each other. The power and beauty of Hayden's Afro-Modernism emanates from his ability to merge the streams and to discipline the tumult which resulted from the intensity of a vision which speaks to the most disruptive voices of the modernist tradition.

In his essay "The Five Major Rubrics of Nietzsche's Thought," Martin Heidegger explains Nietzsche's insight into the twentieth century as an "era whose upheavals could not be compared to anything previously known" (5). According to Heidegger, the key to Nietzsche's insight is that these upheavals will be newly ambiguous processes with unprecedented potential for liberation and destruction. He summarizes Nietzsche's vision of the eroding possibilities for withdrawal from and resistence to accelerating modern change which is "no longer experienced as sheer annihilation and deplored as wasteful and wrong, but is rather greeted as a liberation, touted as an irrevocable gain and perceived as fulfillment" (5). Hayden certainly shared Heidegger's sense that the basic impulses of literary modernism have to do with meditation upon and response to the inescapable, accelerating changes brought on by modernity.

Similarly, from their beginnings, most articulations of African-American modernism—such as the pragmatism of Du Bois and Alain Locke—have embraced the anti-romantic push toward the future. Black Americans' experiences of slavery and segregation clearly belied romantic images of an idyllic and pastoral past on the old plantation. In *Just Above My Head*, James Baldwin quotes the lyrics from a spiritual to underscore the ways psychological and historical realities inform the urge to push forward. Meditating on the elusiveness of personal memory and the realities of historical suffering, Baldwin writes: "You cannot see when you look back: too dark behind me. And the song says, merely, with a stunning matter-of-factness, 'There's a light before me. I'm on my way' " (60). Black American history offered scant opportunity for romantic nostalgia. Like Baldwin in Harlem, when Hayden was growing up in one of the harshest Detroit ghettoes prior to World War II, the imperatives for historical progress were clear and present.

The Bahá'í faith approaches history as a progressive and cyclical test of mankind's ability to change and evolve in ways deeply compatible with the African-American and Nietzschean embrace of personal and historical change, innovation, and upheaval. While Bahá'í believe in the necessity of each historical epoch and the contributions of each of the major prophets (Abraham, Moses, Christ, Muhammad), they consider the modern to be the most important era in the history of humanity. Therefore, Bahá'í is a quintessentially modern faith which teaches that any "religious" belief that doesn't maintain reasoned accord with scientific pursuits amounts to empty superstition. Hatcher notes that, "according to Bahá'í Writings, the transition which mankind is currently experiencing is the most significant transformation he will ever undergo.... This transition ...necessarily involves the abandonment of archaic systems and attitudes, the attendant loss of identity, and the acquisition of insecurity and trepidation, even though the outcome of that trepidation will be a radically advanced, refined and fulfilled organism" (160). Without question, Hayden's faith encouraged him to confront the modern upheavals described by Shoghi Effendi in terms that recall Heidegger's comments on Nietzsche. In *The Promised Day Is Come*, Effendi writes:

> A tempest, unprecedented in its violence, unpredictable in its course, catastrophic in its immediate effects, unimaginably glorious in its ultimate consequences, is at present sweeping the face of the earth. Its driving power is remorselessly gaining in range and momentum. Its cleansing force, however much undetected, is in-creasing with every passing day. Humanity, gripped in the clutches of its devastating power, is smitten by the evidence of its resistless fury. It can neither perceive its origin, nor probe its significance, nor discern its outcome. (3)

In "A Certain Vision," Hayden explains how his Bahá'í beliefs sustained him in the maelstrom of the wasteland and underwrote his world view and his unique approach to the craft of poetry:

> I think that today when so often one gets the feeling that everything is going downhill, that we're really on the brink of the abyss and what good is anything, I find myself sustained in my attempts to be a poet and my endeavor to write because I have the assurance of my faith that this is of spiritual value and it is a way of performing some kind of service. Indeed, I feel that very deeply now—I'm not praising my own poetry; I don't mean that I think my poetry is of all that great consequence to the world—but what I do mean to say is that there is a certain vision of the world that I have. I believe in the essential oneness of all people and I believe in the basic unity of all religions. I don't believe that races are important; I think that people are important. I'm very suspicious of any form of ethnicity or nationalism; I think that these things are very crippling and are very divisive. These are all Bahá'í points of view, and my work grows out of this vision. (111)

Beyond these general moorings, Hayden's specific approach to writing is succinctly set forth in his "Counterpoise Manifesto," published in 1948 as a leaflet announcing his co-authored volume *The Lion and the Archer.* Almost a prose poem itself, the manifesto asserts Hayden's effort to fully engage the modern social and political tempest with aesthetic innovation and artistic rigor. Making it plain that he will defer his creative impulses and craft to no political platform or subordinate his politics to aesthetic constraints, Hayden's manifesto deserves quotation in full:

> we are unalterably opposed to the chauvinistic, the cultish, to special pleading, to all that seeks to limit and restrict creative expression
>
> we believe experimentation to be an absolute necessity in keeping the arts vital and significant in contemporary life; therefore we support and encourage the experimental and the unconventional in writing, music and the graphic arts, though we do not consider our own work avant-garde in the accepted sense of the term
>
> as writers who belong to a so-called minority we are violently opposed to having our work viewed, as the custom is, entirely in the light of sociology and politics
>
> to having it overpraised on the one hand by those with an axe to grind or with a conscience to salve
>
> to having it misrepresented on the other hand by coterie editors, reviewers, anthologists who refuse us encouragement or critical guidance because we deal with realities we find it neither possible nor desirable to ignore
>
> as poets we naturally believe that it is more profitable for our generation to read good poetry than it is to listen to soap opera, since poetry has humanistic and spiritual values not to be ignored with impunity
>
> we believe in the oneness of mankind and the importance of the arts in the struggle for peace and unity. (Hayden, "Counterpoise" 41–42)

Announcing the era of his mature writings, Hayden's tract counters the obstacles which threaten all artistic autonomy, but which have afflicted African-American writing with particular tenacity. Having secured the perimeter, Hayden is poised to employ his skills as a poet to solve for the "x" in the modern self and in its relationship to history. Hayden's characteristically restrained claim that "poetry has humanistic and spiritual values not to be ignored with impunity" anticipates William Carlos Williams more emphatic lines from his 1955 "Asphodel, that Greeny Flower":

> It is difficult
> to get the news from poems
> yet men die miserably every day
> for lack
> of what is found there. (318)

Like Ellison's Invisible Man, the personae that comprise Hayden's Afro-Modernism continually seek visions of unity through departure. Hayden attempted to protect his creative process from the entropic *energy leaks* which occur in relationships framed by the institutions of what Max Weber called the "disenchanted world" (301). Hatcher records methodological notes Hayden jotted down during the early 1950s. Together they comprise a major statement of Afro-Modernist poetic sensibility. I refer to his statement as the "diver's manifesto." Guarding against any unnecessary social exchanges—as well as a few that in retrospect may have been necessary—Hayden challenges himself to:

> 1. Refrain from criticism of others. A *poet* should be above this.
>
> 2. No longer share what is most personal with anyone—neither wife, friend, nor child. Express it only in poetry and in an indirect or objective way.
>
> 3. No longer discuss my writing or my hopes for it with anyone. It is too special and sacred to me; no one should be expected to understand how I feel about it.
>
> 4. Seek solitude and stand alone.
>
> 5. Do not let fatigue, disappointment, professional routine and academic trivia betray finer instincts.

> 6. Cease complaining. And do not any longer make excuses or explanations to anyone.
>
> 7. Read and think more and talk less. Or not at all, unless in a fairly objective and impersonal way. (25)

Hayden's poetry, then, is firmly grounded in his faith in the paradoxical Afro-Modernist notion of a deeper engagement with experience through withdrawal. His ability to put descendental processes in service of his deeply democratic, redemptive artistic vision re-connects Afro-Modernism with the Whitmanian impetus which, as the essays which comprise the collection *Walt Whitman & the World* demonstrate, played an important role in early modernisms throughout the world.

When considering Hayden's Afro-Modernist method and vision, the key poem is "The Diver." Hayden's conspicuous placement of "The Diver" in his evolving corpus signals its importance. Although first published in 1962, the poem was omitted from the original published version of *A Ballad of Remembrance*. Instead, it first appeared in Rosey Pool's collection of African-American poets *Beyond the Blues*, published in England. Nonetheless, in the 1966 *Selected Poems*, the 1975 *Angle of Ascent*, and the 1985 *Collected Poems*, "The Diver" is placed at the beginning of each collection or as the first poem in the *Ballad of Remembrance* section. If the "Counterpoise Manifesto" signals the beginning of Hayden's mature writings, "The Diver" is the poetic preface to his best work, from "A Ballad of Remembrance" to "American Journal."

The vertical emphasis of "The Diver" is clear in the narrow, single stanza which cuts a path down the page. Immediately, the reader enters a world in which the rational distinctions, or identities, which organize and separate phenomena fail to apply. To dive into Hayden's Afro-Modernism is to enter a poetic world of tremendous precision in which would-be stable distinctions become elusive and transitional. The title-line sits above the stanza like a diver on the edge of the dock or boat. The title both is and isn't part of the opening sentence:

> The Diver
>
> Sank through easeful
> azure.

While the pull of the syntax suggests the plunge, the capitalized S in "Sank" frustrates the continuity of identity between "The Diver" above the surface and "[that which] Sank through easeful / azure" (3). Most of the actions which occur on the dive have at least dual significance. The action takes place in overlapping, yet distinct, realms. The suggestion of 'sky-blue' in the word *azure* complicates the unidirectional nature of the diver's descent. On the way down, the diver attains both greater heights and depths.

The poem's structure troubles the distinctions that provide the foundations for modern social and psychological order. In *Figures of Division*, James Snead discusses how stable social and psychological frameworks depend on clearly demarcated categories of space and experience. Indeed, he argues that "separation is one of the founding paradigms of Western thought. ... It seems [that like societies] the mind uses various figures of division to defend itself against chaos" (7). Snead suggests that figures of division represent devices that suggest stable distinctions to efface the multi-leveled realities of connection, inter-dependence, and flux. As Du Bois noted, and as Ellison shows in his essay "What America Would Be Like Without Blacks," American culture is *essentially* interracial, a reality that casts the social divisions that uphold its order into doubt. As Snead argues, in order to efface uncomfortable realities of connection, rhetorical figures of division can, especially in cases of "economic and other kinds of duress[, be taken to] a pathological limit" (14). Yet, from Whitman to the present, democratically inclined poets have sought to span the regional and racial divisions which order and threaten the nation. This spanning might well be the "thesis" image of *Leaves of Grass*, as it appeared on the first page of the first edition in 1855:

> Or I guess it is a uniform hieroglyphic,
> And it means, sprouting alike in broad
> zones and narrow zones,
> Growing among black folks as among
> white,
> Kanuck, Tuckahoe, Congressman,
> Cuff, I give them the same, I receive
> them the same. (31)

Hayden's Afro-Modernism responds to Whitman's call by searching out levels of experience and modes of perception in which figures of division cannot operate. It charts regions of dangerous possibility and seeks a vision which obeys the laws of a *democratic unconscious*. In "The Poet and His Art: A

Conversation," Hayden describes "The Diver" as one of his most "deeply personal" poems, which he "consciously made rather obscure" (161). He explains that "the act of diving and the temptation the diver feels to really let go, to yield to death, really represent, are symbolic of something very personal. The entire poem is actually a metaphor" (161–62). Certainly, the romance of death might recall Keats, even Dickinson, but by the time he wrote "The Diver" Hayden was some twenty years beyond what he'd termed his "Keats period" (132). Instead, "The Diver" points toward a level of experience beyond rational compartmentalization. As Freud's view of the unconscious suggests, distinct but interrelated spheres of reality or experience obey different, even incompatible, structures. All movement between them involves transitions which warp data and frames of reference. In his posthumously published essay "Dream Work and Interpretation," Freud writes that the "governing rules of logic carry no weight in the unconscious; it might be called the Realm of the Illogical. Urges with contrary aims exist side by side in the unconscious without any need arising for an adjustment between them" (44).

Hayden seeks to establish and redeem connections by embracing a similar vision. In "The Diver," "lost images / fadingly remembered" continually invoke the failure of figures of division by joining rationally incompatible terms. Yet many of Hayden's critics attempt to re-inscribe the division: Hatcher, Wilburn Williams, and Maurice O'Sullivan all identify death with depth, and pit descent against life and the "measured rise" which begins on the final line of the poem. But Hayden's systematically irrational twinning of terms frustrates such decisions even as it recognizes the associated risks. Snead discusses how "the escape from division can take dangerous forms: madness ...social exclusion ... or even death" (15). The descendental twinning of rationally incompatible qualities such as freedom and danger recalls Federico Garcia Lorca's notion of a non-rational, dangerously, even perilously free spirit, *duende*, at the core of the creative process.

In "The Poet and His Art," Hayden, a Spanish major at Detroit City College, claimed Garcia Lorca as an influence picked up along with Rukeyser, Auden, and others at an important stage in his development in the early 1940s (134). In his lecture "Theory and Function of the *Duende*," Garcia Lorca associates *duende* with depth, with the sound that "surges up from the soles of the feet," and with the sound of the "*Delba*, a variant of the Andalusian cante jondo (deep song)" (91–92). He continues: "These 'dark sounds' are the mystery, the roots thrusting into the fertile loam known to all of us, ignored by all of us, but from which we get what is real in art" (91). For

Garcia Lorca, *duende* is the ever-changing essence of the creative impulse, "not the forms ... but the marrow of forms" (92). Emphasizing the ungraspable and improvisational nature of *duende*, he writes that it "is a power and not a behavior, it is a struggle and not a concept" by which to "help us seek .... there is neither map nor discipline" (92–93). It "breaks with all styles, rejects all the sweet geometry one has learned," and "always presupposes a radical change of all forms based on old structures" (93, 95). In addition to its destabilizing qualities, Garcia Lorca associates *duende* with ever-present danger, death, and renewal:

> As soon as the muse is aware of death, she shuts her door.... The duende, on the other hand, does not appear if it sees no possibility of death. If it does not know that it will haunt death's house, if it is not certain that it can move those branches we carry, which neither enjoy nor ever will enjoy any solace.... The duende wounds, and in the healing of this wound which never closes is the prodigious, the original work in man.... whoever beholds it is baptized with dark water ... and this struggle for expression and for the communication of expression reaches, at times, in poetry, the character of a fight to the death. (99–100)

In conclusion, Garcia Lorca writes: "The duende—where is the duende? Through the empty arch comes an air of the mind that blows insistently over the heads of the dead, in search of new landscapes and unsuspecting accents; an air smelling of a child's saliva, of pounded grass, and medusa veil announcing the constant baptism of newly created things" (103). Hayden's Afro-Modernist quest to "experiment with forms and techniques I have not used before—to arrive at something patterned, wild, and free" echoes Garcia Lorca's artistic engagement with *duende* (75).

In "The Diver," the images combine the risk of descendental movement with the forces of beauty and renewal which Garcia Lorca describes as the "constant baptism" in "dark water." The irrational combinations abound: "freefalling, weightless / as in dreams of wingless flight," the "dead ship, / carcass that swarmed with / voracious life," "drowned instruments / of buoyancy," "in languid / frenzy strove / as one freezing fights off / sleep desiring sleep," "fled the numbing / kisses that I craved." Every physical and psychological force vies with and accompanies its counter-force, resulting in the poem's shifting "dance of gilded / chairs" and its "eldritch hide and / seek of laughing / faces."

The images recall Hayden's diver's manifesto, especially those of withdrawal from entropic exchanges which, as Hatcher notes, went contrary to Hayden's social impulses. The Eliotic images of a social and cultural wasteland in "The Diver" become clear when read with awareness of Hayden's personal ambivalence about social and professional interaction: "Do not let ... professional routine and academic trivia betray finer instinct. / Read and think more and talk less. Or not at all." The diver is drawn toward the enthralling dance of the dead. In ways that recall and invert Prufrock's impotence, Hayden's diver navigates the throes of sensuality, even necrophilia, as he "explored her ... entered / the wreck, awed by her silence, / feeling more keenly the iron cold ... probing."

In "The Diver," Hayden signals his simultaneous awareness of the need to embark and the pitfalls which occur on the internal quest. Yet his poetry never accepted a stable division between the personal/psychological and the political/historical. In a letter written to Hayden and dated May 6, 1975, Michael Harper voices his frustration with the tendencies of poets and readers to insist on the rationalized separations which Hayden's work disturbs. Confident that Hayden will understand his feelings, Harper describes his travels through the South, where he encountered "some mindless performances by our people, the students who don't read or think, but 'politic'—questions from the gallery about how poems relate to the people, and faculty catering to this nonsense, an attack on May Miller ... [poets claiming they] could only write the political poem—consciousness is political!" (995). Hayden certainly agreed with Harper that "consciousness is political." But his poetry explores (as does Harper's) the modernist complexities which frustrate all such identities. The crossroads between public politics and the excavation of consciousness is a shifting and treacherous site of awareness and action.

A central image of mediation between black consciousness and American politics of any *color* is the mask, and the most famous articulation of the politics of the mask is Paul Laurence Dunbar's "We Wear the Mask." In this poem Dunbar excavates terrible pressure and pain that is part and parcel of masking. Contemporary criticism tends to convert Dunbar's poem into a tactical agenda in which the (would-be political) "grins and lies" of masking can be separated from the (personal/cultural) excavation of the self. Hayden knew that these binary divisions, which imply a fully knowable self forced into deception by racist oppression, were not possible in his creative quest. Rather than an "authentic self" pitted against an outside threat and masked by a "tactical self," Hayden imagined a labyrinth of selves all of which wear—even exchange—masks. As he was aware, this internal complexity does not negate exterior forces of confinement. But he viewed them in a specifically modernist manner. In "A 'Romantic Realist,' " he reiterates Eliot's notion of depersonalization. Hayden writes: "I resist whatever would force me into a role as a politician, sociologist, or yeasayer to current ideologies.... Frequently, I'm writing about myself but speaking through a mask, a persona.... Reticence has its aesthetic values too you know" (120). Failing to recognize the validity of Hayden's perspective generates impasses in the understanding of Afro-Modernist processes.

In "Adorno, Ellison, and the Critique of Jazz," James Harding points out the "idealistic conception of the self" in Stepto's *From Behind the Veil* and Baker's *Blues, Ideology and Afro-American Literature.* Building on Stepto's notion that *Invisible Man* shows that "there is a self and form to be discovered beyond the lockstep of linear movement within imposed definitions of reality," Baker develops a cultural theory in which "the private session of jazz and blues singers—when the white oppressor is absent—is where the real playing occurs" (168). These formulations of a "real" self/culture protected by a "masked," tactical self/performance neglect the areas of *overlap,* both social and metaphorical, which Du Bois describes in his formulation of double-consciousness. The unrecognized idealism of such approaches has spawned a host of "post-colonial" theories of cultural "safe-spaces" where the authentic life of what William James would call "The Self and Its Selves" happens. Despite critical simplifications such as Farah Griffin's image of blues clubs as safe spaces, the work of August Wilson, Toni Morrison, James Baldwin, Gayl Jones, Yusef Komunyakaa, and others recovers the danger of the cultural "safe-spaces" as they sound the fissures and excavate missing spots in the faces behind the mask.

These issues are not solely of historical interest. In a brief 1996 essay written in response to a photo exhibition featuring portraits of "High Risk" students in the Indianapolis Public Schools, Yusef Komunyakaa, from his own diver's angle of vision, observes that the students "throw back frightened reality" and wear "masks ... invented to intimidate because the wearers don't feel safe." Troubling the relationship between the face and the mask, he speculates that "many of the faces cannot even guess when the masks were created." Komunyakaa emphasizes the multiple dangers of unreflective masking. Unable to perform the type of resistance Hayden intimates, Komunyakaa wonders if "these 'high risk' students [are] surprised to find themselves wearing masks that society created for them, to find their features have hardened into caricatures of their real selves." However necessary the performances might be, he suggests that the masks project images which have no pasts, parents, or interior lives. Instead of a prism at the crossroads of the self and the world, the mask becomes a "psychological caul." The result is a kind of alienation in which "their survival masks are devouring them" (60).

Hayden's Afro-Modernism focuses precisely on the anguish created by simplistic conceptions of stable divisions among self, mask, and world. Published in *American Journal*, Hayden's elegiac poem "Paul Laurence Dunbar" mourns as it honors the painfully split dimensions of Dunbar's experience:

> Poet of our youth—
> his 'cri du coeur' our own,
> his verses 'in a broken tongue'
>
> beguiling as an elder
> brother's antic lore. (15)

In "The Diver," Hayden enters the non-resolving interaction between the alternate spheres of experience. The contradictory impulses descend into and express the multiplicities of the self in a way that reverberates with Yeats's "The Mask":

> I would but find what's there to find,
> Love or deceit.
> It was the mask engaged your mind,
> And after set your heart to beat,
> Not what's behind. (263)

Preserving Yeats's sense of contradictory couplings, Hayden links the interior quest with a critique of Afro-Modernism's inward-looking self-indulgence:

> I yearned to
> find those hidden
> ones, to fling aside
> the mask and call to them,
> yield to rapturous
> whisperings, have
> done with self and
> every dinning
> vain complexity. (4)

As Yeats implies, safe spaces in which to "fling aside the mask" are difficult to find, and may not exist at all. Hayden makes the oxymoron clear: There are no one-way mirrors, no safe revelations. Further, the vertical impulses behind Hayden's notion that poems "say what cannot be said any other way—and, in some poems, you are trying to say what cannot be said at all"—emphasize the improvisational risk of excavation. Beyond idealized divisions and ideological stabilities, one continually sounds the valences of consciousness which echo, unsettle, and renew (unmask) readily available phrasings. Yet Hayden's process does not surrender entirely to secluded indeterminacy. Hayden's poems seek to share the deeply sought. His is a solitary poetics of communion. Harper, whose own poetry echoes Hayden's impulses, is right: Such a poetics "is political." Just as surely, it can never fully emerge into the public sphere, certainly not as it exists in the modern era.

Hayden excavated cultural traditions as he attempted to adhere to his diver's manifesto of creative seclusion. The poems that follow "The Diver" in *Selected Poems* sift together and order these impulses as Hayden turns the diver's terribly beautiful depth perception from the purposes of the interior to those of social excavation. The concluding image of the poem, the "measured rise," does not take place in "The Diver." Instead, it happens in the poems which follow. "Veracruz" reiterates the diver's manifesto to observe the intersection of consciousness and experience:

> Leap now
> and cease from error.
> Escape. Or shoreward turn,
> accepting all—
> the losses and farewells,
> the long warfare with self,
> with God. (30)

Hayden's Afro-Modernism employs metaphorically Freudian depths of veiled and unresolvable realities and sifts Whitman's democratic connections out of modern figures of division. He uncovers the metaphysical heartbeat of Weber's *pneuma* and Garcia Lorca's *duende* pulsing beneath Jim Crow's disenchanted wasteland. In part II of "Veracruz," Hayden images what he called a "romantic realist" sphere of experience in ways that speak to the core of Afro-Modernism (121):

> Thus reality
>   bedizened in the warring colors

of a dream
parades through these
arcades ornate with music and
the sea.

Thus reality
become unbearably a dream
beckons
out of reach in flyblown streets
of lapsing rose and purple, dying
blue.

Thus marimba'd night
And multifoliate sea become
phantasmal
space, and there,
light-years away, one farewell image
Burns and fades and burns. (30)

In *Selected Poems*, the two poems that follow "The Diver" image the relationship of cultural tradition (stories, lore, and religious faith) to the forces of modern rationalization and disenchantment. Hayden dedicated "Electrical Storm" to his friends and neighbors in Nashville, the devout Seventh Day Adventists Arna and Alberta Bontemps, who appear as lifesavers in the poem. The poem tests the relationship among (scientific) understanding, (religious) belief, and cultural practice as they contend with the intensities and contingencies of modern experience. This first stanza describes the God-fearing elders' beliefs as they cower from a thunderstorm in a Fated universe:

He don't like ugly.
Have mercy. Lord, they prayed,
seeing the lightning's
Mene Mene Tekel
hearing the preaching thunder's deep
Upharsin. (13)

Hayden's use of Old Testament imagery recalls James Weldon Johnson's expansion of "dialect" into the prophetic tongues of *God's Trombones*. The call-and-response rhythms are interrupted by the wrath/lightning. Hayden's concision sheers, "He don't like ugly," from its flip-side response (in my experience, something like, *and He ain't too particular about pretty!*), allowing him to cut to the quick. At the ambiguous center of the first stanza is the ethos of inadequacy and unworthiness which Hayden images in the Old Testament verse. In "The Poet and His Art," he explained his use of the refrain from the story of Belshazzar: "*Mene Mene Tekel Upharsin*—these were the words that God wrote on King Belshazzar's palace wall, meaning 'thou art weighed in the balance and found wanting'" (148). Embedded in the scene, Hayden's Old Testament imagery connects with a black cultural vocabulary and conserves the ambiguities of the diver's Afro-Modernist vision. The tension between would-be "folk" superstition (or even colonized internalization of shame) and the improvised confrontation with the reality of the human condition it invokes is unresolved. No matter how the tension plays out, the self-scrutiny mitigates against hubris and pride in ways which provide a foundation for communal and universal tolerance and forgiveness. Despite or because of the irresolution, the poem clearly redeems the deep implications of this particular feature of Old Testament poetics and the sensibility of cultural elders.

Hayden shifts perspective to emphasize the rational and scientific nature of modern subjectivity. In the second stanza, the persona is *grown*, "colleged (as they said)." He understands the scientific explanations of "pressure systems, / colliding massive energies / that make a storm" (13). The third stanza puts the intellectual *progress* to the test of experience. Much like Flannery O'Connor's hyper-rationalist "schoolteacher" in *The Violent Bear It Away*, the persona in "Electrical Storm" is comfortable with the peace/piece of mind offered by his scientific understanding. As he drives through a storm, the energy of the scene begins to outstrip the understanding of the persona. The pure science of the storm becomes "warring weather. / Wind and lightning havocked / berserked in wires, trees." The intensity of sensation and random danger of the storm force the persona to recall "Jehovah's oldtime wrath." The final image in the stanza recalls a dangerous event in Hayden's life, transformed in the poem through what he termed his "detachment and philosophical calm" (148). Returned home to find the house intact, a message from on High confronts the persona's understanding:

> Fallen lines we could not see at first
> lay in the yard when we reached home.
> The hedge was burning in the rain. (13)

Hayden leaves the persona in a quandary. Repeating the baffled question—"Who knows?"—which has muted his scientific knowledge, he wonders if there's a difference between "heavenly design" and "chance." In "The Poet and His Art," Hayden recalls spending the night of this particular storm sleepless, thinking about "Human vulnerability—what is chance, what is accident?" (148). He concludes with a blues image of the ultimate failure (or at least incompleteness) of rational knowledge. Like the speaker in Frost's "Design," Hayden's persona remains at a loss to explain what "brought us and our neighbors through—/ though others died—/ the archetypal dangers of the night?" Hayden's line recalls the stormy scene and title of Hurston's *Their Eyes Were Watching God* and Bessie Smith's "Backwater Blues." Hayden distills the "archetypal" blues he recalled hearing Bessie sing "at the old Koppin Theater one night—a Detroit movie and vaudeville house patronized largely by us ghetto folks" (144). The poem's coda reinforces the unique power of belief to order experience. Although Hayden doesn't name it, he implies that by Grace alone does one come through archetypal dangers of the night. His persona answers his own question from what he knows and says nothing of what he believes:

> I know what those
> cowering true believers would have
>   said. (15)

The poem begins with the believers cowering in fear. It ends with the "colleged" persona at a loss to respond to his experience. In the coda, Hayden removes the opposition. Now all that the persona has learned is reduced to what he *knows* the "true believers" believe. He intimates the lasting power of the "folk elements in 'Electrical Storm' [that] are there because they are still a part of me, even though I've been 'colleged' and know that dogs and cats don't 'draw' lightning" (149).

Many of the poems in *Selected Poems* are arranged in pairs which offer alternate takes on shared themes. "Full Moon," images the interaction between myth and science in unmistakably political and, nearly overt, racial terms. Hayden's persona opens with an image of the full moon eclipsed by science and technology: "No longer throne of a goddess to whom we pray." He remembers how, before modern science, the rhythms of the moon ordered experience in accord with beliefs:

> Some I love who are dead
> were watchers of the moon and knew its
>   lore;
> planted seeds, trimmed their hair,

> Pierced their ears for gold hoop earrings
> as it waxed or waned. (15)

In relation to modernity, the moon has become the "brilliant challenger of rocket experts, / the white hope of communications men," just another in a series of great white hopes. Hayden's commentary on the importance of Jack Johnson to the residents of his home neighborhood in Detroit in his poem "'Summertime and the Living ...'" clarifies the racialized nature of the battle between tradition and science. Like Jack Johnson, the full moon, once the province of lore and ritual, has become a tool of political modernity. Hayden witnesses the deep cultural and racial implications of the lunar eclipse. But, rather than calling forth a bygone time of wholesome innocence, Hayden's remembrance of "belief" provides the basis for trenchant critique. Offering a skeptical appraisal of the social priorities evidenced in then-President Kennedy's pro-American space mission, Hayden writes:

> Already a mooted goal and tomorrow
>   perhaps
> an arms base, a livid sector,
> the full moon dominates the dark. (15)

In "The Poet and His Art," Hayden describes the relationship between image and politics reflected in his modernism. He concludes that he "aimed to write a poem that would give the lie to the bigots. But I wanted it to be a *poem* and not vindictive rhetoric, not propaganda" (173).

In "The Rabbi," Hayden places his persona's childhood interracial friendships amid exchanges that reflect adult prejudices. The young black man is curious about Jewish religious practice: "Once there, did [the Rabbi] put on / sackcloth and ashes? Wail?" Signaling the connection between religious institutions and segregation, he remembers, "He would not let me in to see / the gold menorah burning." Not allowed in the synagogue, the young man picks up a mix of culture and prejudice in the street:

> Mazuzah, Pesach, Chanukah—
> there were timbred words I learned,
> were things I knew by glimpses.
> And I learned schwartze too
>
> And schnapps, which schwartzes bought
> on credit from "Jew Baby." (17)

The kids aren't fully aware of, or interested in, the racism and exploitation that influence their culturally eclectic, improvised games:

> Tippling ironists laughed and said
> he'd soon be rich as Rothschild
>
> From their swinish Saturdays.
> Hirschel and Molly and I meanwhile
> divvied halveh, polly seeds,
> were spies and owls and Fu Manchu.

In the final stanza, the institutional spaces inhibit the kids' interactive play. One culturally exclusive institution replaces another, and Hayden images the religious leader as a culturally paternalistic kidnapper.

> But the synagogue became
> New Calvary.
> The rabbi bore my friends off
> in his prayer shawl. (17)

The final image collects the petty insults and exploitations from above and shows the *increasingly* segregated conditions of early- and mid-twentieth-century black urban life that Hayden recalls from his childhood. Despite the religious cloak, the final moment of the poem shows Jewish movement out of the "ghetto" and toward the American economic mainstream. The persona is left behind.

Published immediately after "The Rabbi," "Belsen, Day of Liberation" juxtaposes the relative social mobility of Jewish people in the United States with the situation in WWII Europe. The second poem describes the liberation of a death camp by Allied troops. The dedication to Dr. Rosey Pool is itself an image of interracial cooperation. John Hatcher notes the importance of Pool's support to Hayden's career. Pool, whose parents were executed by the Nazis and who was herself imprisoned in a concentration camp, once told Hayden that "she and her fellow prisoners, wishing to pray together in secret yet lacking a common faith, used lines from Negro spirituals instead" (31). The pair of poems bears witness to the power and fluidity of human connection threatened by figures of division, and even systematically murdered by modern institutions of social control.

Another pairing of poems cuts to the terrible core of the battle between human dignity and racial abstraction for the soul of Whitman's vision of a vibrant and inclusive America. "The Ballad of Sue Ellen Westerfield" depicts the internal and external dangers inherent in interracial connections. The poem was inspired by his foster mother, Sue Hayden, who, as Hayden notes, "had once worked on a Mississippi River Steamer and had been married to Jim Barlow, a man she never forgot" (5). In "The Ballad," Hayden twists his impression of his foster mother's lost love into a diver's meditation on the entwined politics of gender and race. The poem systematically introduces stock historical themes and then complicates them with subtle amendments and intimations. The opening line invokes Old Testament poetics as well as a Faulknerian notion that acknowledging the history of the interracial "family" opens up new angles of vision into the complexities of the nation:

> She grew up in bedeviled southern
>   wilderness,
> but had not been a slave, she said,
> because her father wept and set her
>   mother free.

The theme of plantation rape is everpresent, but, importantly, never explicitly stated in the poem. The image of the (presumably white) father weeping further complicates the relationship. Later the persona finds work as a maid on Mississippi river boats. If a whisper of rape sounds beneath the opening scene, something else lurks in the rest of the stanza:

> She hardened in perilous rivertowns
> and after The Surrender,
> went as maid upon the tarnished
>   Floating Palaces.
> Rivermen reviled her for the rankling
>   cold
> sardonic pride
> that gave a knife-edge to her comeliness.
>   (21)

Hayden's portrait sits in uneasy proximity to the "Temptress/Sapphire/Redbone" stereotype of light-skinned and/or mixed-race black women. The *sharp* pride and "hardened" attitude are familiar features of the stereotype. If Hayden recalls that "it was W.H. Auden who once said to me that writing a poem is like solving for x in an equation," the same is true for reading Hayden's poems. The variable (or missing quantity) in the opening passage is plantation rape. In the second part, it's interracial love and consensual sex.

Obviously, the historical reading of "The Surrender" is the North's victory in the Civil War. But, in Hayden's words, "a poem should have silences," and "a poem should have drama, should have tension" (192, 151). The historical chiché mutes the tension between the "hardened" woman and "The Surrender." There's a lurking sense of sexuality, even prostitution, behind the poem's equation.

Similarly, the second stanza opens with an image of silence, the importance of things unsaid. The woman has told the speaker stories "of the dangers lived through on the rivers," but when it comes to certain aspects of the past, she falls into silence. In fact, she employs a version of Hayden's creative approach to conserving the intensity of experience. In his diver's manifesto, Hayden challenged himself to "no longer share what is most personal with anyone—neither wife, friend, nor child" (25). In "The Ballad," he writes: The woman "never told of him, / whose name she'd vowed she would not speak again / till after Jordan." The conservation of energy preserves the intensity and private intimacy of her imagined connection through the years. The woman's voice breaks through the narration to confess to herself "Oh he was nearer nearer now / than wearisome kith and kin." Her method of keeping her remembered companion closer than her family (kin) or community (kith) violates the racial and marital prescriptions as yet unmentioned in the poem.

Lest the reader become engrossed in sentimentality, Hayden immediately splices this image of imagined interracial intimacy with the silences (rape and prostitution) of the first stanza. Upon their first meeting

> His blue eyes followed her
> as she moved about her tasks upon the
> *Memphis Rose.*
> He smiled and joshed, his voice
> quickened her.
> She cursed the circumstance .... (21)

If the reader associates the "he" who was "nearer nearer" with the "He" who "smiled and joshed," the "blue eyes" fall in line with the power to "set her mother free" as racially suggestive markers. The voyeuristic, stalking images of the eyes that "followed her" preserve the tension that existed in the plantation relationship between Sue Ellen's mother and father. Despite the silence surrounding the images, the connotations of "his voice quickened her" underscore the intimacy of her remembrance. The "circumstance" she cursed refers to the human connection which society will not allow. The silent themes suggest a more intimate conflict, but reading *quickened* as 'startled,' or 'harassed,' runs counter to the central senses of the term which imply a restoration of vigor, inspiration, animation. To complicate the scene even further, an archaic sense of the term associates *quickened* with pregnancy.

Hayden emphasizes the fugitive status of this human connection which exiles the figures from the social context of the poem. The man rescues the woman twice. Amid a burning and sinking ship, "he fought his way to her ... and helped her swim to shore." As he rescues others from the "hellmouth water," Sue Ellen feels her psyche coming apart. She wanders through the chaos, attempting to help others, until he returns:

> A woman screaming under the raddled
>   trees—
> Sue Ellen felt it was herself who
>   screamed.
> The moaning of the hurt, the terrified—
>   she held off shuddering despair
> and went to comfort whom she could.
> Wagons torches bells
> and whimpering dusk of morning
> and blankness lostness nothingness for
>   her
> until his arms had lifted her
> into wild and secret dark. (22)

Wandering for "How long how long was it," they become "fugitives whose dangerous only hidingplace / was love." She makes the final choice not to pass for white and "forfeit what she was," along with her connection to "kith and kin." Completing the cycle, the man "wept as had her father once," they part, and "Until her dying bed," she "cursed the circumstance" (22). Denying none of the historical tropes, Hayden extends the "fugitive" status of interracial connection in American history which can be recovered only through Afro-Modernist descent. Fugitives from the social order, the images of connection become private, then secret, now silent. Hayden structures the interracial horrors into the silent frame of the poem and excavates the private sense of loss and remembrance.

In "Night, Death, Mississippi," which immediately follows "The Ballad of Sue Ellen Westerfield," Hayden again mutes the clichéd scenes of historical brutality, but to a drastically different effect. He emphasizes that descent alters perceptions and remembrance, but it leaves the white supremacist world above intact. While its silences preserve the tensions, "The Ballad" is sentimental in structure. The forces of humanity, love, connection, and valor are pitted against the forces of tragedy, accident, and the racial "circumstance." In "Night, Death, Mississippi," the muted horrors frame a scene of the human condition thoroughly steeped in racial hatred and blood-thirst. Hayden portrays the power of racial hatred in an elder white man's interior. Rather than threaten love and connection, racial hatred here encodes and sustains the bonds between "kith and kin." Hayden's "Night, Death, Mississippi" looks beyond the abject image of human destruction in lynching. Even in this extreme situation, Hayden maintains his diver's vision and focuses in on the troubling dilemma that there's no easy division between the human and violent elements of the psyche or the nation. Hayden critiques the (largely Northern) liberal notion that it's "monsters" who enact these gothic horrors. Monstrous certainly, but not monsters. As the tragic best writing of Carson McCullers, Lillian Smith, Flannery O'Connor, and William Faulkner points out, it's mostly fathers, husbands, and sons out there in the Southern night. And as grisly events from 1999 indicate, the Southern night extends from the New Jersey Turnpike to Jasper, TX, from Albany, NY, to Evanston, IL, to Bloomington, IN.

In an interview with Tom Johnson, Yusef Komunyakaa commented that "poetry is really distilled empathy" (126). Empathy depends on connections which blur and join identities, often going beyond stable borders between "self" and "other," interior and exterior. No poem of Hayden's uses the structure of the democratic unconscious to extend the implications of this poetic empathy into more troubled waters of twentieth-century culture than "Night, Death, Mississippi." Grown too old to participate in the lynching rituals, the poem's protagonist paces his house, eagerly listening. Suddenly, he hears "A quavering cry. Screech-owl? / Or one of them?" (23). Reveling in the sounds—"Time was. A Cry? / A cry all right."—he lives vicariously through his son's participation. Feeling the close bond of shared ritual, the old man imagines meeting his son after the rite. Remembering the time he "Unbucked that one" and now "fevered by groinfire," he takes pleasure in the bond between father and son now reformed as that of monstrous man to monstrous man:

> Have us a bottle,
> Boy and me—
> he's earned him a bottle—
> when he gets home. (23)

Hayden, who confessed to having once written "a very bad play" about Harriet Tubman titled *Go Down, Moses,* seems to have Faulkner's novel by that title in mind as well. The ritualized hunting scenes and the old man's repetitions of "Time was. Time was" recall the tension in Faulkner's opening story "Was," a strangely wrought, beguiling, and problematic slapstick fugitive slave narrative told by one young Southerner, McCaslin Edmonds, to another, Ike McCaslin. One stanza of "Night, Death, Mississippi" recalls the most famous section of Faulkner's *Go Down, Moses,* "The Bear."

> Christ, it was better
> than hunting bear
> which don't know why
> you want him dead. (24)

Throughout the 1950s and '60s, James Baldwin's essays continually argued that black Southerners knew, basically, what was at stake in Southern race relations. White Southerners, Baldwin argued—extending his point to most white Northerners as well—could not face the psychological consequences *they* would have to face in order to end segregation. In a 1961 interview with Studs Terkel, Baldwin observed:

> As a Negro, you represent a level of experience which Americans deny. This may sound mystical, but I think it's proven in great relief in the South. Consider the extraordinary price, the absolutely prohibitive price, the South has paid in order to—as it's quaintly put—keep the Negro in his place; and he has not succeeded in doing that, but has succeeded in having what is almost certainly the most bewildered, demoralized white population in the Western world.... [It's this] torment that goes on in a Southerner .... it seems to me [that] is the key to those terrifying mobs. It isn't hatred that drives those people in the streets. It's pure terror. (7–8)

Apparently, Hayden understood what Baldwin meant when he said that "Faulkner ... can really get at the truth of what the black-white relationship is in the South" (7). While complicating the binary dilemma by adding a crucial American Indian theme into the "black-white" situation in "The Bear," Faulkner implies that the ones who don't know what's really at stake on the hunt for the "bear" are the white hunters themselves.

Hayden's allusion conserves this crucial irony. Like Faulkner's "white" bear hunters, Hayden's "hunters" are the ones who don't understand what Baldwin called "pure terror," muted by the mob and the hunt. Spliced between italicized Christ/lynching imagery which recalls Langston Hughes's 1931 poem "Christ in Alabama," Hayden's final stanza delivers a crushing blow. Mirroring the inter-generational exchanges of "The Ballad of Sue Ellen Westerfield," but leaving the generation unspecified, a mother calls to her children as a father returns from a hunt. Probably recalling his own childhood, the old man hears someone's (his? or his son's?) Southern mother say:

> You kids fetch Paw
> some water now so's he
> can wash that blood
> off him ....

In the final line, the night itself seems trapped in a deathly evil design:

> *O night betrayed by darkness not its own*
> (24)

From his diver's vantage point, in "'Summertime and the Living...,'" he excavates the complex flux of vitality and violence in his childhood neighborhood. In "The Poet and His Art," he commented on the tension which gives the location Robert Stepto called the "symbolic South" (164) it's complex importance in African-American art:

> For ghetto life as I knew it was full of contrasts. Violence and ugliness and cruelty. We kids were exposed to the grim realities, to coin a phrase, in spite of all our elders could do to protect us. But there was beauty, there was gentleness too. There was a vividness of life, and intensity of being. (141)

In "'Summertime,'" Hayden writes in the third person, which allows him to be "a little more objective, exteriorize up to a point." Drawing on Eliot's notion of the creative "point of view" which is at once interior and exterior to artists, Hayden comments about the use of the third person: "I could get a perspective and be both inside and outside of the poem at the same time. And, too, I was looking at another self—seeing myself in a different time dimension. You know the feeling you get when you see pictures of yourself as a child" (140).

Hayden describes the poetics of recollection in terms of descent and emergence which recall "The Diver": "Most of [the images] were down in my subconscious—that's where most of what I need for a poem is—and when I came to write 'Summertime,' why they just rose to the surface" (140). In "From *The Life*," written in 1977, when he returned to his old neighborhood as part of a film project, Hayden described the scene as a public crossroads:

> Paradise Valley, that ironically named area of the old east side ghetto. St. Antoine: Saint Anthony: pronounced by Detroiters St. Anto-wine. Detroit's Beale Street. Respectable people shunned it as the devil's. It was often described as a sort of crossro'ads of the "colored world." You stand on St. Antoine and sooner or later everybody you know or ever heard of will be passing by. (18)

In a half-muted satirical tone, Hayden intones that everyone goes down to the crossroads, "sooner or later." St. Anto-wine, like crossroads throughout the diaspora, represents the meeting place of good and evil, of the depths of the self and the energy of the street. Hayden remembers its vibrant and destructive energy:

> Kaleidoscopic in memory now, its sordidness all but forgotten. Restaurants, barbershops, pool halls, cabarets, blind pigs, gamblin' joints camouflaged as "Recreation Clubs." Shootings, stabbings, blaring jazz, and a liveliness, a gaiety at once desperate and releasing, at once wicked—Satan's playground—and good-hearted. (19)

His recollection of the main artery of Paradise Valley invokes images of every- and anything, except those of a safe space, or a mystical locus of an "authentic" self. In a passage which echoes Curtis Mayfield's classic excavation of the symbolic South, "The Other Side of Town," Hayden writes:

> The good old days in the Detroit slums had never been good.... these streets recalled for him voices, faces he had loved and ... a way of life forever part of his consciousness as an artist, forever a source for his poems, and forever a source of joy and pain never to be assuaged by awards, published books, prestige, accomplishment, such as it was, nor by the security that had come to him in the latter years of his life—a security distrusted and perhaps even feared. (21)

Hayden recalls that "the contrasts" of the poem "developed out of the material without my deliberately working toward them at first" (141) The key phrase is *at first.* Hayden refined the intense calm of the verses by using his algebraic technique to craft links to the jazz standard "Summertime" and to Gwendolyn Brooks's *A Street in Bronzeville.* Extending the jazz tradition of "quoting" standards in the course of improvised verses, Hayden's title is itself quoted directly from the lyrics. "'Summertime and the Living...'" condenses the opening line of the song: "Summertime and the living is easy." By cutting the phrase short, Hayden's title ends on a capitalized image of vitality but frees the "grim realities" from the happy-go-lucky stereotypes associated with *easy living* (141). The pattern of quotation emphasizes the call-and-response rhythms which pattern exchanges in black cultural spaces. Hayden's poem also recalls that the song is essentially a lullaby sung, almost always sung by a woman, to a child. The line"your daddy's rich and your mama's good looking" reinforce a child's needful perception of his parents who, as Hayden notes above, can protect him or her, at best, only partially and temporarily from the street. The tension appears as the syrupy lyrics simply assume the "grim realities," the blues of the symbolic South. Hayden uses the placid satin backdrop as one aspect of a complex reality that includes "elders, / so harshened after each unrelenting day / that they were shouting-angry." The cool tones of the music waft into "The fevered tossings of the dusk, the dark" (53).

Like modernist poetics of allusion, jazz quotations often sound ironies and punch-lines of implied jokes not quite shared with the audience. The opening lines of "'Summertime and the Living ...'" focus on wild plants and children growing up side-by-side:

> Nobody planted roses, he recalls,
> but sunflowers gangled there some
> times,
> tough-stalked and bold
> and like the vivid children there
> unplanned. (53)

The images of wild, "tough-stalked" plants (weeds really) and "vivid" ghetto kids voice Hayden's autobiographical connection to the "children there unplanned." Hayden, born Asa Bundy Sheffy, was himself raised by the Haydens as a fosterchild. The "gang" root of the word *gangle,* along with its rhythmic and tonal similarity to *gangrel*—'loose-jointed' and/or 'vagabond'—emphasizes the kinship between the wild urban plants and children in

Hayden's memories of Paradise Valley. Hayden's images call directly to the "back yard" described by Gwendolyn Brooks's young, middle-class persona:

I've stayed in the front yard all my life.
I want a peek at the back
Where it's rough and untended and
  hungry weed grows.
A girl gets sick of a rose.

I want to go in the back yard now
And maybe down the alley,
To where the charity children play.
I want a good time today. (28)

But, Hayden writes from the "charity children['s]" side of the fence. The images of the "circus-poster horses curveted / in trees of heaven," and the elders who "would sit on broken steps," locate this poem on the front or street-side of the houses. The playful allusion in these images and the title of Hayden's poem becomes clear when one considers that Brooks's poem is entitled "a song in the front yard." Hayden's line "No roses there in summer—/ oh never roses except when people died—" recalls Brooks's classic "The Sundays of Satin-Legs Smith":

No! He has not a flower to his name.
Except a feather one, for his lapel.
Apart from that, if he should think of
  flowers
It is in terms of dandelions or death.
  (43)

In "'Summertime and the Living ...,'" Hayden's description of the moments of deep cool on Beacon Street suggest a public sense of connection very different from the modernist images of rupture and disruption in the symbolic South. Hayden figures communal presence as a shared calm. The calm makes a drastic contrast, suggests a great distance, between the evening calm on Beacon Street and the hustle of St. Antoine. Splicing together tones and voices, he moves from comments laced with irony to a touching elegy:

But summer was, they said, the poor
    folks' time

of year. And he remembers
how they would sit on broken steps amid

The fevered tossings of the dusk, the dark,
wafting hearsay with funeral-parlor fans
or making evenings solemn by
their quietness. Feels their Mosaic eyes
upon him, though the florist roses
that only sorrow could afford
long since have bidden them
    Godspeed. (53)

In "From *The Life*" Hayden recounts the same impressions with different patterns, but retains the third person and the ironic point of entry. The quotations from the poem recall his comments about poetics and the excavation of memory. Hayden's prose recalls the poem which *is* his memory of the scene:

> A street lamp. A point of reference. Hattie and Elmer and M.C. the tomboy who died in her teens, and he, old Four-eyes.... Summer evening time. It is always summer when he thinks of his life on Beacon Street. The grownups sit on the front porch, taking ease after the demands and vexations of the day. Leaf shadows of trees of heaven. Ma is smoking Piedmont cigarettes. Pa is nodding. Auntie is taking the cool, as people used to say, before she goes to the Chinese restaurant where she is a waitress. (17–18)

Hayden ends the poem on Sunday, returning to St. Antoine to describe the street preachers and parades. The beginning of the stanza invokes the importance of music and performance to sacred rituals, a point Hayden underscores in "Mourning Poem for the Queen of Sunday," which depicts a congregation lost without its lead vocalist, whose songs vied with "the world a-clang with evil" (50). Without the singer, who succumbed to temptation when "Satan sweet-talked her" and died when "four bullets hushed her," Hayden asks:

Who's going to make the old hardened
  sinner men tremble now
and the righteous rock?

Oh who and oh who will sing Jesus
  down
to help with struggling and doing
  without and being colored
all through blue Monday?
Till way next Sunday? (50)

Accenting the power of music in "From *The Life*," Hayden recalls that "it is the tambourines that attract the children, not the preacher, for what the preacher says is scary. When the women pass through the crowd with the preacher's hat asking for money for their church, the sinner men and women drop in a coin or two in expiation of their sins" (18). Again, the resonance between the autobiographical and the compression of poetic memory is clear in the opening of the final stanza of "'Summertime'":

Then grim street preachers shook
their tambourines and Bibles in the
  face
tolerant wickedness; (53)

From his diver's point of view, Hayden continues to excavate the deep foundations of communal energies which flow in the call-and-response rhythms of the culture.

Hayden develops the implications of freedom and flight by weaving the African-American and Greek mythologies of flight and repatriation together in "O Daedalus, Fly Away Home":

My gran, he flew back to Africa,
just spread his arms and
Flew away home. (71)

In "'Summertime and the Living ...'" Hayden's images of flight draw subtly on the energy of the street and the lyrics of the song "Summertime." The song lyrics portray a parental vision of hope for a child: "One of these mornings / you're going to rise up singing / spread your wings and take to the sky." Wedged into the brutal confines of the symbolic South, Hayden's "'Summertime'" draws on the power of 1920s' political and popular cultural mythology to expand the song's image of personal flight into a communal vision of hope:

then Elks parades and big splendiferous
Jack Johnson in his diamond limousine
set the ghetto burgeoning
with fantasies
of Ethiopia spreading her gorgeous
wings. (53)

Hayden's modernist vision implies a hint of skepticism. But whether the skepticism is understood as Hayden's depends on the reader's response to Garveyism's Old Testament propaganda. Hayden was undoubtably aware of the numerous pitfalls suppressed by adoration of Garvey and the "burgeoning ... fantasies" of redemption and return. Nonetheless, Hayden's poem invokes the power of the communal patterns of life in the symbolic South which confirm Garvey (or his Afrocentric heirs) as much more than a huckster and Jack Johnson (Joe Louis or Muhammad Ali) as more than a boxer. In "The Poet and His Art," Hayden notes that "Jack Johnson was something of a folk-hero, and ghetto people admired him as a symbol.... His victories were their own vicarious triumphs over the oppressor. And they saw his eventual fall as the result of a plot to destroy him because he had dared to defy the conventions of the white world" (142).

The brilliance of Hayden's Afro-Modernist poetic technique lies in how he sifts together the various levels of experience in his diver's vision. As it happens, the ironic distance and sense of critique are not solely the product of the diver's modernism. In Hayden's "'Summertime,'" the distance comes through in words which seem to overburden the line: "splendiferous," and "diamond limousines" as chariots of repatriation and redemption. In "From *The Life*," Hayden witnesses the communal critique as he recalls a typical scene in which the ironies are debated and bantered back and forth in the audience of the parade. The scene suggests Garcia Lorca's understanding that *duende* can be supplied by *hearers* as well as singers. Noting the role of call-and-response in "Theory and Function of the *Duende*," he writes: "Often the composer's duende passes to the interpreter. It is also worth noting that even if the composer or poet is false, the interpreter's duende can create a new marvel bearing little resemblance to the original work" (96). Likewise, Hayden understood the crucial role of audience and communal processes to a full sense of black performance. Hayden's account reads as if it's lifted out of a Hurston short story or one of Hughes's Jesse B. Simple vignettes:

> In the hot sunshine of a Sunday afternoon the followers of Marcus Garvey, storm center of the Back to Africa movement

> (United Negro Improvement Association) during the 1920's, might be seen there marching in purple and green, carrying banners with black stars on them; chevaliers with plumed hats, black star nurses, children in trucks festooned with crepe paper. People stood along the curb watching, outraged or reassured. "Damn fools," one man might say. "I sure ain't lost nothing to Africa and I'm sure as hell ain't going back there to look for nothing." "Just like a zigaboo to talk like that," another might say. "Garvey trying to bring our race together and here you go low-rating him. Man, he talks good sense. We the onlies nation in the world don't have a country of our own and don't have a flag of our own." (19)

Rather than let the different voices intersect as Hughes did in the Simple stories or his own modernist epic *Montage of a Dream Deferred*, Hayden, through his crossroads poetics, distills the dissonance and communion in the space of a few words. He remembers moments of consensus as well: "But nobody quarreled when the Colored Elks or the Colored Masons or Woodmen stepped it off along St. Antoine. The music, the precision of the drill teams, the polish and gleam and sparkle, the ribbons and badges. Ethiopia spreading her gorgeous wings" (19). One of these mornings—

In "Covenant of Timelessness and Time," Wilburn Williams discusses how Hayden dealt with the difficult relationship of his modernist poetics to his social and historical interests. Williams argues correctly that, in order to resolve the dilemma, Hayden turns his realist's interest in history into a modernist's interest in "time." In his deeply Heraclitan poem "Theme and Variation" Hayden underscores the reality that awareness (past and present) is in a state of constant change:

> all things alter even as I behold,
> all things alter, the stranger said.
>
> Alter, become a something more,
> a something less. Are the reveling
> shadows
> of a changing permanence. Are, are not
> and same and other, the stranger said.
> (59)

In an interview entitled "A 'Romantic Realist,'" Hayden discusses his use of present tense in historical poems. For Hayden, imaging the past in the present tense pulls it loose from its stable moorings, keeps it *becoming:* "I think I may be using it to achieve dramatic immediacy and because in a sense there is no past, only the present. The past is also the present. The experiences I've had in the past are now a part of my mind, my subconscious, and they are there forever" (124).

In "Latin-American Poetry," Octavio Paz discusses the disjunction between poetics which engages history and modernist and symbolist poetics which abandons, or descends, from it. For Paz, "When history and poetry are consonant, the name of this coincidence is, for instance, Whitman; when there is discord between the two, the dissonance bears the name Baudelaire" (215). Paz then discusses the pitfalls of abandonment and withdrawal. He argues the need to remain in contact with social and historical concerns because abandonment "can only withdraw into itself ... [and the] dangers attendant upon [it] are irresponsible song or silence" (215). Seen from this angle, Hayden's method of a deeper engagement through withdrawal set forth in "The Diver" offers a combination of Paz's modes.

Hayden's modernist interest in the "time" of history and his meditations on the "past-present" bring historical narratives and imagist poetics together. "Runagate, Runagate" shows both the presentness of the past and the entanglement of historical and imagistic themes. Breaking to some extent with the principles outlined in his diver's manifesto, Hayden foregrounds interactive exchange in the composition of "Runagate, Runagate." Interestingly, the revised version of the poem published in *Selected Poems* and subsequent volumes was inspired when Hayden heard Rosey Pool read an earlier version to an audience. Hayden had written the first version and decided that it was not worth revising. Unbeknownst to him, it was published in England. Pool brought it to Fisk where she read it for an audience that included Hayden. Hayden recalls:

> Now I hadn't dared look at this poem for years, and as Rosey read it I was amazed and gratified to discover that most of it was much better than I'd thought. And as Rosey read—she is one of the finest readers of poetry I've ever heard—I realized the poem was worth saving, worth working on some more.... I went back to "Runagate," revised it drastically, though I kept the form I had used in the other versions. (183)

One stanza exemplifies the interaction at the crossroads between the imagistic descent and the historical engagement. Hayden splices realistic, matter-of-fact chronicles of brutality—actual slave owners' advertisements in nineteenth-century newspapers—with phrases from childhood games ("catch me if you can") and a meditation on the labyrinthine nature of underground quests. He frames the stanza with slaves' voices singing from the spirituals "No More Auction Block for Me," with its famous refrain "many thousands gone," and "Oh Freedom!" as they light out for "O mythic North / O star-shaped yonder Bible city":

> No more auction block for me
> no more driver's lash for me
>
> If you see my Pompey, 30 yrs of age,
> new breeches, plain stockings,
> negro shoes;
> if you see my Anna, likely young
> mulatto
> branded E on the right cheek, R on
> the left,
> catch them if you can and notify
> subscriber.
> Catch them if you can, but it won't be
> easy.
> They'll dart underground when you
> try to catch them,
> plunge into quicksand, whirlpools,
> mazes,
> turn into scorpions when you try to
> catch them.
>
> And before I'll be a slave
> I'll be buried in my grave (76)

If Whitman's discord with history mellowed as he aged and revised his *Leaves of Grass*, Hayden's revisions whetted the cutting edge of his cultural critique. Hayden's *Angle of Ascent*, *Words in the Mourning Time*, and *Collected Poems* show how he continued to hone his poetics into more lyrical and resonant combinations of black and world cultures, modernist process, and Bahá'í faith. In 1977, upon his arrival in Paradise Valley, he thought to himself "wryly ... so I've become a grey eminence.... But not, I hope, a good grey poet" (17). Not. But while, by almost all accounts, his work sharpened, the costs of the algebraic descents had mounted on Hayden's psychic life. Evincing the costs of the descendental path, in July of 1975, he wrote a hauntingly confessional letter to his younger friend Michael Harper, an excerpt of which serves as an epigraph to this essay. Momentarily flinging "aside the mask," Hayden wrote:

> I got up one morning, not too long ago, and felt I could not go on with my life. The diver had to admit that he couldn't surface again, alone, without help. And the long and short of it is that I am now going to a psychiatrist—certainly, for me, an admission of almost complete defeat. I have lived through days of sheer spiritual horror, and but for my beautiful [wife] Erma I could not have borne it. Well, this sounds like melodrama, sure enough, but it's ice-cold reality of which I speak. (Nicholas 997)

In a Shem-like response to his elder's suffering, Harper's reply looks the other way and congratulates Hayden for his decision to go against his diver's manifesto: "Remember: you had the sense to get someone to talk to" (999).

Hayden's letter makes it clear that even—possibly especially—the most brilliant Afro-Modernists rarely elude the "ice-cold reality" of the problems associated with poetic withdrawal and descent. As much as any mid-century writer, Robert Hayden bore the risks associated with exploring the modernist awareness of the contingent and contested intersection between culture and consciousness. Posthumously published, Hayden's *Collected Poems* begins with "The Diver" and ends with "American Journal." From the diver's depth, the "measured rise" becomes a satellite's scope on American culture. "American Journal" is a near-perfectly executed balance of detachment and engagement, critique and faith, knowing and belief. All is calibrated to keep the reader solving for Auden's "x," by now, fully Hayden's "own, wild, and free":

> elan vital and that some thing essence
> quiddity i cannot penetrate or name
> (195)

Works Cited

Baldwin, James. *Just Above My Head.* New York: Dial, 1979.

Baker, Houston. *Blues, Ideology and Afro-American Literature: A Vernacular Theory.* Chicago: U of Chicago P, 1984.

Brooks, Gwendolyn. *Blacks.* Chicago: Third World P, 1987.

Conniff, Brian. "Answering 'The Waste Land': Robert Hayden and the Rise of the African American Poetic Sequence." *African American Review* 33 (1999): 487–506.

Dunbar, Paul Laurence. *The Complete Poems of Paul Laurence Dunbar.* New York: Dodd, Mead, 1967.

Effendi, Shoghi. *The Promised Day Is Come.* Rutland, England: Bahai Publications Trust, 1996.

Faulkner, William. *Go Down, Moses.* 1942. New York: Vintage, 1990.

Fetrow, Fred. *Robert Hayden.* Boston: Twayne, 1984.

Freud, Sigmund. *The Interpretation of Dreams.* 1900. New York: Macmillan, 1927.

—. "Dream Work and Interpretation." *An Outline of Psycho-Analysis.* Ed. and trans. James Stachey. New York: Norton, 1949. 23: 38–96.

Harding, James M. "Adorno, Ellison, and the Critique of Jazz." *Cultural Critique* 31 (1995): 129–58.

Hatcher, John. *From the Auroral Darkness: The Life and Poetry of Robert Hayden.* Oxford: George Ronald, 1984.

Hayden, Robert. *American Journal.* New York: Liveright, 1982.

——. *Angle of Ascent: New and Selected Poems.* New York: Liveright, 1975.

——. "A Certain Vision." Hayden, *Collected Prose* 90–114.

——. *Collected Poems.* Ed. Frederick Glaysher. New York: Liveright, 1985.

——. *Collected Prose.* Ed. Frederick Glaysher. Ann Arbor: U of Michigan P, 1984.

——. "Counterpoise Manifesto." Hayden, *Collected Prose* 41–42.

——. "From *The Life:* Some Remembrances." Hayden, *Collected Prose* 17–27.

——. "The Poet and His Art: A Conversation." Hayden, *Collected Prose* 129–204.

——. "A 'Romantic Realist.'" Hayden, *Collected Prose* 115–28.

——. *Selected Poems.* New York: October House, 1966.

——. "Something Patterned, Wild, and Free." Hayden, *Collected Prose* 74–78.

Heidegger, Martin. *Nietzsche, Volume III: The Will to Power as Knowledge and Metaphysics.* New York: HarperCollins, 1987.

Komunyakaa, Yusef. *Blue Notes: Essays, Interviews, and Commentaries.* Ed. Radiclani Clytus. Ann Arbor: U Michigan P, 2000.

——. "Masks." *Indiana Review* 19.1 (1996): 59–60.

Lorca, Gabriel Garcia. "Theory and Function of the *Duende.*" *Poetics of the New American Poetry.* Ed. Donald Allen and Warren Tallman. New York: Grove P, 1973. 91–103.

Nicholas, Xavier, ed. "Robert Hayden and Michael Harper: A Literary Friendship." *Callaloo* 17 (1994): 976–1015.

O'Connor, Flannery. *The Violent Bear It Away.* 1955. New York: Noonday, 1998.

O'Sullivan, Maurice. "The Mask of Allusion in Robert Hayden's 'The Diver.'" *CLA Journal* 27.1 (1973): 85–92.

Standley, Fred L., and Louis Pratt, eds. *Conversations with James Baldwin.* Jackson: UP of Mississippi, 1989.

Whitman, Walt. *Whitman: Complete Poetry and Collected Prose*. Ed. Justin Caplan. New York: Library of America, 1982.

Williams, Wilbum. "Covenant of Timelessness and Time: Symbolism and History in Robert Hayden's *Angle of Ascent*." *Chant of Saints: A Gathering of Afro-American Literature, Art, and Scholarship*. Ed. Michael S. Harper and Robert B. Stepto. Urbana: U of Illinois P, 1979. 66–84.

Yeats, William Butler. *The Variorum Edition of the Poems of W. B. Yeats*. Ed. Peter Allt and Russell K. Alspach. New York: Macmillan, 1966.

Chronology

1913	Born Asa Bundy Sheffey on August 4 in Detroit, Michigan; adopted by Mr. and Mrs. Robert Hayden following parents' separation.
1919	Joins Second Baptist Church.
1930	Graduates from Northern High School in Detroit.
1932	Enters Detroit City College (Wayne State University).
1938	Begins studies at the University of Michigan summer program; wins Hopwood Award for *Heart-Shape in the Dust*.
1940	Marries Erma Inez Morris; publishes *Heart-Shape in the Dust*.
1942	Wins second Hopwood Award for *The Black Spear*; daughter Maia born; becomes a member of the Bahá'í World Faith; receives bachelor's degree from Detroit City College.
1944	Granted Master's degree from the University of Michigan.
1946	Named Assistant Professor of English at Fisk University; meets Arna Bontemps and Mark Van Doren.
1947	Receives Rosenwald Fellowship in Creative Writing.
1948	Publishes *The Lion and the Archer* with Myron O'Higgins.
1954	Travels to Mexico on a fellowship from the Ford Foundation.
1962	Publishes *A Ballad of Remembrance*.

1966	Publishes *Selected Poems*; presented with the Grand Prix de la Poésie at the First World Festival of Negro Arts in Dakar, Senegal.
1968	Publishes *Kaleidoscope: Poems by American Negro Poets*; defends his work at the Black Writers' Conference at Fisk University.
1969	Resigns professorship at Fisk and is appointed Bingham Professor at the University of Louisville; awarded citation by the Pan-American Association in Washington, D.C.
1970	Publishes *Words in the Mourning Time*, which is nominated for the National Book Award; becomes Professor of English at the University of Michigan.
1971	Teaches at the University of Connecticut and Denison University as Visiting Professor.
1972	Publishes *The Night-Blooming Cereus*.
1975	Elected Fellow of the American Academy of Poets; appointed consultant in poetry at the Library Congress (later known as Poet Laureate); publishes *Angle of Ascent*.
1977	Reappointed consultant in poetry at the Library of Congress.
1978	Publishes *American Journal*.
1979	Inducted into the Academy of American Poets and Institute of Arts and Letters.
1980	Honored by President Jimmy Carter at the White House; On February 25, Robert Hayden dies of cancer.

Contributors' Notes

HAROLD BLOOM is Sterling Professor of the Humanities at Yale University. He is the author of over 20 books, including *Shelley's Mythmaking* (1959), *The Visionary Company* (1961), *Blake's Apocalypse* (1963), *Yeats* (1970), *A Map of Misreading* (1975), *Kabbalah and Criticism* (1975), *Agon: Toward a Theory of Revisionism* (1982), *The American Religion* (1992), *The Western Canon* (1994), and *Omens of Millennium: The Gnosis of Angels, Dreams, and Resurrection* (1996). *The Anxiety of Influence* (1973) sets forth Professor Bloom's provocative theory of the literary relationships between the great writers and their predecessors. His most recent books include *Shakespeare: The Invention of the Human* (1998), a 1998 National Book Award finalist, *How to Read and Why* (2000), *Genius: A Mosaic of One Hundred Exemplary Creative Minds* (2002), and *Hamlet: Poem Unlimited* (2003). In 1999, Professor Bloom received the prestigious American Academy of Arts and Letters Gold Medal for Criticism, and in 2002 he received the Catalonia International Prize.

CONSTANCE J. POST has taught at the College of Staten Island and is the author of *Signs of the Times in Cotton Mather's* Paterna: *A Study of Puritan Autobiography*.

LEWIS TURCO has taught at Cleveland State University, Hillsdale College, and SUNY-Oswego. A poet and critic, he is the author of *The New Book of Forms* and *The Shifting Web: New and Selected Poems*.

FRED M. FETROW is Professor of English at the United States Naval

Academy, where he teaches African-American literature, Shakespeare, and 18th-century British literature.

ROBERT B. STEPTO is Professor of English, African-American Studies, and American Studies at Yale University. His books include *From Behind the Veil: A Study of Afro-American Narrative* and *Blue as the Lake: A Personal Geography*.

WILBURN WILLIAMS, JR. is the author of *The Desolate Servitude of Language: A Reading of the Poetry of Melvin B. Tolson*.

CHARLES T. DAVIS served as Chair of the African-American Studies Department at Yale University. He co-edited *The Slave's Narrative* with Henry Louis Gates, Jr. and *On Being Black: Writings by Afro-Americans from Frederick Douglass to the Present* with Daniel Walden.

FRITZ OEHLSCHLAEGER is Professor of English at Virginia Polytechnic Institute. He is co-editor of *Toward the Making of Thoreau's Modern Reputation* and co-author of *Articulating the Elephant Man: Joseph Merrick and his Interpreters*.

VERA M. KUTZINSKI is Professor of English, African-American Studies, and American Studies at Yale University. Her books include *Against the American Grain* and *Sugar's Secrets: Race and the Erotics of Cuban Nationalism*.

PONTHEOLLA T. WILLIAMS is the author of *Robert Hayden: A Critical Analysis of his Poetry*.

BRIAN CONNIFF is Chair of the English Department at the University of Dayton. His essays have appeared in *Religious Studies Review* and *African American Review* among other journals.

FRANK RASHID is Professor of English and Chair of the English and Modern Languages Department at Marygrove College. He specializes in American literature, and 19th- and 20th-century poetry.

EDWARD M. PAVLIĆ is Associate Professor of English and Africana Studies at Union College. He is the author of a collection of poetry entitled *Paraph of Bone and Other Kinds of Blue*.

Bibliography

Aubert, Alvin, ed. (special issue devoted to Robert Hayden) *Obsidian: Black Literature in Review* 8, no. 1 (Spring 1981).

Bell, Bernard W. *The Folk Roots of Contemporary Afro-American Poetry*. Detroit: Broadside Press, 1974.

Bontemps, Arna. "Negro Poets, Then and Now." *Phylon* 11 (1950): 356–57.

Boyles, Ann. "'The Angle of Ascent': Process and Achievement in the Work of Robert Hayden." *Journal of Bahá'í Studies* 4, no. 2 (December 1991–March 1992): 1–28.

Campbell, Charles R. "A Split Image of the American Heritage: The Poetry of Robert Hayden and Theodore Roethke." *Midamerica* 12 (1985): 70–82.

Chamblee, Angela E. "Frederick Douglass in the Painting of Jacob Lawrence and the Poetry of Robert Hayden." *Proteus* 12, no. 1 (Spring 1995): 18–23.

Collins, Michael. "On the Track of the Universal: 'Middle Passage' and America." *Parnassus: Poetry in Review* 17, no. 2, and 18, no. 1 (1993): 334–59.

Conniff, Brian. "Answering *The Waste Land*: Robert Hayden and the Rise of the African American Poetic Sequence." *African American Review* 33, no. 3 (Fall 1999): 487–504.

Cooke, Michael G. "Robert Hayden: At Large, At Home in the World." *Afro-American Literature in the Twentieth Century*. New Haven: Yale University Press, 1984.

———. "Christopher Okigbo and Robert Hayden: From Mould to Stars." *World Literature Written in English* 30, no. 2 (Autumn 1990): 131–144.

Darcy, Zabel. "Hayden's 'Runagate, Runagate.'" *Explicator* 60 (Winter 2002): 100–02.

Davis, Arthur P. *From the Dark Tower: Afro-American Writers 1900–1960.* Washington, D.C.: Howard University Press, 1974.

Davis, Charles T. "Robert Hayden's Use of History." *Black is the Color of the Cosmos: Essays on Afro-American Literature 1942–1981.* Ed. Henry Louis Gates. New York: Garland, 1982.

Dean, Michael P. "Magnolias, Mayhem, and Malice: Two 'Mississippi Poems' by Robert Hayden." *Publications of the Mississippi Philological Association* (1986): 1–12.

Faulkner, Howard. "'Transformed by Steeps of Flight': The Poetry of Robert Hayden." *CLA Journal* 21, no. 1 (1977): 282–91.

Fetrow, Fred M. "'Middle-Passage': Robert Hayden's Anti-Epic." *CLA Journal* 22 (June 1979): 304–318.

———. *Robert Hayden.* Boston: Twayne, 1984.

———. "Portraits and Personae: Characterizations in the Poetry of Robert Hayden." *Black American Poets between Worlds, 1940–1960.* Ed. R. Baxter Miller. Knoxville: University of Tennesee Press, 1986.

———. "Reading the Man: Robert Hayden and Frederick Douglass." *CLA Journal* 44, no. 2 (December 2000): 189–203.

Friedlandeer, Benjamin. "Robert Hayden's Epic of Community." *Melus* 23, no. 3 (Autumn 1998): 125–43.

Gallagher, Ann M. "Hayden's 'Those Winter Sundays.'" *Explicator* 51, no. 4 (Summer 1993): 245–47.

Gibbons, Reginald. "Robert Hayden in the 1940's." *Triquarterly* 62 (Winter 1985): 177–86.

Glaysher, Frederick. "Re-Centering: The Turning of the Tide and Robert Hayden." *World Order* (Summer 1983): 9–17.

Goldstein, Laurence and Robert Chrisman, eds. *Robert Hayden: Essays on the Poetry.* Ann Arbor: University of Michigan Press, 2001.

Greenberg, Robert M. "Robert Hayden." *African American Writers.* Ed. Valerie Smith, Lea Baechler, and A. Walton Litz. New York: Scribners, 1991.

Hansell, William H. "The Spiritual Unity of Robert Hayden's *Angle of Ascent.*" *Black American Literature Forum* 13 (Spring 1979): 24–31.

Harper, Michael. "Remembering Robert Hayden." *Michigan Quarterly Review* 21, no. 3 (1982).

Hatcher, John. *From the Auroral Darkness: The Life and Poetry of Robert Hayden*. Oxford: George Ronald, 1984.

Henderson, Stephen. *Understanding the New Black Poetry: Black Speech and Black Music as Poetic References*. New York: Morrow, 1973.

Jones, Norma R. "Robert Hayden." *Afro-American Writers, 1940–1955*. Ed. Trudier Harris and Thadious M. Davis. Detroit: Gale Research, 1988.

Komunyakaa, Yusef. *Blue Notes: Essays, Interviews, and Commentaries*. Ed. Radiclani Clytus. Ann Arbor: University of Michigan Press, 2000.

Kutzinski, Vera M. "Changing Permanences: Historical and Literary Revisionism in Robert Hayden's 'Middle Passage.'" *Callaloo* 9, no. 1 (1986): 171–183.

Lewis, Richard B. "A Literary-Psychoanalytic Interpretation of Robert Hayden's 'Market.'" *Negro American Literature Forum* (Spring 1975): 21–24.

Major, Clarence. *The Dark and the Feeling: Black Writers and Their Work*. New York: Joseph Okpaku, 1974.

Nicholas, Xavier. "Robert Hayden." *Bulletin of Bibliography* 42, no. 3 (1985): 140–53.

———. "Robert Hayden and Michael Harper: A Literary Friendship." *Callaloo* 17 (1994): 976–1015.

Nielsen, Aldon L. "The Middle Passage." *Writing Between the Lines: Race and Intertextuality*. Athens: University of Georgia Press, 1994.

Novak, Michael Paul. "Meditative, Ironic, Richly Human: The Poetry of Robert Hayden." *Midwest Quarterly* 15 (Spring 1974): 276–85.

O'Brian, John, ed. *Interviews with Black Writers*. New York: Liveright, 1973.

Oehlschlanger, Fritz. "Robert Hayden's Meditation on Art: The Final Sequence of *Words in the Mourning Time*." *Black American Literature Forum* 19 (Autumn 1985): 115–19.

O'Sullivan, Maurice J. "The Mask of Illusion in Robert Hayden's 'The Diver.'" *CLA Journal* 17 (September 1973): 85–92.

Parks, Gerald. "The Bahá'í Muse: Religion in Robert Hayden's Poetry." *World Order* 15 (Spring-Summer 1981): 37–48.

Pavlić Eric M. "Something patterned, wild, and free": Robert Hayden's Angles of Ascent and the Democratic Unconscious." *African American Review* 36, no. 4 (Winter 2002): 533–555.

Pool, Rosey E. "Robert Hayden: Poet Laureate." *Negro Digest* 15 (June 1966): 39–43.

Post, Constance. "Image and Idea in the Poetry of Robert Hayden." *CLA Journal* 20, no. 2 (December 1976): 164–175.

Rashid, Frank. "Robert Hayden's Detriot Blues Elegies." *Callalee* 24, no.1 (2001): 200–226.

Rice, William. "The Example of Robert Hayden." *New Criterion* 8, no. 3 (November 1989): 42–45.

Richards, Phillip M. "Robert Hayden (1913–1980): An Appreciation." *Massachusetts Review* (Winter 1999–2000): 599–613.

Stepto, Robert B. "After Modernism, After Hibernation: Michael Harper, Robert Hayden, and Jay Wright." *Chant of Saints: A Gathering of Afro-American Literature, Art, and Scholarship*. Ed. Michael S. Harper and Robert B. Stepto. Urbana: University of Illinois Press, 1979.

Turco, Lewis. "*Angle of Ascent*: The Poetry of Robert Hayden." *Michigan Quarterly Review* 16, no. 2 (Spring 1977): 199–219.

Williams, Pontheolla T. *Robert Hayden: A Critical Analysis of His Poetry*. Urbana: University of Illinois Press, 1987.

Walcott, Ronald. "Calling the Names and Centering the Call in Robert Hayden's 'American Journal.'" *CLA Journal* 43, no. 3 (March 2000): 320–37.

Williams, Wilburn. "Covenant of Timelessness and Time: Symbolism and History in Robert Hayden's *Angle of Ascent*." *Chant of Saints: A Gathering of Afro-American Literature, Art, and Scholarship*. Ed. Michael S. Harper and Robert B. Stepto. Urbana: University of Illinois Press, 1979.

Wright, Jay. "Desire's Design, Vision's Resonance: Black Poetry's Ritual and Historical Voice." *Callaloo* 10, no. 1 (1987): 13–28.

Wright, John S. "Homage to a Mystery Boy." *Georgia Review* 36 (Winter 1982): 904–11.

Acknowledgments

"Image and Idea in the Poetry of Robert Hayden," by Constance J. Post. From *CLA Journal* 20, no. 2 (December 1976): 164–175. © 1976 by the College Language Association. Reprinted by permission.

"*Angle of Ascent*: The Poetry of Robert Hayden," by Lewis Turco. From *Michigan Quarterly Review* 16, no. 2 (Spring 1977): 199–219. © 1977 by The University of Michigan. Reprinted by permission.

"'Middle Passage": Robert Hayden's Anti-Epic," by Fred M. Fetrow. From *CLA Journal* 22, no. 4 (June 1979): 304–318. © 1979 by the College Language Association. Reprinted by permission.

"After Modernism, After Hibernation: Michael Harper, Robert Hayden, and Jay Wright," by Robert B. Stepto. From *Chant of Saints: A Gathering of Afro-American Literature, Art, and Scholarship*, eds. Michael S. Harper and Robert B. Stepto. © 1979 by the Board of Trustees of the University of Illinois. Reprinted by permission.

"Covenant of Timelessness and Time: Symbolism and History in Robert Hayden's *Angle of Ascent*," by Wilburn Williams, Jr. From *Chant of Saints: A Gathering of Afro-American Literature, Art, and Scholarship*, eds. Michael S. Harper and Robert B. Stepto. © 1979 by the Board of Trustees of the University of Illinois. Reprinted by permission.

"Robert Hayden's Use of History" by Charles T. Davis. From *Black is the Color of the Cosmos*, ed. Henry Louis Gates, Jr. © 1982 by The Estate of Charles T. Davis. Reprinted by permission.

"Robert Hayden's Meditation on Art: The Final Sequence of *Words in the Mourning Time*," by Fritz Oehlschlaeger. From *Black American Literature Forum* 19, no. 3 (Fall 1985): 115–119. © 1985 by Indiana State University. Reprinted by permission.

"Changing Permanences: Historical and Literary Revisionism in Robert Hayden's 'Middle Passage,'" by Vera M. Kutzinski. From *Callaloo* 9, no. 1 (Winter 1986): 171–183. © 1986 by Charles H. Rowell. Reprinted by permission.

"*A Ballad of Remembrance* (1962)," by Pontheolla T. Williams. From *Robert Hayden: A Critical Analysis of His Poetry* by Pontheolla T. Williams. © 1987 by the Board of Trustees of the University of Illinois. Reprinted by permission.

"Answering *The Waste Land*: Robert Hayden and the Rise of the African-American Poetic Sequence," by Brian Conniff. From *African American Review* 33, no. 3 (Fall 1999): 487–504. © 1999 by St. Louis University. Reprinted by permission.

"Robert Hayden's Detroit Blues Elegies," by Frank Rashid. From *Callaloo* 24, no. 1 (2001): 200–226. © 2001 by Charles H. Rowell. Reprinted by permission.

"'Something patterned, wild, and free': Robert Hayden's Angles of Descent and the Democratic Unconscious," by Edward M. Pavlić. From *African American Review* 36, no. 4 (Winter 2002): 533–555. © 2002 by Edward M. Pavlić. Reprinted by permission.

Index

Characters in literary works are indexed by first name followed by the name of the work in parentheses.

DATE DUE

NOV 28 2011			